The Reckoning of Pluralism

The Reckoning of Pluralism

POLITICAL BELONGING AND THE
DEMANDS OF HISTORY IN TURKEY

Kabir Tambar

Stanford University Press
Stanford, California

Stanford University Press
Stanford, California

Printed in the United States of America on acid-free, archival-quality paper

Library of Congress Cataloging-in-Publication Data

Tambar, Kabir, author.
  The reckoning of pluralism : political belonging and the demands of history in Turkey / Kabir Tambar.
      pages   cm — (Stanford studies in Middle Eastern and Islamic societies and cultures)
  Includes bibliographical references and index.
  ISBN 978-0-8047-8630-0 (cloth : alk. paper)
  ISBN 978-0-8047-9093-2 (pbk. : alk. paper)
    1. Alevis—Turkey. 2. Religious minorities—Turkey. 3. Religious pluralism—Political aspects—Turkey. 4. Islamic sects—Turkey. 5. Islam and state—Turkey. 6. Nationalism—Turkey. 7. Secularism—Turkey. I. Title. II. Series: Stanford studies in Middle Eastern and Islamic societies and cultures.
DR435.N67T36 2014
322'.109561—dc23
                                                                                        2013036396

CONTENTS

ACKNOWLEDGMENTS

THIS BOOK COULD NOT HAVE been written without the support of a number of friends and mentors at various stages. At the University of Chicago, I appreciated the critical engagement by Hussein Ali Agrama, Jean Comaroff, Cassie Fennell, Susan Gal, Brian Horne, Rocío Magaña, Saba Mahmood, William Mazzarella, Ayşe Polat, Elizabeth Povinelli, Danilyn Rutherford, Michael Silverstein, Martin Stokes, Michel-Rolph Trouillot, Nükhet Varlık, Jeremy Walton, and Lisa Wedeen. I thank Anne Ch'ien for her tireless support. While teaching at the University of Vermont, I had the opportunity and space to reconceptualize the project, and the book itself was drafted during a subsequent year spent at the Institute for Advanced Study in Princeton, NJ. The process of writing, thinking, and rewriting was catalyzed by colleagues who read and improved manuscripts headed for journals or responded to public presentations. I am grateful to Michael Allan, Vicki Brennan, Benjamin Eastman, Matthew Engelke, Zeynep Gürsel, Sherine Hamdy, Angie Heo, Banu Karaca, Burcu Karahan, Burçak Keskin-Kozat, Emily Manetta, Ceren Özgül, Ayşe Parla, Andrew Shryock, Jonah Steinberg, and Berna Turam for their feedback at these junctures. I revised the text while teaching at Stanford University, and I thank my colleagues in the Department of Anthropology for their support and collegiality.

I am especially indebted to a number of friends and colleagues who read the manuscript in its entirety. Joseph Hankins and Kelda Jamison read numerous drafts of chapters and offered intellectual companionship across the many years that I have worked on this text. Laura Helper-Ferris sharpened the writing. Thomas Blom Hansen, Sarah Muir, and Esra Özyürek offered discerning and spirited critiques, and Joan W. Scott pressed me to think at the edges of anthropology's disciplinary conventions.

The bulk of the research conducted for this project took the form of ethnographic study in Turkey, and this work depended heavily on the support of various friends and colleagues. Aykan Erdemir, Mustafa Şen, and Ahmet Tasğın provided early assistance and encouragement. Mark Soileau shared his erudition generously. Ahmet Kerim Gültekin, Erden and Melahat Özer, and Cihan Pak offered the joy of friendship without suspicion, for which I remain grateful beyond words. I also thank Durmuş Aslan, Altan Demir, Teoman Şahin, and Ali, Mehdi, and Ali Rıza Üremiş for welcoming me into their lives and communities.

Middle East Technical University and Bilkent University offered affiliations and library access in Ankara. Research and writing were funded by the Fulbright Hays Dissertation Research Abroad Fellowship, the Wenner-Gren Foundation, the Institute of Turkish Studies, and the Charlotte W. Newcombe Fellowship. The Institute of Turkish Studies also provided a subvention grant to help cover the costs of publishing the book. I was fortunate to work with Stanford University Press, and I thank Kate Wahl for her commitment to the project.

My parents, Prem and Indra Tambar, have never demanded a return on their support, and their unflinching confidence in my intellectual perambulations, even when seemingly most random and least coherent, has always provided me with a ground and orientation. Siddharth Tambar and Sonal Chandra were the first to encourage me to study anthropology, and so this book is ultimately in their debt.

From ethnography to writing, Kelda Jamison has shared the life-world of this project. The world this text seeks to represent is one she has helped me imagine, conceptualize, and understand. Her influence on the work exceeds delineation. Arav and Rohan joined this project quite late in the day, and happily they return me to the world beyond it.

NOTE ON ORTHOGRAPHY

MODERN TURKISH IS WRITTEN WITH the Latin alphabet. Most letters loosely correspond to characters found in English, but there are a few differences. The Turkish *c* is pronounced like the English *j* as in *jam*. *J* is pronounced like the final "ge" of the French *rouge*. *Ç* is pronounced "ch" as in *child*. *Ş* is "sh" as in *show*. *İ* and *ı* (i.e., with and without a dot) are comparable to "ee" and "uh" respectively. *Ğ* lengthens the vowel preceding it but is not pronounced separately. Umlauts (as in *ö* and *ü*) are akin to those in German.

Throughout this book, I make use of modern standard Turkish orthography for most technical Islamic terms. For instance, I use *cemaat* rather than *jamā'a*. Where relevant, I note the standard transliteration of Arabic in parenthesis. Exceptions to the use of Turkish orthography include words that are commonly represented in English: I use Shi'i rather than either Shī'ī (formally transliterated Arabic) or Şii (Turkish). I have also rendered proper names of figures from early Islamic history with conventional English spellings, for example, Husayn rather than Hüseyin (Turkish). All translations are my own unless noted.

The Reckoning of Pluralism

1 IN THE TIME OF PLURALISM

THE POLITICS OF PLURALISM IS an oxymoron, at least within a certain imaginary of modern political community that has been dominant in Turkey for much of the past century. Within this imaginary, political communities are isomorphic with territorially circumscribed nation-states, and nation-states in turn are imagined as internally homogeneous. Whatever differences—of culture, religion, ethnicity, gender, and class—may exist within such communities, they are supposed to be sublated to a feeling of common purpose that would bind a people together in fraternity and ensure their equal treatment. Politics, in this framing, is a field of action that transcends the pluralities that would otherwise fracture a polity. It is grounded in the sense of a shared past and a collective destiny. As with many nation-states in the past two centuries, the Turkish state sought to cultivate this conception of political belonging by standardizing the language and history of the nation.

In Turkey today the issue of pluralism ignites explosive debate, particularly when it takes form in a historical register. Various social actors, organizations, and international political bodies claim that, from its founding, the Turkish state has policed the uses of language and regulated the writing of history in ways that have promoted discrimination rather than fraternity or equality. These groups denounce the forms of historical erasure, of cultural domination, and of political violence that were deemed necessary to build the nation-state. They prompt questions about the very legitimacy of the modernist project that emerged in the early twentieth century, after the collapse of the multi-religious and multi-ethnic Ottoman Empire. The Turkish Republic today faces an unprecedented challenge to the ideologies of homogeneous nationalism that justified its initial formation. Pluralism represents a historical reckoning with the dominant imagining of Turkey's political modernity.

A brief vignette suggests that this reckoning remains both contentious as a political project and unsettling in its effects. On October 6, 2004, the European Commission released its annual report on the progress of political and economic reform in Turkey. The report argued that recent policies implemented by the Turkish state largely conformed to EU regulations and recommended that full member accession talks be initiated. The positive recommendation notwithstanding, the report offered a range of criticisms against the Turkish state in areas where reform remained sluggish. One of these areas concerned the Alevi population:

> As far as the situation of non-Sunni Muslim minorities is concerned, there has been no change in their status. Alevis are not officially recognized as a religious community, they often experience difficulties in opening places of worship, and compulsory religious instruction in schools fails to acknowledge non-Sunni identities. . . . Most Alevis claim that as a secular state Turkey should treat all religions equally and should not directly support one particular religion (the Sunnis) as it currently does through [the Directorate of Religious Affairs]. (European Commission 2004: 44–45)

The report continued, bringing these observations to their political upshot: "Alevis are still not recognized as a Muslim minority" (2004: 54).

Abdullah Gül, who was then serving as Turkey's minister of foreign affairs, expressed concern about the report's formulation of the concept of minority. "Europe's concept of minority is different from our concept of minority. The EU defines minority in terms of ethnic identity, while we use religious identity" (*Zaman* 2004b). Gül was referring to the fact that under the authority of the Treaty of Lausanne (1923), the only formally recognized minorities in Turkey were Christians (Armenian and Greek) and Jews.[1] The long-standing position of the state with regard to Alevis is that, in constitutional terms, they are no different from the Sunni majority. They are, in effect, within the fold of the dominant religious identity in Turkey—they are Muslims, a category for which the state does not recognize sectarian distinction. As such, they cannot be legally considered a minority. In more specific terms, the state has refused to recognize Alevi traditions and practices as deserving special legal recognition as forms of worship. For the past few decades, state officials have instead designated Alevi rituals as historical elements of the nation's "culture" or "folklore."

The state's efforts to classify Alevi practice have not gone uncontested. Both Alevi and non-Alevi actors have disputed state rhetoric in various venues of debate—more often than not, outside of the formal mechanisms of political representation. For instance a popular Turkish musician of Sunni descent, Zülfü Livaneli, published a critical commentary in a national daily about the unwillingness of state officials to view Alevi ritual as worship. "Our Alevi citizens can open a *cemevi* [a site to perform the *cem*, a central Alevi practice] as a 'social and cultural association' but not as a 'place of worship' (*ibadet yeri*). As this situation is contrary to human rights and to democracy, it is probably not necessary to state that it is also contrary to the principle of secularism" (Livaneli 2005: 6). For Livaneli and the European Commission, the problem is that the Turkish state misrecognizes Alevi ritual, and this misrecognition places unwarranted political constraints on its expression. These arguments contest the state's authority to stipulate the terms of social and religious difference.

Yet almost from the outset of my research, I encountered statements from Alevis themselves that confounded this political challenge to state authority. Stumbling blocks were already visible in the debate over the concept of minority in 2004. While many Alevi intellectuals and activists agreed that, contrary to state policy, sites of communal ritual ought to be classed as places of worship, there was pronounced disagreement over the category of minority. Some came out in favor of this designation as an effective way of attaining various rights and exemptions (for instance, exemptions for children from attending mandatory courses on religion and morals in public schools). A considerable number of other Alevis, however, began voicing hostility toward the report's application of the category to their community. Ali Rıza Selmanpakoğlu, the mayor of the provincial town of Hacıbektaş, publicly opposed the report, claiming that the Alevi community has been a foundational component (*asli unsur*) of the Turkish Republic, a cornerstone (*temel taşı*) of Turkey's democracy, secularism, and enlightenment (*Hürriyet* 2004).[2] The trope of *asli unsur*, that Alevis are an essential and constitutive element of the republic, was expressed by a number of Alevi commentators in the course of the debate. The head of the Şahkulu Dergah Association (an Alevi organization), Mehmet Çamur, accused those Alevis who favored the minority designation of seeking to "prioritize subidentities, divide the nation-state, and Balkanize Turkey"

(Özyürek 2009a: 135). At the threshold of a political discourse about pluralist reform, many Alevis themselves responded by appealing to the nation-state's authorized self-image, positioning themselves within the official narrative of the republic's founding.

I encountered this ambivalent pluralism not only in the discourse of some Alevi spokespersons—activists, public intellectuals, municipal officials, and the like—but also in public performances of Alevi ritual. Since the 1960s, but accelerating rapidly after the 1990s, Alevi organizations have sponsored gatherings, festivals, and protests in public squares and streets. Commentators have tended to view these events as a politically effective appropriation of public space, in which Alevis represent their cultural differences and forward their political interests (e.g., Yavuz 2003b; Şahin 2005; Sökefeld 2008). Many of my Alevi friends similarly understood such performances as raising awareness within the national public at large about Alevi traditions. It is not uncommon to find participants in such events holding up posters of Ali ibn Abi Talib, the cousin and son-in-law of the Prophet Muhammad. Ali is a figure from early Islamic history who is honored by most Muslims, but is given special reverence by Alevi and Shi'i Muslims. At such events, his image is emblematic of Alevi identity. What is perhaps less expected is that, alongside the image of Ali, participants often wave Turkish flags and display photographs of Mustafa Kemal Atatürk, the leader of the nationalist forces under the early republican regime and its paradigmatic icon. The display of these images reverberates with a sense of loyalty to the statist project of secular nationalism, echoing the claim that the community stands as a cornerstone of the republic. Alevi public visibility, often cast as signifying a nascent pluralist politics, is itself mediated by the most potent indices of the Turkish state.

This book examines how Turkey's Alevi community has raised a politics of pluralism. In the past two decades, numerous Alevi groups have questioned the ways in which their community was marginalized from public life in both the Ottoman and Turkish republican eras. In these acts of questioning, history operates as a key discursive practice. It enables Alevis to contest the forms of organized domination that existed in the past, and it emboldens them to give political voice to their grievances in the present. Yet for many Alevi organizations and intellectuals, pluralist politics operates on a volatile fault line. In its discursive and aesthetic embodiment, the practice of history remains dependent upon the institutional scaffolding of the modernist project. It reinforces, even as it puts into question, the state's authority to define political community.

In the chapters ahead, I contextualize the practice of history. I specify the genres of speech and writing that mediate its expression, the modes of address that allow it to hail a public audience, and the political authorities that regulate its limits. I examine the icons, images, and forms of spectatorship that define its spaces of appearance. The analysis interrogates the production of political voice at its points of institutional articulation, asking how that voice remains beholden to, even incited by, state power.

The politics of pluralism commonly represents a criticism of the modern state's violent efforts to assert the ethnic and religious homogeneity of the nation. What, then, are the limits of pluralism when it is organized within the institutional and ideological frameworks of the nation-state? How are the conditions of political criticism regimented by those framings? Where might we locate forms of engagement that, rather than remain vocal within the existing dispensation of citizenly participation, challenge the conditions of political enunciation?

FORMATIONS OF POLITICAL MODERNITY

I approach the concept of pluralism as an ethnographic object: its political significance is defined by the historical and political context of its invocation. One consequence of this approach is that I do not begin my analysis with a strong, prescriptive definition of pluralism. The problem with beginning in that manner is that it would simply lead us to mark the deficiencies of its actual use, rather than to an understanding of what its invocation contextually signifies. Abstracting the notion of pluralism from its context of use elides the crucial analytical task of interrogating the normative charge that the concept sustains for actors who deploy it.

Pluralism is a charged concept because it directs attention to the history of Turkish citizenship and the mechanisms of political power formative of that history. In Turkey, as elsewhere, the political imaginary of citizenship has not been static. It has evolved in the course of a tumultuous history, which included the development of legal protections of life and property in the nineteenth-century Ottoman Empire, culminating in the promulgation of an imperial Constitution in 1876.[3] The Constitution was suspended only two years later, and although it was reinstated in 1908, the empire itself disintegrated by the end of the following decade. The Turkish Republic, which emerged on the heels of the demise of the Ottoman Empire, was the product of one of the most spectacular transitions of political sovereignty in the Muslim world. Political leaders who guided the foundation of the republic touted national citizenship for the social and political freedoms it enabled. As with the leaders of many emergent national states in the twentieth century, Turkish republicans inscribed themselves within a political tradition that claimed the values of equality and liberty, but only by identifying political rights with national sovereignty.

The localization of rights within the nation was deeply problematic rather than self-evident. The late Ottoman and early republican regimes that propounded the notion of citizenship also policed the conditions of loyalty and belonging to the nation, often in violently exclusionary terms. Determinations about who constituted a national of a given state, and who was to be excluded from such nomination, were decided by assertions of state sovereignty and the unstable results of imperial warfare. From the late nineteenth century to World War I, the Ottoman Empire hemorrhaged much of its territory, from the Balkans, to the Levant and the Arabian peninsula, and across North Africa. Sizable non-Muslim communities, particularly Armenian and Greek Christian populations, were "exchanged," exiled, forcibly relocated, or systematically killed. In the process, a massive influx of Muslim refugees entered Anatolia from Greece and the Balkans. The first decades of the Turkish Republic continued this method of political intervention, forcibly displacing Kurdish populations for the sake of assimilating them to the linguistic and cultural norms that state authorities saw as befitting citizens of the new nation-state (Üngör 2011). This series of events, disturbingly regular as a form of state action, constituted the historical context for defining the Turkish nation, the political subject whose freedoms it protected, and the collective whose well-being it ensured. The freedoms heralded by national citizenship were premised on the violent repudiation of the ethno-religious pluralities that characterized Ottoman social and political life.

The dilemmas of political modernity in late Ottoman and early Turkish republican contexts were symptomatic of a broader political dynamic. Writing about the late nineteenth and early twentieth centuries, Hannah Arendt (1966: 272) detailed the historical consequences of "[combining] the declaration of the Rights of Man with national sovereignty": the development of refugees, asylum seekers, and the stateless as mass phenomena; the increasing exercise of state sovereignty in the practice of mass denationalization and expulsion; and the establishment of the category of minority as a permanent legal institution, in which the recognition of certain populations as remaining outside of normal legal protections was considered an enduring and lasting situation rather than a temporary exception to the norm. Nation-states across a wide geography, including those in western Europe and North America that are commonly seen as models of democracy, normalized the use of emergency powers as a means of politically dispossessing those now classed as internal enemies.[4] The consequent political form promised liberties and entitlements, but only to those defined as existing within the national community. For Arendt, the appearance of masses of individuals divested of political rights and unable to secure entitlements and protections signaled an impasse for a political tradition that aspired to provide inalienable rights of man.[5] The late Ottoman and early Turkish republican regimes were exemplary of, rather than exceptional to, the global norm.

For many commentators in Turkey today, the history of violence and exclusion that led to the establishment of the nation-state remains a crucial problem for democratic politics. Ergun Özbudun—a legal scholar and (at the time of writing) president of the academic committee charged with drafting a constitution to replace the one established after the 1980 military coup— submits that "the most fundamental problem facing the present-day Turkish democracy is to reconcile . . . social pluralism with an authoritarian state tradition that seeks to impose an artificial homogeneity, even uniformity, on the society" (Özbudun 2012: 70). Forced to negotiate between claims to social difference and the project of enforced homogeneity, democratic politics in the modern state contends with the legacies of a historical contradiction.

For political sociologist Çağlar Keyder, political liberalism offers the possibility of addressing this contradiction. Political liberalism, he claims, stands opposed to the authoritarian tradition of the republican state but does so without abandoning the project of political modernity altogether: "The current struggle in Turkey seems to be between the old authoritarian-modernizationist, paternalistic state, with its crumbling nationalist and populist legitimation, and a modernist conception of political liberalism and citizenship" (1997: 48). On this account, political liberalism loosens the grip that the paternalist state holds over the definition of national belonging, disarticulating citizenship from the arbitrary exercise of sovereign power. Liberalism, Keyder maintains, offers a credible response to the rise of Kurdish, Alevi, and Islamic movements, a response that would tame the demands of those movements away from separatism or militancy toward the exercise of rights within the framework of the law. He continues, "If the project of modernity is to divest itself of its modernizationist encumbrance, then political liberalization, ushering in civil rights and the rule of law, is the next step" (49). The task, then, would be to liberalize the historical project of modernity, or as Fuat Keyman (2007: xxvi) puts it, to make "Turkish modernity more societal, liberal, plural, and multicultural, [and to transform] Turkish democracy into a more consolidated and substantial democracy."[6]

What is striking is the fact that in the present day, liberalization is touted as a necessary means of democratization not only by certain minority groups and critical intellectuals, but also by the reigning regime. Mainstream Islamist political groups in Turkey that were once antagonistic to political and economic liberalization have come to adopt policy platforms that indicate an accommodation to, if not full embrace of, these processes.[7] For their part, secularist political groups that were long representative of the statist elite have begun to develop practices of self-representation defined within the framework of liberalization.[8] The concept of pluralism, moreover, has been at the center of these liberalizing rhetorics. Since 2001, the ruling Justice and Development Party (Adalet ve Kalkınma Partisi, AKP) has included "pluralism" (çoğulculuk) among the principal values of its official platform. More recently the major opposition party, the Republican People's Party (Cumhuriyet Halk Partisi, CHP), mentioned the term in its party agenda. Even the right-wing Nationalist Action Party (Milliyetçi Hareket Partisi, MHP), which sponsored violent assaults on Alevi communities in the late 1970s, has begun issuing statements about how best to recognize and institutionally accommodate religious plurality (Milliyet 2009). Pluralism has come to be invoked both by minorities and intellectuals critical of state practice and by those who wield the powers of the state. This variegated field suggests that the discourses of pluralism and liberalization are not simply about augmenting minority freedoms; rather, the political liberties they support are elements of a new mode of regulating social difference.

In the face of an apparent consensus about pluralism as a governing ideal, it is worth remaining vigilantly concrete about the institutional forms that liberalization has taken and the practices of political freedom it has enabled for minorities. Rather than imagining that pluralism has resolved, or even holds open the possibility of resolving, the historical tensions of Turkish modernity, we ought instead to investigate how discourses of pluralism have contributed to the reconfiguration of those tensions. What do contemporary formations of pluralism owe to the history of political violence they are otherwise meant to transcend? What forms of power animate the pluralist political subject?

TACTICS OF INCLUSION

The book centers its attention on the Alevis, who reportedly constitute approximately 15 percent of Turkey's total population.[9] Most Turkish citizens belong to the Sunni majority. Scholars of religious history argue that Alevism displays the influence of a number of different socio-religious traditions: Shi'i Islam, various forms of Islamic mysticism (especially Bektaşi Sufism), Central Asian shamanism, and expressions of Christianity found in Anatolia (Ocak 2004; Mélikoff 1998).[10] Many Alevis themselves disagree on how best to define their religious identity, and recent decades have witnessed the development of a heated community-internal debate about the nature of Alevi religious history, belief, and practice. The debate has led to the development of a number of relatively discrete orientations. To name just a few of the different stances that have been advocated by rival Alevi groups and organizations in recent years, one position identifies Alevism with Sufi Islam, another foregrounds the significance of Shi'ism, and yet another claims that Alevism is outside of Islam altogether.[11]

Until the second half of the twentieth century, most Alevi communities inhabited rural regions of southwestern, central, and eastern Anatolia. In both ethnic and linguistic terms, there is in fact no single Alevi community. The term "Alevi" is attributed to groups that cross ethnic lines, including Turks, Kurds, and Arabs. This preliminary typology can be segmented further. Among Kurdish Alevis, linguistic distinctions can be drawn between Zaza and Kurmanji speakers. Turkish Alevis are also internally differentiable on tribal and regional grounds. Some of the rituals of Alevis in southwestern Anatolia (often referred to as Tahtacıs) differ from those observed in central Anatolia. Given this variability, an anthropologist keen to avoid the dangers of essentialism might be encouraged to avoid the term "Alevi" altogether. However, the category has become socially legible and politically inescapable in contemporary Turkey. Indeed, the varied groups identified under its name have themselves embraced it in the course of the twentieth century.[12]

Many Alevi leaders today often insist that the community has been a cornerstone of Turkish secularism and democracy, supporting the nationalist revolution from its earliest days. Selmanpakoğlu's proclamation that Alevis constitute a foundational element of the Turkish nation-state represents one such claim. The claim can be misleading, however, to the extent that it projects back a ready association between Alevis and the early republican secularist elite. Very few, if any, Alevis were part of the political elite that constituted the nationalist vanguard in the 1910s and 1920s. Moreover, not all Alevi communities championed the Turkish state's nationalist modernization project. In the 1930s, the state's efforts to "Turkify" its population led to a massive military campaign against largely Kurdish Alevi communities in the eastern region of Dersim. Many Alevi communities were not, of course, subjected to this degree of military violence, but they nonetheless lacked the social, political, or economic capital to participate in state planning or national administration. Alevis were in fact objects of scrutiny and investigation by the late Ottoman and early republican state.

From the 1960s onward, the Turkish state heavily promoted processes of industrialization and urbanization. Many rural communities—both Sunni and Alevi—began migrating to city centers, finding work in industrial labor. For at least some Sunni migrants (or children of migrants), this would be a period of rapid growth. It was at this point that a new group of pious (*dindar*) Sunni businessmen, intellectuals, and politicians began to emerge, leaders who would eventually pose a serious challenge to the secularist elite. Over the past few decades, a religious Sunni middle class has integrated itself into mainstream Turkish society, active in public spheres previously dominated by secularist modes of consumption, fashion, and politics. Heiko Henkel (2005: 487–488) explains that "the most tangible aspect of this transformation is the triumph of the post-Islamist Justice and Development Party (AKP), which won a landslide victory in the 2002 elections [and again in 2007 and 2011] with a platform combining commitment to its roots in the Islamic tradition with a program of political liberalization." A political and economic elite constituted by pious Sunni Muslims has established itself in Turkey today, sitting at the head of several major corporations, business associations, media conglomerates, and political parties.[13] The same cannot easily be said of Alevis.

Certainly, newly urbanized Alevis in the 1960s entered institutions of mass education in larger numbers than ever before. They began to organize themselves in the idioms of modern politics, even establishing a short-lived political party.[14] Alevi youth grew increasingly active through the 1970s, especially through associations on the political Left. From the late 1980s on, as migrations to the city rapidly accelerated, Turkey witnessed a veritable explosion of Alevi intellectuals and organizations. While some continued to advocate a leftist politics, others focused on providing support to new migrants, promoting the rights and entitlements of Alevi communities against existing state policies, enacting and performing Alevi rituals in public urban spaces, and combatting negative representations of Alevism among the Sunni majority.[15]

Advances in education and political participation have not, however, led to the formation of an Alevi governing elite, as was the case with segments of the Sunni population. For many Alevis, the sense of political possibility opened up by the structural transformations of urbanization and mass education has been tempered by a concomitant history of sectarian violence and discrimination targeting the urbanizing minority. The late 1970s saw an escalation in civil violence around the country, particularly around Cold War binaries of leftist and right-wing groups. By the end of the decade, left-right conflicts manifested themselves in ethno-sectarian terms: in cities across central and eastern provinces, such as Çorum, Sivas, Malatya, and Kahramanmaraş, Alevi communities fell victim to systemic discrimination, harassment, and violence.[16] Although the military coup of 1980 and the period of martial law it imposed brought these events to an end, the episodic recurrence of communal violence in the 1990s suggested to many Alevis that sectarian animus had not, in fact, comfortably yielded to an ethos of social tolerance.[17]

The Alevi experience of Turkey's twentieth century—the century that witnessed the formation of the nation-state and its key ideologies of secularization, nationalization, and developmental modernization—has been decidedly uneasy, despite claims about the community's foundational role in those processes. Few, if any, individuals of Alevi descent were among the architects of the Turkish nation-state. Alevis have, of course, played a role in its development, but largely due to the fact that they have been targeted for militant attacks by those who viewed their exclusion as a condition of the nation's unity, courted by opportunistic political parties as an electoral constituency, or celebrated by state officials as bearers of national folklore. Alevis have been subjected to various governing strategies. If Turkey represents one of the Middle East's most aggressively forged secular nationalist states, the management of Alevi difference has formed one of its volatile edges for nearly a century.

While some Alevi intellectuals are outspoken critics of state policies and discriminatory attitudes on the part of the Sunni majority, the experience of vulnerability to violence has led many Alevis to abide by, rather than flout, norms of public expression regulated by the state. The sense of vulnerability goes some way to explaining why some Alevis invoke emblems of the modernist nation-state precisely when one might expect a challenge to its characteristic ideology of homogeneous citizenship. In a period of uncertainty, doing so secures a recognizable position within a statist discourse of governance.

In the twentieth century, Alevis were not subjected to physical repression alone. The violence and structural exclusion that shaped Alevi experiences of Turkish modernity were accompanied by a concomitant discourse of inclusion and belonging. They were located within an entire array of institutional deployments and forms of knowledge that enabled the construction of an image of Alevi religiosity congruent with nationalist discourses. Concerned to establish the historical and cultural legitimacy of the nascent Turkish nation's political sovereignty, late Ottoman and early republican intellectuals championed the Alevis as bearers of the nation's heritage (see chapter 3). Identifying Alevism as a token of the nation's past was one way of providing positive empirical evidence of the nation's historical depth and duration. The concerted effort to locate Alevism within the history of the Turkish nation only intensified in the second half of the twentieth century. Alevis were increasingly integrated into the industrial capitalist economy and became publicly visible in provincial and metropolitan centers. In the process, Alevi religion has become an openly debated topic of public discourse, although the forms of this discourse—its narrative structures, iconic tropes, and historical reference points—often presuppose institutionally entrenched notions of national history (see chapter 5). The governance of Alevi difference must be distinguished from the management of other structurally marginalized groups, such as Greek and Armenian Christians, who were by and large defined in the late Ottoman and republican periods as foreign to the nation. In contending with Alevi religious difference, the Turkish state has for the most part not sought to remove them but, rather, to set the terms of their domestication.

The growing inclusion of heterogeneous populations in public deliberation is neither simply an index of expanded political opportunity for disadvantaged groups nor a widening of the space of politics whereby power can be contested. It is the ground and target of a governmental logic that often perpetuates the political vulnerability of such groups. Increasingly and in many locales, the discourse of inclusion represents a modality of governance that disciplines the boundaries within which social difference is permitted to authenticate itself (Povinelli 2002; Hale 2002; Shryock 2004; Comaroff and Comaroff 2004; Sullivan 2005; Hankins 2012). It represents an element in the regulation of social, religious, and ethnic differences.

Within Turkey specifically, the tactics of inclusion have been reported in a number of contexts. For instance, Turkey's Jewish community is often pressured to display itself publicly as patriotic, and in the context of relations between Turkey and the European Union, it is called upon to demonstrate that it is in fact a tolerated minority (Brink-Danan 2010, 2011). Similarly, the Roma population in Turkey has recently found elements of its musical and dance repertoires embraced by the Turkish state as the " 'safe face' of cultural/ political pluralism" (Potuoğlu-Cook 2010: 101). Undocumented Bulgarian Turkish migrants have found avenues of limited political inclusion by claiming ethno-religious identification with the Turkish Muslim majority, a tactic that both fails to guarantee their social and economic rights and contributes to the vulnerability of other migrant groups (Parla 2011a, 2011b). In these cases, as with the Alevi examples discussed in this book, the rhetoric of inclusion consolidates rather than undermines social hierarchies, and it extends the state's authority to define the proper limits of social difference.

Throughout the twentieth century, the status of Alevis was defined in terms of both a history of violence and a discourse of inclusion. The latter has quite obviously failed to prevent the former. Yet I would also caution against a critique of existing rhetorics of inclusion as an ideological mask or as a limit to a more robust pluralism. Such a critique would too quickly look past the predicament that many Alevis find themselves compelled to confront: for the first time in Turkish republican history, they have attained a relatively stable footing in public spaces but only by means of nationalist discourses that have historically put the community in positions of vulnerability and risk. Many Alevi groups and individuals have to work through the terms of engagement that governmental apparatuses establish, the urban spaces they apportion, and the institutional mechanisms they make available, even as those discourses, spaces, and institutions carry the unsettling traces of a violent past.

The contradiction at work in the governance of Alevi difference—between a history of violence and exclusion, on the one hand, and a concerted development of technologies of inclusion and domestication, on the other—suggests that the tensions of political modernity discussed above have been restructured rather than overcome. Although apparently marginal in the nation, Alevis provide a privileged vantage point for scrutinizing the claims of pluralism and the mechanisms of power articulated around its invocation. They allow for a detailed exploration of the complex interlinkages that bind the freedoms of liberalization to the management of populations.

To conceptualize pluralism as a tactic of inclusion within a regime of governance requires attention to the regulated forms of social difference—its key terms, its discursive and affective modalities, and its sites of institutional manifestation and mooring. For many Alevis today, this assemblage of elements at once binds and empowers them. It creates tools of political maneuver and possibilities of political engagement for a community that has long been excluded from participation in state planning and policy formulation. Yet these empowering forces also set the terms of reference necessary for Alevi discourse to be validated as legitimate. They incite but also monitor and regulate displays of collective difference. Focused on the ambivalence of Alevi participation in public life, this book explores the intimate coupling of violence and modern political belonging, of domination and political inclusion. I examine the practice of pluralism, the forms of political authority that sustain it, and the limits it demarcates for those struggling within and against its discipline.

HISTORICISM AND THE TIME OF GOVERNANCE

The tensions of modernity are strikingly apparent in debates about the place of the Alevi community within Turkish national history. As indicated above, Alevis have acquired a legitimate public footing in the country today to the extent that they abide by the notion that their community represents the historical past of the nation. Far from being restricted to scholarly concerns alone, historicist interpretations of Alevism are freighted with tremendous ideological potency by state officials, politicians, journalists, and some community organizers alike. I examine this potency across the chapters of this book, and as such my use of the concept of historicism warrants a preliminary discussion.

Dipesh Chakrabarty (2000: 23) describes historicism as a "mode of thinking" that "tells us that in order to understand the nature of anything in this world we must see it as an historically developing entity, that is, first, as an individual and unique whole—as some kind of unity at least in potentia—and, second, as something that develops over time." Historicism defines a way of understanding the birth and evolution of social and political phenomena—whether these are legal statutes, ritual practices, or political communities. Its objects of investigation are conceived to be contextually particular, emergent at specific times and places, rather than transcendent of human action. They are understood to evolve over time in a linear fashion that can be represented

chronologically.[18] This mode of thinking not only undergirds historical scholarship; it has become a key element of modern politics and a premise of statist
narratives of national belonging in much of the world (B. Anderson [1983]
1991).

In this very broad sense of the term, historicist forms of knowledge have
been relevant in Turkey and in the Ottoman Empire that preceded it for at
least two centuries. By the middle of the nineteenth century, Ottoman historians had already begun to compose official imperial narratives that bore
a distinctly historicist cast (Hanioğlu 2008: 98).[19] In the late nineteenth and
early twentieth centuries, Ottoman intellectuals and officials promoted folkloric studies, seeking to recuperate and record the heritage of Anatolian peasants. Moreover, late Ottoman intellectuals like Ziya Gökalp and Mehmet Fuat
Köprülü studied the development of Turkic cultural and religious patterns
within a broadly evolutionary theoretical frame, inspired in part by western
European hypotheses about primitive religions. By the first decades of the
Turkish Republic, the state concertedly institutionalized historical narratives
of the nation, establishing councils and congresses whose explicit mandate
was to develop an official historiography.[20] Finally, in discussing Alevis themselves, we should not discount the significance that Marxist theories of historical progression attained for many urbanizing Alevi youth in the 1960s. Many
Alevis who were siding with the political Left at the time accused traditional
Alevi religious leaders (dedeler) of exercising a feudal mode of exploitation.
The significance of historicism lies less in any single attitude or political interest than in a palimpsest of associations, motivations, political movements,
and historical moments. Given the shifting terrain of historicism's social and
institutional presence, this study does not attempt to isolate its origin but
explores the regime of governance that it is made to support today.

It is well known that nation-states selectively appeal to history, often fab-
ricating and falsifying the historical record, creating and erasing historical
memories.[21] The construction of historical narrative is commonly understood
as part of the process by which states produce an image of a homogeneous
national people, united in a bond of fraternity. However, this notion of a
national people, posited by state pedagogy as the product of a deep and continuous historical development, remains contingent upon the conditions of its
invocation in the present. Any effort to fix the boundaries of a nation and its
people is vulnerable to the vicissitudes of contextual enactment. The historicism of the state's pedagogy remains dependent on performative conditions

that it cannot fully control (Bhabha 1994; Duara 1995). As a result, assertions of national unity often confront conflicting counternarratives, particularly of groups that claim contentious historical identifications.

Given the institutional entrenchments of the discourse of history in Turkey, it should not surprise that it has become a divisive political battleground. Contemporary Islamist political groups, for instance, have claimed a counternarrative of the nation's history in accordance with an Islamic rather than secularist past—by commemorating the Ottoman conquest of Istanbul or by claiming that early nationalists were in fact pious rather than aggressively secularist (Çınar 2005; Özyürek 2006). As numerous commentators have insisted, such efforts to redefine national history do not represent a reaction against modernity on the part of Islamist political groups; rather, they are better interpreted as constructing a form of modernity—an alternative modernity—that challenges the secular-nationalist elites who had occupied positions of administrative authority for much of the nation-state's history.[22] The production of a rival modernity entailed a process of commandeering the institutions of sovereign power in order to reconstruct the terms of citizenly belonging. But what of those for whom notions of modernity and citizenship continue to conjoin political liberties to mechanisms of state coercion, in an extraordinarily ambivalent embrace?

For the most part, the Alevi groups examined in this study are not overtly contributing to the project of an alternative modernity that is founded on a critique of the early republican state. On the contrary, they often appeal to the iconographic and historiographical forms authorized by the modernist, secular nation-state. The issue, I suggest, is not that Alevis have failed to understand the limits of the Kemalist state's dispensation of political life, but that they have not been in a position to dictate the terms of political modernity.[23] Their public expressions of collective memory are in significant measure made to comply with statist accounts of the past.

My claim is that, for nearly a century, state authorities have mobilized Alevism as an evidential sign, providing proof of the historical past of a Turkish national society. Alevism became relevant to institutions of modern governmentality in the past tense: neither as an emblem of the nation's present nor as an index of its future aspirations, but as a trace of its historical trajectory. Many Alevi organizations have been reluctant to fashion an antagonistic alternative to the already instituted secular-nationalist variant of Turkish modernity in part because their religious traditions have been slotted to serve as evidence of that modernity's historical formation.

This effect is not unique to the regime of governance found in Turkey. Modern modes of power have often exhibited a similar effect, managing expressions of social alterity by stipulating their temporal location. European colonial powers often legitimated their imperial presence by defining the colonized as belonging to an earlier historical era and in need of moral and political guidance (Fabian 1983; Comaroff and Comaroff 1991; Trouillot 2003; on contemporary settler colonialism, see Povinelli 2011). In the case of the Turkish nation-state, the temporal regimentation of social difference does not establish spatial distance, as in colonial regimes that imagined both a geographical and historical chasm between the metropole and the colony. Rather, Alevi difference is situated within the spatial imaginary of the nation. A critical analysis of citizenship in an era of pluralism requires attention to the ways in which cultural difference is spatially and temporally located within available narratives of the nation.

If the modern nation-state confronts narratives counter to its own ideological claims, it attempts to regulate that confrontation by allocating positions in its imagined past and present to its various populations. Public performances of Alevi tradition are often pressed into the service of confirming statist narratives of the nation's historical past. Governing powers calibrate the tense relationship between the pedagogical and performative temporalities of the nation that might otherwise serve as a source of political turbulence. What we find is neither a repression of Alevi difference in public space (an expectation born of a liberal imagining of pluralism) nor the eruption of a liberating counternarrative, but an incitement to publicly display communal traditions in the register of national historicism.

THE POLITICS OF MOURNING

In his genealogy of the secular, Talal Asad (2003: 43) maintains that in many nation-states "secular history's linear temporality has become the privileged measure of all time." The secular temporality of the nation has come to be authorized as the standard for judging the validity and authenticity of manifold social practices, including expressions of religious memory.[24] The somewhat sweeping nature of the claim (that it is the measure of *all* time) ought to be read, I argue, not as a definitive conclusion but rather as a provocation to further specify its points of application. Indeed, the authority of historicism commonly lurks as a tacit standard. A critical challenge is to identify sites where that authority is institutionally materialized and made visible.

By means of what sentiments, rhetorics, and practices has historicism's linear temporality become, not merely legitimate, but required as a condition of intelligibility for constituting a modern political subjectivity? What other forms of belonging and subjectivity are destabilized or rendered unsustainable in the process?

In order to approach these questions, I focus considerable attention on certain rituals that Alevis share with a community of practitioners that far exceeds the space-time of the Turkish nation. The rituals align with an Islamic geography that the state neither controls nor authorizes. Such practices involve an extensive array of devotional parables, rituals, and emotions with which to mourn the death of early Muslim martyrs, especially the death of Muhammad's grandson, Husayn, in the desert of Karbala. The narratives and parables of Karbala have occupied a central role in a major strand of the global Islamic revival, commonly associated with Shi'ism. Accounts of Husayn's martyrdom were invoked in the popular uprising against the shah of Iran in the late 1970s and by Lebanese Shi'i activists who protested Israel's invasion in the early 1980s. Ritual commemorations of his death have also become iconic of political possibilities and constraints for Shi'i communities in Pakistan, India, Iraq, Afghanistan, and elsewhere.

In contrast to what has otherwise emerged as a global resurgence of the rituals of Karbala, practices of lamentation in many Alevi milieux are sparsely attended. They do not form a primary site of political mobilization, as in other parts of the Shi'i world. Indeed, some of my Alevi interlocutors simply expressed disinterest in lamenting the deaths of early Muslim martyrs, viewing the act of ritual mourning as outdated and anachronistic in the present day. It might be tempting to view the relative disaffection with ritual mourning as the product of a secular outlook among many Alevis. Given the political stance of urban Alevis in recent decades, first as aligned with leftist politics in the 1970s and then in opposition to the rise of Islamist politics in the 1980s and 1990s, such an assessment seems to capture an important facet of Turkey's recent political history. However, it risks naturalizing the notion of a secular sensibility as such, viewing it as an achieved result, rather than a fraught and ongoing production in the present day. What disciplinary practices bolster the feeling that ritual lament is out of place in contemporary Alevi life and belongs to a different historical era? What institutional norms orient Alevi dispositions toward the past and present of their community? Attitudes to ritual lament and the apparently secular sensibility they manifest are constituted within a dense network of discursive forms, social practices, and political authorities (see chapter 2).

Despite the fact that ritual mourning is not overtly politicized by Alevi groups, questions about whether the lives and deaths of Shi'i martyrs are formative of the Alevi past and relevant to the Alevi present remain deeply contentious. In their connection with a Shi'i geography, Alevi mourning rituals have not been readily supported by the forms of Sunni Islam practiced by Turkey's majority population and the forms of religiosity that the Turkish state sanctions as properly Islamic. Over the past few decades, state agencies, journalists, scholars, and public intellectuals have paid close attention to public expressions of the community's rituals. The presence of these mostly non-Alevi figures at Alevi events is touted by some state officials as a sign of growing tolerance and acceptance of sectarian difference, but it is perceived by many Alevi organizers as a form of institutional surveillance. When under the gaze of state authorities or standing before a journalist's lens, Alevi leaders often discourage emotionally charged devotional practices that involve cursing figures of Islamic antiquity who are revered by pious members of the Sunni majority. The regimentation of public enactments of ritual mourning represents a crucial element in the domestication of Alevi difference.

Rendering communal difference intelligible as an object of national historicism manifests itself *as a sociopolitical task* in disputes over the propriety and significance of public displays of Alevi lament. Precisely because such practices derive from a community of practitioners whose geography and history do not coincide with narratives of the Turkish nation and its projected historical past, they have continually posed a problem to the forms of knowledge and of moral unity promoted by the Turkish state (see chapter 3). Practices of mourning unsettle institutionally recognized modalities of Alevi difference, eliciting concerted intervention by state authorities. As an element in a strategy of governance, the absenting of mourning from contemporary Alevi life allows for a clear demarcation of Turkey's Alevis from the wider Islamic geography that otherwise shares in this tradition of devotional expression. It generates a frontier against which to claim Alevism as a foundational element of the Turkish nation.

Focusing on the apparatuses of management mobilized around ritual lament enables an interrogation of the political energy invested in establishing Alevi difference as a sign of the nation's past. It allows us to reframe this political project, not merely as fostering tolerance and unity, but as actively silencing forms of ethical and political belonging that exceed the boundaries of the nation.

TRAJECTORIES

Across the chapters of this book, I explore various ways in which Alevis are encouraged to assert their presence in public life through state-authorized narratives of political belonging. I begin in chapter 2 by examining the ambivalent embrace of modernity among Turkey's Alevis. Many Alevis, especially urban youth, position themselves as secular and modern. They often view religious rituals, including community specific traditions of lamentation, as irrelevant to the sociopolitical demands of the present day. Yet this self-positioning is more uncertain than the rhetoric of irrelevance suggests. It is implicated in the institutional regulation of social difference, a point that I elaborate by turning to the management of public displays of Alevi tradition. Such events are commonly attended by journalists and political officials, and their presence often discourages Alevi participants from performing practices of devotional mourning. Several of my Alevi interlocutors felt that the act of mourning was inappropriate in a context documented by news media and attended by state dignitaries. In a more apprehensive tone, an Alevi organizer maintained that absenting lament from public display was one method of furthering national unity. The ethnographic material indicates how institutional pressures orient Alevi sensibilities toward their ritual traditions.

If some Alevis justify the absenting of lament in moments of public display by claiming that they need to demonstrate national harmony, it is worth asking why they are burdened with this requirement in the first place. In part, the concern with self-presentation may be understood as a tactic of a persecuted minority—a way of avoiding majoritarian hostility or state repression. Yet a functionalist explanation elides a pressing historical question: how did the discourse of national unity first emerge and how was it made to apply to representations of Alevi religiosity? What do discourses of pluralism today owe to political conditions established in the course of that history?

Chapter 3 attends to these questions by providing a genealogy of modern citizenship in Turkey, turning back to the late nineteenth and early twentieth centuries, when the Ottoman Empire collapsed and the Turkish nation-state emerged in its wake. The analysis emphasizes the forms of knowledge that anchored the production of new terms of political belonging in the national republic. I examine the moment when late Ottoman administrators and intellectuals, actors who would eventually become ideologues of the new nation-state, directed their attention to the Alevi community, viewing it as a trace of the nation's cultural history. They began to produce historiographical and ethnographic knowledge of Alevism, locating the religious history of the community within the developmental trajectory of the nation. Elements of Alevi religiosity that did not conform to this temporalization, particularly those that involved Shiʻi traditions of lament, were effectively eliminated from the institutionalized production of knowledge about Alevism. The silencing of Alevi mourning suggests that national citizenship is premised not only on the production of certain emblems of loyalty, but also on the elision of alternative emotive repertoires. Alevism came to be championed by early nationalist elites, who were bent on disqualifying modes of commemorating Alevi pasts that did not conform to emerging narratives of the nation.

Chapter 4 moves the historical account forward to the second half of the twentieth century. It reframes the political-economic liberalization project that Turkey has undertaken in the past three decades. Rather than viewing this liberalization as easing restrictions on minority expression, I demonstrate how it has entailed a concerted reinvestment of governmental resources in the management of communal differences. I focus on how the traditional Alevi dance of the *semah* is commonly promoted by public officials as an element of Turkey's folkloric heritage, often performed as an act of entertainment that is widely perceived to be palatable and pleasing to a national audience. The governance of Alevi difference functions, not merely through explicit ideological assertion, but through the aesthetics of its public enactment—where it is sited and circulated, who performs it, and with what adornments and associated sensibilities. The ethos and aesthetics of public Alevi performance reveal a disciplining of national belonging in precisely those moments that are otherwise seen to signal a pluralization of the public sphere. Processes of liberalization have, to a degree, enabled demands for collective rights in the name of equal citizenship, but this expansion of the discourse of rights must be understood in relation to its conditions of social and material expression. Governmental powers invest in the way that liberalizing energies can be released, congealed in aesthetic form, and put on public display.

Chapter 5 reveals a central mechanism of political power at work in discourses of pluralism, in which modern forms of historical knowledge are operationalized to govern religious difference. If in the early twentieth century nationalist elites actively sought to historicize Alevism in their efforts at constructing a Turkish nation, by the late twentieth century, with mass migrations of Alevis into urban settings, a new governmental imperative emerged: to demand that Alevis themselves historicize their pasts within the narrative trajectory of the nation. I trace connections between various practices of historicization, including the use of religious and national icons that create visual historical narratives, the writing of communal histories by a new class of Alevi intellectuals, and authorized public enactments of Alevi collective memory. Taken together, these practices indicate a form of self-fashioning through a modernist consciousness of history. A close ethnographic examination of such practices also reveals the persistence of certain forms of emotional expression (such as ritual cursing and weeping) that unsettle historicist renditions of the religious past. Various scholarly and political authorities committed to a rigorous historicization of Alevi religiosity seek to regulate, and in some cases to silence, these traditions of affective subjectivity. The chapter examines how the iconographic forms and textual genres that have enabled the historicization of Alevi pasts have also provided mechanisms for regimenting the terms of acceptable difference.

Having described in the course of the preceding chapters the production of legitimated modes of Alevi expression and the historicizing disciplines this has required, I turn my attention in chapter 6 to efforts by an Alevi group to scrutinize the discursive and aesthetic media of their public participation. The group that I focus on in this chapter is one that appeals to Shi'i traditions of devotional piety, including especially the forms of ritual lament commonly excluded from public Alevi performance. I describe how this group attempts to gain critical leverage on the forms of subjectivity that national historicism has made available to them. Repeatedly performing practices of lament across the calendar year, the group seeks to produce a form of collective memory that does not abide by the historicist temporalities of the nation. The group's practices provoke a tremendous amount of controversy, among state officials and many other Alevi organizations alike, not for expressly violating the law but for transgressing legitimated forms of collective belonging.

As a whole, the book offers a reflection on modern political authority in an era of pluralism. The modernist trope of a homogeneous national body—one that does not support distinctions of race, religion, ethnicity, and so on—has been central to the discourse of equal citizenship in Turkey. The constitutional discourse of equal rights of citizenship was mounted upon a form of political authority invested in promoting social cohesion and a unitary national body. The recent rise of pluralism as a salient political discourse has intensified rather than resolved the tension between the rights of citizenship and the state's authority to define the terms of national unity. Liberalization and the forms of pluralism it has enabled have loosened certain restrictions on marginalized groups, but only by means of an institutional solicitation of their commitment to statist narratives of national modernity. This paradox of contemporary pluralism places such groups in an extraordinary bind, in which the available practices of self-representation are secured by institutional powers that contribute to their political vulnerability.

In identifying some of the limits of pluralism, my purpose is not to denounce the failures of a political project. Rather, my goal is to open a space for conceptualizing a certain kind of politics that arises in relation to these limits. The politics in question contests the way that forms of public speech and spaces of public visibility are distributed unequally and unevenly within the social body. In the Conclusion, I describe these modes of politicization as challenges to the normative formation of republican citizenship.

ETHNOGRAPHIC LOCATIONS

This book is based on ethnographic field research conducted largely between 2005 and 2007. My fieldwork began in Ankara, but most of the research was conducted over seventeen months in the provincial town of Çorum. Located south of the Black Sea and east of Ankara, Çorum has approximately two hundred thousand inhabitants. I initially selected Çorum as the primary site of my research because the city is spatially organized along sectarian lines. Most Alevis who inhabit the urban space reside within a single, delimited area, constituting what locals refer to as an "Alevi neighborhood" (*Alevi mahallesi*). The neighborhood is located in the eastern end of the city, bounded to the northwest and the southwest by perpendicular avenues that intersect in the center of town. While it is not uncommon to find urban spaces divided along sectarian lines in many cities around the country, Çorum is unique to the degree that it is separated into two sides along a single divide. As one friend explained to me, "it is as though the Berlin wall divides the city."

Most Alevis either migrated from villages to the city or were born to parents who undertook this migration. Relatively few are more than one generation removed from rural origins. During the 1960s and 1970s, Alevis and many Sunnis migrated to urban spaces, such as Çorum, larger Turkish cities like Istanbul, Ankara, and Izmir, and cities abroad, in Europe and the Arabian peninsula. Rapid state-led industrialization was the principal motor of this pattern of migration, and industrial labor was the primary vehicle. The state protected domestic industries by imposing high tariffs on imports. In Çorum, the state's policies first resulted in the production of a cement factory. Later, brick and tile factories and a large state-run sugar factory were opened, and countless flour mills and egg-production facilities followed. Çorum today continues to find a role in the national economy as a producer of bricks, tile, and industrial machinery, and as a known source of construction workers. It is not uncommon to find retired laborers who spend half of the year in Germany with their now-grown children and half of the year in Çorum.

It was only in 1980 that the city came to be divided by sectarian affiliation. Civil unrest was widespread throughout the country in the late 1970s. Within provinces of central and eastern Anatolia, where Alevi populations had increasingly resettled in urban settings, Cold War polarizations of Left and Right came to be popularly identified with the denominational categories, Alevi and Sunni. Far-right nationalist organizations, largely organized within the Sunni community, came to view Alevis with suspicion, identifying them with the communist Left. Some of these organizations spawned militia groups, which coordinated a series of attacks on Alevi-owned stores and businesses. Right-wing militias confronted newly urbanizing Alevi communities with tactics of intimidation, physical harassment, and violent assault. Çorum was the last of a series of central and eastern Anatolian towns to witness sectarian violence, reaching its peak in the summer of 1980. Most Alevis in Çorum fled to one barricaded neighborhood in search of protection. The violence was brought to an end only with the imposition of martial law and the military coup in September of that year.

In the 1980s and 1990s, the Alevi neighborhood grew and developed. Progressive migration to the city has increased the population density and the size of the neighborhood. New forms of state investment and private capital have led to an expansion of the telecommunications network, the construction of natural-gas lines, and the building of banks, branches of the post office, cafes, and high-rise apartment complexes. By the mid-1980s, the population of the city outgrew that of the villages of Çorum Province, and it was at that point that the rural village population began to progressively decline. While Sunni villages were affected by this accelerated phase of migration, the presence of Sunni Muslims in the city of Çorum was nothing new. By contrast, the increasing presence of migrants from Alevi villages made the Alevi population numerically significant only from the 1980s onward.

In the aftermath of the 1980 coup, the spatialization of sectarian difference remained, even if overt hostilities had been brought to an end. The Alevi
population has since increased to the extent that it occupies not one but five
adjacent administrative neighborhoods. In the imaginary of many inhabitants, however, the area still retains its singularity as *the* Alevi neighborhood.
In popular parlance, the Alevi neighborhood is spatially denoted as *yukarı
taraf,* or the upper side, a reference to the gently ascending slope on which one
end of the neighborhood rests. The Sunni portions of town, contrastively, are
referred to as *aşağı taraf,* the lower side. These terms are frequently used to
provide a spatial index for sectarian identity.

At its western edge, the Alevi neighborhood stretches the sprawling frontier of the town itself. Streets shooting off of the main avenue often crumble
into dirt paths. Most of the buildings here are of relatively recent origin, the
product of either hasty and poor construction or of a new expansion in finan-
cial investment. A shabby, one-story single family home with concrete floors
and coal-fired heating sits alongside an eight-story apartment building, boast-
ing tiled floors and natural gas. Small fruit stands compete with a large corpo-
rate supermarket. Several small health clinics have opened up in recent years,
and a few elementary schools were built in the 1980s.

One piece of this broad, if uneven, urban development has been the emergence of several organizations claiming to represent Alevism. Some organizations provide after-school activities for local youth, involving lessons in dance
and music long associated with traditional Alevi rituals. Others represent
local branches of national organizations, charged with the task of hosting
important events on the ritual calendar for the Alevi community, including
annual commemorations of the death of Husayn. Also located in the neighborhood is the Alevi group mentioned above that follows the doctrines and
practices of Shi'i Islam. None of these organizations existed prior to the 1980s,
and most emerged only in the late 1990s or thereafter. They are products of the
same history of industrial urbanization that led to the sectarian spatialization
of the town.

Since the 1990s, the state has also constructed several mosques in the area,
organized under the official auspices of the Directorate of Religious Affairs.
From the perspective of the Directorate of Religious Affairs, the mosque is
an institution that adequately represents the religious needs of all of its Muslim citizenry, whether Sunni or Alevi. This stance is by no means politically
innocent. Many Alevi organizations have insisted that the state's mosques

reflect the traditions of the Sunni majority and have argued that the building of mosques in Alevi villages and neighborhoods reflects a politics of assimilation. In the context of a town that has witnessed sectarian violence, followed by a sectarian separation of neighborhoods, the building of mosques has been viewed by critics as a concerted intervention in the governance of an Alevi space.

Çorum is distant from the metropolitan centers of political and intellectual life. Major cities such as Istanbul and Ankara are the loci where an Alevi politics is being most explicitly and vibrantly formulated, where intellectuals meet with officials from the European Union, and where protests against state policy increasingly occupy city streets. However, the provincial focus of this study need not detract from its critical purchase. Michael Meeker (1994a) argues that in the aftermath of decades of urbanization it is the provincial town—rather than either the village or the metropole—that has come definitively to represent Turkey's political present.[25] Moreover, the relocation of ethnographic attention from metropole to province invites a certain analytical displacement: instead of locating the politics of pluralism within ongoing battles over state initiatives—battles, for instance, over legal and constitutional mandates—this book identifies pluralism within its material and pragmatic limbs, in the organization of urban and rural spaces, in the cultivation of an ethos of public performance, and in the supervision and patterned elision of ritual mourning. An analysis of pluralism in a setting where the history of sectarian violence remains palpably inscribed on the urban landscape throws these processes into sharp relief. Assessing pluralism from this provincial edge calls for an excavation of its governing imperatives amid the affective sensibilities it attempts to foster and the silences it seeks to effect.

2 DISCIPLINES OF THE PARABLE

IN THE COURSE OF MY fieldwork I attended a number of Alevi rituals of lament. Participants collectively wept as they listened to accounts of the martyrdom of revered figures from early Islamic history. Weeping was particularly intense when stories centered on the Prophet Muhammad's kin. Practices of mourning drew my attention for a number of reasons. Like many observers of such practices—practices that Turkey's Alevis share with Shi'i Muslims elsewhere in the world—I was struck by the emotional intensity participants brought to the task of listening to narratives of early Islam. As a reciter described the virtuous lives and deaths of the martyrs, audience members would hold their heads in their hands and, often enough, begin to weep. Occasionally participants would cry out curses upon the oppressors of Muhammad and his family.

The emotional display was affecting, even to an outside observer like myself. After attending a few gatherings, I asked a couple of participants if they would allow me to record the laments, also known as *mersiye*. Agreeing to my request, Ayfer hanım and Ali amca met me a few days later at a local Alevi organization's building.[1] Both individuals were elderly and retired. Ayfer hanım spent much of her time volunteering at the Alevi organization, cleaning, cooking, and participating in events both big and small. She lived in a modest, coal-heated house just down the road and was entrusted with the keys to the organization's building. Ali amca was retired from a life of factory work. As with many Alevi men his age, he had worked for a time as an industrial laborer in Germany, then returned to Çorum. At the Alevi organization, he was recognized as an *aşık*, that is, as the reciter of the ritual laments.

We sat in a quiet room, secluded from the sounds of traffic outside. Ali amca recited a few mersiye about the events leading up to the death of Husayn, Muhammad's grandson. He related an emotional account of the torments that Husayn and his companions suffered in the desert of Karbala. Ayfer hanım did not join in the recitation, but neither did she remain silent. She would occasionally interject a curse upon Husayn's oppressors, and eventually she began to weep. Neither the curses nor the weeping appeared to interrupt Ali amca's recitation. They were expected elements of the lament itself.

Cursing and weeping are important components of the formal practice of ritual mourning. Like the narratives of Husayn's death to which they respond, such practices derive from a deep history and a wide geography, not restricted to any given locale or national context, and often connected with traditions of Islam associated with Shi'ism. Given the wide geohistorical foundation of the practice of lament, I was struck by the fact that the mersiye recited by Ali amca was in Turkish. Responding to a question about where the mersiye originated, Ali amca initially explained that they derive from a long history of aşıks, but this answer only called for further explication—where did the aşıks come from? I pressed them to specify a bit more. Were they specific to the cultural and historical milieux of Anatolia? Ayfer hanım took up the question: "No, everyone recites the same mersiye—Muslims in Iran, in Iraq, in Pakistan." She evoked a community of practice that is not restricted to the space-time of the nation but extends across a global geography.

The emotions and interpretations offered by these interlocutors are at once exemplary and out of place among Alevis in Turkey today. They are exemplary in the sense that they reflect ritual understandings that are recognized by most scholars and Alevis alike as belonging to the community's history. Many Alevi intellectuals who have attempted in recent decades to compose social histories of the community often include an account of the battle of Karbala and the death of Husayn. With the recent rise of such communal histories, Alevi narratives of early Islam have acquired a new mode of publication and dissemination, accessible to a national reading public. Given the recent expansion of the narrative's textual circulation, one might expect an upsurge in the scale and frequency of devotional narrations.

Yet the emotions displayed by Ayfer hanım and Ali amca do not appear to be widely cultivated or provoked in contemporary Alevi neighborhoods, like the one in which I conducted fieldwork. Sparsely attended, events organized by Alevi organizations for the sake of ritual lamentation involved anywhere from ten to fifteen participants at the low end and up to several hundred at larger gatherings.[2] In contrast to many other parts of the Shi'i Muslim world, where events of commemoration generate mass public audiences, Turkey's Alevi community has not witnessed a resurgence in performances of ritual lament. Instead, most of my Alevi interlocutors expressed skepticism as to the ongoing propriety and relevance of such practices in the present day. When I questioned Alevis who were not participants in devotional commemorations of Husayn's death, I was often told that weeping for Husayn was common one or two generations earlier, when Alevis still lived largely in rural settings, but that it is no longer relevant in the present day. Many urban Alevis, especially youth, view ritual lamentation as anachronistic, incongruent with and irrelevant to the social and political contexts of the contemporary world.

In this chapter, I examine claims about the irrelevance of lament in order to probe the political ambivalence of pluralism in Turkey. Over the past few decades, Alevis have grown increasingly vocal about ritual traditions that distinguish them from the Sunni majority. For many observers, declarations of Alevi identity and public enactments of Alevi ritual herald the promise of a new pluralism in contemporary Turkey. What, then, accounts for the absence of a principal practice of devotional piety—the ritual of mourning—in a moment of voluble self-assertion? What forms of institutional power are articulated at this conjuncture, where assertive reflexivity on the public stage involves, not just a putting forward of collective identity, but a concomitant redaction?

Lingering on the status of devotional mourning among Alevis today, I juxtapose two ethnographic accounts of the absence of lament. First, I explore the rhetorics by which Alevis of different ages and genders declare the irrelevance and anachronism of mourning practices. The significance of such rhetorics lies in the social and political location they provide for the speaker: the relegation of a certain practice to the community's past provides a flashpoint, a material location for defining one's own modernity in a narrative of historical progress. For some Alevis, the anachronism of lament and the historical break it reveals are preconditions of modern social life and political agency.[3]

Other Alevis, however, encounter the absenting of lament not simply as a rhetorical strategy in a narrative of social progress but as an institutional norm, ballasted by state authorities, political parties, and representatives of news media. In the second half of the chapter, I turn to a commemorative event hosted by a local Alevi organization, where the presence of journalists and state officials effectively silenced the act of mourning. The decision of local Alevis not to mourn while under public scrutiny was guided by the sense that these practices might be perceived to be publicly inappropriate and a threat to national unity. The pressures placed on public displays of Alevism reposition the ritual from one that evokes a potentially global community of practitioners, as in Ayfer hanım's statement, to one that bears the burden of indexing the nation's unity. My reading of the commemorative event suggests that, for some Alevis, sentiments about the irrelevance of lament are regimented by disciplinary powers that demand conformity to statist norms of national cohesion.

The chapter draws together two seemingly distinct, if not completely heterogeneous, experiences of modernity: one characterized by narratives of progressive historical development and the other forged by institutional practices aimed at policing national unity and integrity. My aim in indicating a relationship between these two ethnographic moments is not to annul the salience of the modernist narrative of historical progress but to situate that salience within a field of institutional power. The ethnographic juxtaposition reveals the abiding political anxieties that shadow Alevi engagements with the discourses of modernity. It indicates a disciplinary impetus that orients the possibilities of pluralism in Turkey today.

ECONOMIES OF DISCIPLINE

Historically, Alevis in Turkey have shared with Shi'i communities elsewhere in the world an allegiance to certain narratives of early Islamic history that depict the sufferings of Muhammad's family after his death. Despite regional and historical differences, these various communities maintain a relatively shared understanding of the moral and political calamities confronted by the Muslim community in the aftermath of the Prophet's death. According to these accounts, members of Muhammad's intimate family—often referenced with the phrase *ahl al-bayt*—were physically, financially, or politically mistreated in the post-Prophetic period. Such accounts report that Muhammad's daughter Fatima was stripped of land left to her by her father and physically and verbally abused by political leaders. Muhammad's cousin (also Fatima's husband), Ali ibn Abi Talib, made claims to leadership over the community that were long overlooked. After finally rising to leadership, Ali was soon killed. For the next few centuries, his male descendants would each face similar martyrdom. For many Alevis and Shi'is, Ali and his descendants—known collectively as the Twelve Imams—were the rightful heirs to political leadership of the Muslim community after Muhammad's death and also principal sources of religious knowledge and moral exemplars for Muslims to emulate.[4]

An elaborate martyrology centered on the Twelve Imams distinguishes Alevi-Shiʿi schools of thought from the various forms of Sunni Islam. It establishes a key point of separation between two narrative accounts of Islamic history. More than that, in its narration it also reveals a range of commemorative practices that differentiate Alevis and Shiʿis from their Sunni counterparts. Alevis and Shiʿis have developed a set of rituals in which this history is narrated, accompanied by emotional expressions of mourning, such as weeping, cursing, and flagellation. Across spaces and times, one finds a variety of distinctive practices and, at times, conflicting attitudes toward those practices. Alevis in Turkey form with Shiʿis in other parts of the globe and across history both a community of practice and a community of argument about those practices. What is shared across regional differences is the basic premise that ritually mourning the deaths of early Islamic martyrs is morally virtuous, even if there are extensive and often heated disagreements about how best to do so.

Historical evidence suggests that Alevi communities across Anatolia have long commemorated the martyrs of early Islam. These practices took place in a context in which commemorations for the Twelve Imams not only lacked the sort of state sponsorship found in neighboring Iran but were often actively condemned by Ottoman state authorities, at least in the sixteenth and seventeenth centuries (Cole 2002; Imber 1979; İnalcık 1994; Ocak 1991; Zarinebaf-Shahr 1997). Certain public theatrical representations (ta'ziyeh) that developed in Iran were absent in Turkey. "[I]n Anatolia," Metin And (1979: 238) comments, "there is no tradition of Ta'ziyeh performances, since the Sunni element is predominant there."[5]

Prominent among Alevis are practices of fasting and other forms of abstinence, particularly during the month of Muharram, when the death of Ali's son Husayn in the desert of Karbala is commemorated. Metin And (1979: 244) offers a meticulous description, based on ethnographic observations of an Alevi village in the 1970s:

> While observing the fast, no bad word must be said, nor any harm done to anyone, nor any living thing killed. Therefore, one must abstain from fish, meat, eggs and fowl. . . . During the fasting period when people confront one another,

as a salutation they say, *Yuh Münkire!* (Shame on disbelievers!), and the other will reply, *Lanet Yezide!* (Cursed be Yazid [the figure responsible for killing Husayn]!). . . . There are other abstinences which are acts of mourning. . . . They do not wash or change their underclothing; they do not use soap; they do not shave. . . . [T]hey do not sing, play a musical instrument, dance, laugh or amuse themselves. They do not drink alcoholic beverages, do not kill bugs such as lice and fleas, do not have sexual intercourse, and abstain from inhaling tobacco.

The emphasis on abstention—from certain foods, certain forms of entertainment and pleasure, and certain practices of hygiene—suggests a carefully cultivated ascetic sensibility, driven by an extensive economy of discipline.

Metin And's account from 1979 accords well with a much earlier description of Alevi practices by Yusuf Ziya Yörükan in the 1930s. Yörükan also describes ascetic practices of hygiene and consumption, represented through prohibitions on cleaning one's clothes, on shaving, and on eating meat and fowl. In conjunction with such practices, the disposition and bearing of the self appears to be an element of the repertoire of lamentation: "A man mustn't crave anything while in mourning" (Yörükan 1998: 288). Yörükan's discussion is suggestive, but it remains largely restricted to an understanding of such practices as inhibiting, rather than cultivating, the desires and drives of the subject in mourning.

Traditions of mourning present a complex arrangement of variegated elements, including both historical narratives of early Islam and the narration of such historical accounts in rituals of lament. Michael Fischer's (1980) discussion of the mourning tradition provides a robust conceptual formulation for grappling with the complexity and variety of its constituent elements. He terms this tradition "the Karbala paradigm," in reference to the narrative's emotional climax with the martyrdom of Husayn in Karbala. The valor and death of Husayn are the primary emotional pivots driving most accounts of the narrative, but in its various recitations, the narrative can emphasize aspects of Islamic history that precede or follow his struggles. As Fischer points out, Shi'i communities narrate the story throughout the year in commemoration of a number of events that transpired in the early Islamic community, from episodes in the life of Muhammad down to the struggles and deaths of his descendants across several centuries.

Fischer favors the term "paradigm" to the common alternative, "passion," for the story of Karbala in order to emphasize how it operates as a rhetorical device. The story "provides models for living and a mnemonic for thinking about how to live: there is a set of parables and moral lessons all connected with or part of the story of Karbala which are themselves not obviously contradictory and to which almost all of life's problems can be referred" (Fischer 1980: 21). The story of Karbala provides a reservoir of tales and lessons, which in the telling are related to ethical problems encountered in the present.

The emphasis on rhetoric—that is, on the discursive organization and operationalization of the story—allows for a comparative perspective on the cultural variations that have shaped and voiced the Karbala narratives in the numerous historical and regional contexts in which they have flourished. Invocations of the moral parables of Karbala have, in this sense, borne the marks of a wide variety of ritual occasions. In some Shi'i communities, the narrative is expressed through corporeally expressive practices, such as chest beating or bloody flagellation with chains and razors. Other communities distance themselves from self-flagellation, focusing more heavily on acts of weeping and cursing. The Karbala narrative itself has a rich historical and social life.

Fischer's notion of a paradigm usefully brings together ideas about the morality of the story with the rituals of telling the story, the narratives of early Islamic history with practices of commemorative narration. However, it tells us less about the social labor involved in making these articulations or their multifarious interconnections. What, for instance, are some of the social and ethical consequences of narrating the events of Karbala in the form of a written, academic historiographical text, rather than in sermonic oratory in a mosque? What expectations do hearers or readers bring to the narrative in either case? Are disciplines of mourning and acts of cursing appropriate to any such setting? What obligations and responsibilities is the writer/reciter held to by virtue of the genre of utterance? The excellence of narration in the case of sermonic oratory, for example, may be measured by the intensity of passion elicited in members of the audience—passions that in the context of academic writings and lectures might be construed as signs of immoderation and irrationality.

I mean to draw attention to the dual character of such narratives. As Richard Bauman (1986: 2) succinctly states, "narratives are keyed both to the events in which they are told and to the events that they recount, toward narrative events and narrated events." In Karbala commemorations, the narrated events concern early Islamic history, the martyrdom of the Twelve Imams, and especially the Battle of Karbala. The narrative events—that is, the events of narration in which the parables of Karbala are related—are widely varied: formal academic lectures, elaborate rituals enacted in a mosque, somber scenes in a local civil society organization, publicly staged spectacles, and so on. From one context of narration to the next, conventions for how one ought to recite or respond to the narrative shift. The articulation between narrative text and the traditional disciplines of narration deserves close ethnographic attention. In many Alevi milieux the narrative has come untethered from long-standing ritual practices of narration.

RHETORICS OF ANACHRONISM

There is by now a deep tradition of anthropological scholarship that has sought to raise and answer questions about why social groups engage in ritually orchestrated acts of collective weeping. The issue was central to Durkheim's sociology of religion, where he examined the social function and formal patterning of weeping: "Mourning is not the spontaneous expression of individual emotions. . . . Mourning is not the natural response of a private sensibility hurt by a cruel loss. It is an obligation imposed by the group" (Durkheim 1995: 400–401).[6] Echoing the Durkheimian tradition, Greg Urban (1988) argued that ritual wailing functions both to express the affects of mourning and the "meta-affects" that call attention to the social acceptability of the form of expression. Recent anthropological scholarship has further detailed the variable cultural and discursive anchors of lamentation practices (Abu-Lughod 1993; Feld 1990a) and the potential for such practices to either consolidate or provoke resistance to reigning sociopolitical ideologies (Goluboff 2008; Seremetakis 1991).

Aware of the long dialogue of anthropological work on lamentation, I started attending Alevi rituals of lament when I could find them. At one ritual commemoration that I attended, held in honor of Muhammad's daughter Fatima, I asked some participants why they wept. In the years since I posed that question, I have come to view it as poorly formulated or at least ambiguous as to its aim. Was I seeking a historical explanation of the rituals' origins or an interpretive explanation of the symbolic meaning of weeping? Or did I hope to elicit a response that would situate weeping within a broader economy of moral discipline that participants applied in their daily lives? Perhaps I simply wanted some insight into how participants could be so moved by the story of a figure from the seventh century. One respondent at this event, Muzaffer, patiently indulged my curiosity and offered an explanation to my otherwise unfocused question: "We think of Fatima in the same way that we think of our own mothers. Wouldn't you cry if your mother suffered these abuses?" Rather than clarifying the matter for me, the response raised a new set of questions: Why would one consider the seventh-century figure akin to one's mother? What would be necessary to affix the affective bonds held for one's immediate kin to a personage known only through narratives of deep antiquity?

I was not alone in contemplating such questions. Many of my Alevi interlocutors expressed disinterest in the disciplines of ritual narration, or they reported an inability to fathom the significance that weeping, cursing, and mourning for early Muslim martyrs might hold for their lives today. As I began to reflect on the insistence with which many Alevis distanced themselves from such practices, I came to reconsider the question I had been posing—not the problem of why participants in ritual lamentation weep for Husayn and his companions, but rather why so many others insist that they cannot weep. I started to wonder what work is performed by rhetorically staging the irrelevance of lament.

It is worth emphasizing that there is no single attitude or disposition held by all Alevis toward ritual lament. I seek nevertheless to point to some broad social patterns that I began to notice in the course of my research, specifically regarding the sense that practices of mourning belong to the community's past. Key to my discussion is the fact that such attitudes tend not to involve a dismissal or critique of the story of Karbala as such. Indeed, many Alevi organizations host events that enact the narrative, and Alevi intellectuals and ordinary individuals continue to write or read narrative accounts that depict aspects of Husayn's death at Karbala.[7] These events and writings are elements of a larger process that has taken place over the past few decades, in which Alevis have energetically begun to participate in public discourses on their community's history, religiosity, and politics. In this regard, the Alevi community is undergoing something akin to what scholars have described as a process of "objectification" (Eickelman and Piscatori 1996; Roy 2004; Shryock 1997; Starrett 1998) or "authentication" (Deeb 2006) taking place in many parts of the Muslim world with the introduction of mass education and new technologies of mass communication.[8] Descriptions of Karbala form only one element of a rapidly growing industry of new texts that take the form of social history, newspaper editorials, published books, and pamphlets. Commentators focused on discursive production commonly conclude that Alevis are experiencing a revival of interest in religion, fashioning their traditions in the form of a "public religion" (Ellington 2004; Şahin 2005; Göner 2005; Sökefeld 2008).[9]

This claim, I suggest, is not false so much as misleading. Even as Alevis are exploring new media for the discursive construction of their religious traditions, many urban Alevis, especially youth, are finding the disciplines of devotional piety untenable, uninteresting, and incongruent with contemporary sociopolitical contexts. What I came to notice in the course of my fieldwork was a disjunction between the recent incitement to discourse on Alevi religion, on the one hand, and a growing disaffection with its characteristic disciplines and practices, on the other.

Attitudes toward ritual mourning represent a manifestation of a sensibility I commonly encountered among Alevis toward public performances of a wide range of Islamic practices. In the Alevi neighborhood of Çorum, Alevi residents—young and old, men and women alike—hastened to characterize broad differences in outlook, disposition, and ethos between themselves and Sunni communities. On the Alevi side of town, many residents maintained, I would not see women wearing headscarves, and when cafes and restaurants around town were closed in observance of the fast during the month of Ramadan, teahouses and kebab shops in the Alevi neighborhood would remain open. My interlocutors were pointing out the absence of key practices associated with the Islamic revival in Turkey—what Nilüfer Göle (2002: 173) identifies as the "language styles, corporeal rituals, and spatial practices" that have defined the visibility of Islam in Turkey over the past few decades.

One possible explanation for this absence is that practices of veiling or of fasting during Ramadan are drawn from the Sunni tradition and have not been historically rooted within Alevi religiosity. Some of my Alevi interlocutors themselves offered such an explanation. Yet the absence of a publicly visible Islamic revivalism is not simply a matter of divergent ritual repertoires. The notion that such practices are absent in the Alevi neighborhood sustains a powerful rhetorical presence among its residents. In describing what distinguished their neighborhood from the rest of the town, many Alevis would point to the nonperformance of practices of veiling and fasting. Independently of one another, various Alevi friends said that during Ramadan, Sunnis fearing reproach in their own community come to cafes on the Alevi side of town to eat or drink tea surreptitiously during the day. As an available narrative of communal self-identification, the absence of these religious practices is a social fact.

Many observers—scholars, local intellectuals, and state officials alike—are often struck by the fact that contemporary Alevis tend to adopt a relatively lax approach to religious prescriptions, a relatively liberal mentality toward gender roles, a considerable tolerance and enjoyment of popular entertainment, folk music, and alcohol consumption, and a comfortable accommodation of a secular dispensation of public life. Point for point, the implied comparison in these observations is with the Sunni community and urban spaces in which Sunnis predominate. That this comparison is ideologically motivated is unmistakably apparent in the diasporic German context, in which many Alevis claim to identify more closely with German values (conceived here as secular, democratic, progressive, and tolerant) than to the purportedly fanatical religious values espoused by Turkish Sunnis (Mandel 1990; Dressler 2008). Martin Sökefeld (2008: 185) pointedly reveals the political stakes of this positioning: "In the gross distinction put forward by the German discourse on foreigners which categorizes Muslims as 'antimodern' and the 'most different' of migrants, Alevis position themselves firmly on the side of modernity, that is, on the German side of the divide."

These somewhat varied, if normatively acute, sentiments were rendered tangible for me in the context of another fieldwork encounter. Ercan, an Alevi interlocutor in his mid-forties who taught in a local elementary school, told me that while the neighborhood was largely composed of Alevi residents, there was a growing number of Sunni inhabitants as well. Quickly qualifying his statement, Ercan added that people of Sunni descent who chose to live in the area were usually either leftist in political outlook or simply uninterested in religion. Such individuals moved to the Alevi neighborhood because of the "style of life" (*yaşam tarzı*) it supported. Mesut, a Sunni individual who had moved to the Alevi neighborhood, corroborated Ercan's account. Mesut explained that he elected to live there because he found it more "comfortable" (*rahat*). He maintained, "people in this neighborhood don't put pressure on you to observe religious practices. They have a more modern attitude [*çağdaş zihniyet*]." If, as I suggest, the rhetoric of absence is a social fact, its significance lies not primarily in its referential validity (e.g., whether, in fact, such practices are absent in the Alevi neighborhood) but in its normative charge. As Mesut's comments reveal, the rhetoric establishes a particular claim to modernity.

It is within this context that I wish to examine the relative absence of mourning during the month of Muharram. What rhetoric shapes its significance, and what normative charge does it sustain? In order to understand the social significance of this absence, I began asking Alevi interlocutors about their sentiments toward traditional rituals of mourning. The examples I provide here convey an ethnographic sense of the variety of attitudes maintained by Alevis with regard to such traditions. Despite salient differences, many Alevis frame their conceptions of the practice through a shared historical consciousness of the pastness of its contexts of performance. As I came to learn in the course of my fieldwork, many Alevis who might otherwise differ in their feelings toward the community's religious traditions view ritual lamentation as part of the community's past, unmoored from the social, moral, and political contexts constitutive of contemporary life.

Zehra teyze, a woman in her early fifties, had spent her childhood in a central Anatolian village but had long since moved to Çorum, where she raised a family.[10] Her husband was a civil servant in a local government office. They lived in a modest apartment in the Alevi neighborhood. She had three children: the eldest was teaching in an elementary school at a nearby village, another had completed a university degree in education but failed to pass his certification exam, and the third was still in school. In the course of my fieldwork, I became friends with Serdar, her son who was struggling with his teaching certification, and I frequently joined them for meals at their house.

One afternoon, I asked Zehra teyze whether her family attended Muharram mourning rituals. She responded that her children had never participated in such lamentation practices and were uninterested in doing so. Serdar himself did not explicitly repudiate the rituals. He merely shrugged at the question, claiming that he had never attended them as a child and therefore did not know much about them. Zehra teyze then explained that, unlike her children, she knew many traditional Alevi devotional hymns about Husayn, and she proceeded to sing several of them for my benefit. Intrigued and surprised, I asked whether she continued to participate in rituals of mourning. She answered, "I learned these hymns about the Twelve Imams in my village, but when I left the village, I left the hymns behind as well." For Zehra teyze, the biographical moment of migration was marked by a loss of traditional practices. She retained the memory of the hymns as echoes of her youth.

If for Zehra teyze the pastness of such practices signaled a biographical transition, for the increasing numbers of Alevi youth growing up in Anatolian

cities—including Zehra teyze's own children—lamentation for Husayn con-
jures a sense of the community's historical past, unsuited for and anachronistic within contexts of the present day. Consider the conversation I observed
between two Alevi men in their mid-twenties, Umut and Devrim. Umut was
enrolled in a distance learning program to obtain a university degree, while
Devrim had finished a master's degree in history and was hoping to find a job
teaching in a local school. As with many young Alevis, Umut and Devrim
continued to reside in Çorum beyond their adolescence largely because their
lower-middle class background constrained their mobility and their employment possibilities. Both lived with their parents on the Alevi side of town.

I asked Umut and Devrim about their views on lamentation rituals and
whether they participated in such practices. Intuiting my curiosity about the
apathy of many Alevis toward ritual lament, Umut explained: "My grandparents cry during Muharram, but my parents don't and I don't. I don't really
understand how someone can cry for a person who died more than a thousand years ago. I'm not trying to belittle Alevis who do cry for Husayn, but it
just doesn't make sense [mantıksız]. It seems irrelevant." Umut's generational
reference is significant. While he acknowledged that ritual weeping is undeni-
ably a part of his community's religious history, he did not view it as a model
for practice in the present day. For Umut, lamenting Husayn's death was an
aspect of his grandparents' past but is insignificant in contemporary society.

Reacting against Umut's criticism of the traditional practice, Devrim
countered, "It isn't irrational [mantıksız]—I could weep for Husayn." Con-
fused by the conditionality of his claim, I asked Devrim whether he actually had participated in lamentation rituals. Meeting my question with a wry
smile, Devrim responded, "No, I haven't. The problem is that we lack the right
setting [ortam] these days. Were such stories told as they were in the village,
I would cry." Despite his sympathy for the practice, Devrim indicated that
such rituals were appropriately sited only in rural settings, which he implicitly identified with the past of the community. He acknowledged that his own
capacity to weep for Husayn, for which he otherwise sought to hold out the
conditional possibility, was undercut by the absence of an appropriate setting
in the urban present.

Many other Alevi youth with whom I spoke about the significance of lamentation rituals were less willing than either Umut or Devrim to entertain the
topic of discussion. Erdal, another Alevi in his mid-twenties, resisted my questions. His father, a teacher in an elementary school in Çorum, was a committed

leftist, like many Alevis who came of age in the 1960s and 1970s. Erdal was a doctoral student, studying sociology in Ankara. He was far more interested in discussing Marxist theory with me than Alevi ritual traditions. I had the opportunity to meet with Erdal on several occasions, both in Çorum when he came home for the holidays and in Ankara during the school year. During one conversation in Ankara, I asked him whether he participated in rituals of lamentation. Erdal quickly challenged the value of the question: "Why are you interested in these old practices? What matters for Alevis today are political divisions between the Right and the Left, not weeping for Husayn." Indeed, the conversation that would carry us through the evening was not about the disciplines of mourning; rather, I found myself scrambling to keep up with his extensive account of the relative virtues of Althusser's reading of Marx as compared to that provided by E. P. Thompson. Erdal's rebuke of my query concerning traditions of mourning was guided by the concern that lamentation practices were unimportant and irrelevant to the issues of the present day—in contrast to the continuing significance ascribed to the various lineages of Marxist theory. For Erdal, ritual weeping was at best a curiosity of Alevi history, but distracted from pressing sociopolitical problems.

These interlocutors inflected their responses to my questions about lamentation with a variety of distinct anxieties and concerns—the loss of rituals from one's childhood; an incomprehension of weeping for a moral personage; the sheer irrelevance of such rituals to the political issues of the day—but each respondent shared a sense that the rituals belonged more obviously to the community's past than to its present. The presumption was that the historical conditions that may have once rendered the ritual relevant no longer existed. Even as Alevi organizations and intellectuals that have emerged in the past few decades have developed a growing archive of publications on the community's traditions, including the Karbala narrative, many Alevis feel that ritual expressions of mourning, which once shaped traditional narrations of early Islamic history, are irrelevant, inappropriate, or anachronistic in the contexts of the contemporary world.

STAGING MODERNITY

The persistent claim that ritual lamentation is anachronistic in the Alevi present might lead us to the conclusion that such practices are politically insignificant. Indeed, in comparison with many Shi'i contexts in the contemporary world, Alevis practices of mourning appear remarkably quiescent. In much of the Shi'i world—from the Islamic revolution in Iran to the formation of Hizbullah in Lebanon—the Karbala narrative has been at the center of politics over the past few decades.

Recent scholarship has sought to understand the political significance of the religious narrative by interrogating the ways in which some of its key symbols have been mobilized and manipulated for distinctly modern political ends. In the lead-up to the revolution in Iran, accounts of the Karbala narrative became a crucial vehicle for voicing criticisms of the shah. References to the narrative either explicitly or implicitly associated Husayn's seventh-century oppressors with the shah's regime (Aghaie 2004). The symbolic reinterpretation of the narrative was one crucial mode of modern political engagement in Iran.

The narrative dimensions of the Iranian revolution exemplify what Dale Eickelman and James Piscatori (1996) regard as the symbolic component of modern Muslim politics. In their analysis, symbols provide an "underlying framework of language, ideas, and values" (1996: 16), in which political arguments are made contextually meaningful to local actors. Debate over religious symbols does not represent an appeal to an archaic worldview; it articulates with a political struggle over modern institutions, such as the nation-state. Iranian discourses about the symbolism of the Karbala narrative revealed an important site for challenging the political authority of the shah's regime.

The weight of this line of analysis falls heavily on investigating how symbols are interpreted and contested. Political questions about how social and material resources should be distributed are often at stake in disputed interpretations of religious symbols. From the vantage point provided by this approach, the Alevi case does not seem to be a particularly promising site to pursue an analysis of the politics of religious narrative. Despite the uptick in discursive production among Alevis over the past few decades, there has been very little debate over the central themes and symbols of the Karbala narrative. Moreover, many Alevis explicitly claim the irrelevance of such symbols to the contemporary world.

Yet performances of Alevi ritual are not depoliticized. As described later in this chapter, political parties often dispatch representatives to Alevi ritual gatherings to court potential voters; journalists frequently attend to take photographs for local papers; state officials are also often invited to participate. The attendance of such figures at community events is viewed by Alevi participants themselves with some ambivalence. Their presence appears to demonstrate a growing popular acceptance of sectarian differences, but it also allows Alevi practices to be more carefully monitored and regulated. One result is that Alevi organizers downplay and discourage performances of devotional weeping and cursing.

Alevi lament is positioned within a field of political power, but this positioning cannot be conceptualized as a space of symbolic readings. The central issue, to which I have drawn attention, is the sense that practices of mourning are irrelevant or inappropriate in contemporary social and political contexts. How should we conceptualize the politics of modernity in a situation that turns not primarily on the interpretation of narrative symbols but on the contemporary relevance of the disciplines of narration?

The Lebanese Shiʿi community provides a helpful comparison. On the one hand, certain Shiʿis have engaged in a political reinterpretation of religious symbols—for instance, redefining the symbolic significance of central female figures from early Islamic history, such as Husayn's sister Zaynab, identifying her, not solely as a mourner of her brother's death, but also as a community leader after the Karbala event. Such reinterpretations authorize a more politically active role for Shiʿi women in present day Lebanon (Deeb 2006). On the other hand, debates about religious narrative within that community also concern the contemporaneity of a certain form of narrating the Karbala events in lamentation rituals. Some Shiʿi actors criticize "traditional" approaches to mourning that emphasize weeping for the sake of achieving salvation. For these Shiʿis, preaching at ritual commemorations ought to generate emotions that motivate participants to engage in social and political activism: "Emotion remains important for this recitor [sic], yet emotion is given contemporary purpose in its revision from an end to a means" (Deeb 2006: 143). For those participants and preachers who adopt the activist position, ritual emotion remains relevant to the present only to the extent that the practice of weeping for salvation (as an end in itself) is displaced in favor of a conception of emotion as a means for prompting social activism. The claim about the contemporaneity of a certain style of narration is put forward within a landscape of manifold ethical and political stances.

The debate that arises in the Lebanese context, as in Turkey, invites reflection on the kind of politics that emerges in relation to notions of contemporaneity, or in other words, the political framing that allows certain forms of historical consciousness to be glossed as modern and that disqualifies others from that designation. Timothy Mitchell (2000) opens the way for such an understanding of politics by distinguishing two ways of conceptualizing what he terms "the stage of modernity." He notes that modernity is often understood as a stage of history, preceded by some form of premodernity—for instance, a feudal economy, monarchical rule, or religious law. For some theorists, it is followed by a postmodernity. This understanding of modernity, Mitchell submits, simply posits a developmentalist conception of historical time and so fails to interrogate it critically. Not simply one stage in a historical development, modernity is commonly invoked and claimed by social actors through a staging of history itself that locates some people, practices, and places in the present, and relegates others to the past (see also Chakrabarty 2000; Trouillot 2003; Wilce 2008). Developmentalist conceptions of historical time are neither natural nor an a priori given of human experience, but rather the product of a particular sociopolitical logic that animates and promotes certain imaginings of society and selfhood against others.

Some of my Alevi interlocutors appealed to a modernist narrative of historical development. Recall that Umut and Erdal claimed their own modernity by relegating the act of lamenting Husayn's death to the past of the community, insisting that ritual mourning is no longer relevant to or congruent with contemporary social and political contexts. Sentiments about the incongruence of religious traditions with the modern present have not been uncommon in Turkey, where the state saw itself as radically ruptured from the Ottoman past in order to direct its citizens toward a "new location in historical time" (Parla and Davison 2004: 123; see also Ahıska 2003).[11] Yet it remains analytically crucial not to assume the ideological effectivity or completion of the state-driven modernist project but, instead, to interrogate the practices, disciplines, and institutions that encourage sentiments about the irrelevance of religious traditions. Feelings of anachronism that might be experienced as driven by historical necessity are in fact contingent effects of an ideological framing and require ongoing institutional support for their reproduction.[12] The consciousness of the self as modern and as contemporary has to be orchestrated in practice. It has to be staged.

The sense of pastness ascribed by Umut and Erdal to the ritual is not unequivocally celebrated by all Alevis. If, for instance, Erdal insisted that such practices were simply irrelevant to the present, Devrim's conditional empathy with participants in mourning practices expressed a greater ambivalence about the absence of lament. Zehra teyze's positioning of the ritual to the past was less about epochal shift than about her own biographical transitions. This rather uneven landscape of sensibilities suggests that the historical staging of modernity, along with its ideological distinction of anachronism and contemporaneity, has not achieved an exhaustive hegemony or uniform totalization. The value of the narrative, as a mode of grasping the past and present of the community's engagement with the Islamic tradition, is not a matter of settled consensus.

The project of disciplining historical sensibilities derives from a political history in its own right, and in the course of that history it has been mobilized by various casts of social actors and directed toward a number of practical aims. Subsequent chapters will draw out these institutional itineraries: the studies of late Ottoman and early republican ethnographers and the writings of Alevi public intellectuals in the present are marked by historicist renderings of the community's traditions, and enactments of Alevi rituals in urban centers today are commonly designated by journalists, state officials, and public audiences as signs of the medieval past. Narratives of the nation and its history mediate these intellectual and social practices, and in that form political and scholarly authorities alike have promoted a certain arrangement of Alevi ritual. The sense that Alevi traditions of lament belong to the past has not led to the abandonment of the practice; the historicist sensibility it reveals is as an object of institutional investment.

In order to examine this investment, I want to recontextualize the claim about the irrelevance of lament away from the explicit and reflexive rhetoric of my Alevi interlocutors and position it within settings that are more densely mediated by state institutional practices. What come into view are spatial sensibilities that an exclusive focus on the temporal implications of historicism would overlook, specifically those centered on a national geography, its internal unity, and the threat of its fragmentation along sectarian lines.

MOURNING AND NATIONAL UNITY

One primary reason I chose to focus my ethnographic field research in Çorum is that Alevis have by and large inhabited a single region of the town. I had expected that the spatial cleavage of sectarian differences would present a situation where Alevi organizations would frequently and publicly host ritual performances. This somewhat naive expectation was not borne out. Ritual performances were held with less regularity in Çorum than in larger cities such as Ankara and Istanbul, and when they were enacted, they were rarely announced formally or publicly.

The rituals of mourning held by Alevi groups during the month of Muharram tended to be relatively quiet affairs, secluded from public view. For the first ten evenings of the month of Muharram, one of Çorum's local Alevi organizations hosted an *iftar*—a breaking of the fast, which is conducted in honor of Husayn's struggles. These ten days commemorate the time that Husayn and his companions spent in the desert of Karbala without food or drink. It was on the tenth day, or Ashura, that Husayn was finally slain. At the events that I attended, participation was low, particularly for the first nine evenings. It included about ten to twelve mostly elderly men and women, all of whom were either actively involved in the day-to-day workings of the local organization or kin to those who were.

The iftar gatherings that I attended were not advertised through street posters, newspaper announcements, or on local television. For the first nine evenings, there was no press coverage of the events. Alevi commemorations are, in this regard, altogether different from the Shi'i contexts mentioned above, in which there is thoroughgoing mass mediation and mass participation. In those contexts, community leaders often seek to harness the energy of large crowds gathered for ritual mourning for the sake of political action. The texture, sounds, and sights of daily life are completely transformed during the ritual period. In the Turkish case, by contrast, normal quotidian life is largely undisturbed.

It is not that Alevis lack the organizational capacity to mobilize national media. At other times of the year, Alevi organizations in major metropolitan centers effectively assemble public protests of state policies and gather together large crowds of supporters. Especially significant are annual rallies held on July 2, in commemoration of an attack on an Alevi gathering in the town of Sivas in 1993 where more than thirty individuals were killed in the hotel where they had convened. Every year, Alevi organizations sponsor rallies that commemorate the Sivas incident with demonstrations in public squares in major urban centers. Alevi groups have also campaigned to make the hotel in Sivas into a museum to preserve the memory of the event. Such protests and campaigns are often accompanied by extensive editorial commentary in national newspapers and by responses from government officials. Muharram, however, is decidedly *not* the time of year when Alevi organizations launch political campaigns.

The iftar events that I witnessed were somber affairs, in part because the events involved a handful of participants, not unruly crowds, but also because the gatherings were meant to bring to mind Husayn's trials and suf-ferings at Karbala. The somber tone was established from the start with the fast and by the meal that concluded it. As discussed above, fasting during Muharram is a long-standing practice among Alevis, and it takes a particu-lar form: just as Husayn was unable to obtain water or food in the desert of Karbala, Alevis abstain from consuming water and meat. The meal prepared for iftar at the Alevi organization was consistently modest. In contrast to the celebratory feasts that often break the Ramadan fast, participants in the Muharram iftar ate a simple salad, rice, and lentils. As several attendees explained, the meal continues rather than breaks the austerity fostered dur-ing the fast.

The emulation of Husayn's experience includes other practices. Some male participants did not shave or bathe for the first ten days of Muharram. They engaged in these forms of ascetic practice in order to emotionally and corpore-ally commit themselves to a lived experience of the Karbala parables, abstain-ing from that which was refused Husayn. Before arriving for the evening iftar, these individuals had already begun to narrate the Karbala paradigm in their practices of self-abnegation.

Not all attendees engaged in such abstentions. The men who shaved during Muharram acknowledged that they should refrain from doing so. Yet they found it impossible to abide by the ritual prescriptions, given the day-to-day social expectations of self-presentation, particularly in employment settings. The sense that such abstentions would fail to meet social conventions high-lights the fact that public life in Turkey is not oriented around Muharram rituals. Other than an occasional newspaper article or television news report about Alevi practices, there was very little public discussion about the Karbala narrative in Turkey.

Following the meal that breaks the fast, we moved to the office of the orga-nization's director, Bayram. An avuncular man in his late sixties, Bayram was always ready to comment on daily political intrigue or Alevi social and religious life. He had lived for short periods in Germany and Saudi Arabia, working as an industrial laborer and picking up bits of the local languages. In general, however, like many early migrant laborers, he had been largely unintegrated into the social and linguistic life of the host country. In his office, Bayram held court. When I posed questions to his friends and colleagues at the local Alevi association, he often assumed the authority to respond. His companions tended to defer to his opinion.

Bayram's office was long and narrow, with chairs and sofas lining two of the walls, enough to seat a dozen or more people comfortably. The middle of the office held two small tables, leaving enough space for Ali amca, the aşık mentioned at the beginning of this chapter, to recite dirges (*mersiye*) about the battle of Karbala. Like many of the others in attendance, Ali amca was a retired factory worker. He was not formally trained to recite these dirges, a point that bears some emphasis, as Alevis in Turkey have no formal mechanisms to educate and train religious officiants. When I asked him how he had come to learn the mersiye, he said that at a rather late age, he had started teaching himself, but without specifying how he had done so. Neither his singing voice nor his abilities in playing the saz were polished.[13]

Chanted in Turkish, Ali amca's recitations of the mersiye built upon the emotions cultivated in the fast, seeking to draw participants into a collective act of mourning. Listeners were not passive participants. Many in attendance began to weep or call out curses upon Yazid, the tyrant that Husayn had sought to overthrow. These rituals provided an emotional climax to the day. The days themselves emotionally progressed, building to the tenth of Muharram, the day on which Husayn was finally killed. The scale of participation endowed these evenings with a quality not only of sobriety but of intimacy. The passion expressed by the dirges and the acts of mourning they elicited were moving, if subdued and constrained.

These intimate expressions of emotion prevailed for the first nine days of Muharram. The tenth day, or Ashura, was altogether different. The Ashura gathering, which was meant to be a much bigger affair, was covered by the local media. The Alevi organization planned to hold it in the main hall of the building (rather than in Bayram's office), lining the room with rows of long tables and plastic chairs. The organization sent invitations to local politicians and state officials, including the head of religious affairs for the province (*müftü*). The presence of journalists, politicians, and the müftü transformed the Muharram gathering from an intimate communal affair into an event with a distinctly public address. Also in attendance were hundreds of local Alevis from a wide range of age groups. Some participants clearly knew one another, sharing warm greetings. Many others found themselves seated at tables with others they did not know, exchanging minimal glances and polite nods before turning directly to their meals. The event sustained an overall air of stranger sociability.

The ritual occasion on the tenth of Muharram was distinguished not only by its scale and the sociopolitical profile of its attendees but also by the practical form of the ritual's performance. Dirges were not recited, and participants did not weep. There was little effort to describe the battle of Karbala. Only once was Husayn's name even mentioned, when Bayram asked that participants remember his struggle. The rather sparse mentions of Husayn did not describe his valor or his death. The proceedings were not oriented toward an emotional climax that would induce tears in the audience. The brief mention of Karbala transpired apart from the recitational practices that might have encouraged emotional responses. What had shifted was not the symbolic interpretation of the narrative but the practice of narration.

Ali amca explained to me why they were not performing rituals of mourning. "The setting today is mixed," he said, as he brought his hands together, fingers interlaced, to indicate the joint presence of Sunnis and Alevis. Tersely formulated, the comment implied that neither the narrative of the battle of Karbala nor the emotions elicited by its narration were appropriate for such a mixed audience. Overhearing our conversation, several others quietly nodded in agreement.

Seeking further elaboration, I asked Bayram why he had invited public and political dignitaries to the Ashura commemoration. His response was similar to Ali amca's explanation, but Bayram intoned his statement with a more pronounced sense of political expediency. He claimed that the presence of such officials enables a show of unity (*birlik ve beraberlik*) between Alevis and the Sunni majority. Indeed, all of the party politicians and state officials in attendance were of Sunni origin. It is just such a show of unity, he explained, that allows for harmony between the two communities and that will prevent future episodes of sectarian discord, like those that took place in Çorum in 1980.

The transition from the ninth to the tenth of Muharram revealed a transformation in the pragmatics of the commemorative event. The aim of the gathering shifted on the tenth of Muharram from a practice of mourning to a demonstration of national fraternity. Bayram's comments suggest that Alevis are burdened with the task of enacting their traditions in ways that demonstrate and act out national cohesion.

UNITY AS A JURIDICAL DISCOURSE

Bayram's invocation of the notion of "national unity" corresponded to a broader tendency found among many Alevi spokespersons. The trope has figured prominently in the discourses of Alevi leaders and groups since the late 1980s (Massicard 2006). The ideological force that the trope carries derives from a set of juridical discourses that have been issued from various institutional locations over the past few decades, including military proclamations, constitutional texts and amendments, and the decisions of the Constitutional Court. The juridical discourses of "unity" do not only refer to a sense of solidarity across religious lines for the sake of promoting the common good. They conjoin that sense of national fraternity to problems of territorial sovereignty and the state's political authority. A few prominent examples indicate the stakes of the concept.

On September 12, 1980, the day of the military coup d'état in which parliament was disbanded and martial law extended across the country, General Kenan Evren announced that "the purpose of this operation is to preserve the integrity of the country, to secure national unity and togetherness [*milli birlik ve beraberliği sağlamak*], to avert a probable civil war and fratricide, to reestablish the authority and existence of the state and to eliminate all factors that impede the functioning of the democratic order" (Milli Güvenlik Konseyi Genel Sekreterliği 1981: 193). Evren's allusion to the possibility of civil war was a reference to the escalation of sectarian conflict that had taken place in central and eastern Anatolia in the years leading up to the coup. Crucially, Evren upheld national unity against the looming danger of civil war not only to shelter vulnerable populations but in order to protect the very existence of the Turkish state. The restoration of unity, in this justification of military action, was an element of state action meant to reinforce the viability and authority of the regime itself.

Both before and after the 1980 military coup, the Constitutional Court assumed the prerogative to define threats to national unity and to the regime. Since the 1960s, the Court has closed down numerous socialist and communist political parties on the grounds that they endangered "the unity of the state with its territory and nation." In the past two decades, the Court has banned various political parties associated with Kurdish and Islamist movements, claiming that they sought to destroy "the unity of the country and the nation." Legislative activity in recent decades has consolidated and extended the same rhetorics of unity. Antiterror laws, such as the one passed in 1991, define terrorism as an activity aimed at "damaging the indivisible unity of the state with its territory and nation." Laws on Associations, on Political Parties, on the Duties and Authority of the Police, and on Turkish Radio and Television each stipulate a similar restriction on activities that threaten national unity (Koğacıoğlu 2003, 2004; Belge 2006; Oran 2007).

This body of legislative and juridical discourse does not propound a naked repression of religious and ethnic difference. It often claims to support expressions of such differences, but only insofar as they remain within the boundaries of "culture" that the state itself defines and regulates. In the verdict that closed down the pro-Kurdish Democracy Party in 1994, the Constitutional Court claimed that "the purpose of legal regulations" is not "the prohibition of diversity and of their languages and cultures. . . . What is banned is not the expression of cultural differences and cultural wealth; it is the employment of these with the aim of destroying the unity of the nation and in connection with this, the construction of a new state order based on divisions by means of creating minorities on the land of the Turkish Republic" (Oran 2007: 49). "Culture," the Court argued, only becomes an object of legal regulation when its expression raises a credible threat to national unity. Here, again, the vulnerability of the nation to fraternal disunity is further conjoined to threats to the authority and territorial integrity of the Turkish state.

The juridical discourse on unity shuttles between a number of concerns: (1) threats to the bonds of fraternity that tie together the populations that make up the national body; (2) threats to the indivisibility of the state with its people; and (3) threats to the sovereignty of the state over its territory. One set of concerns does not lead to the next set as a matter of logical necessity. They are brought together as a political act. Invocations of "national unity" often bundle connotations of each—even within a single court decision (Koğacıoğlu 2004). In the contexts of its use, the notion of unity links concerns about fraternal solidarity to an aggressive discourse on state sovereignty. The preservation of unity justifies state intervention.

Bayram's goal of strengthening national harmony by creating a display of sectarian unity must be interpreted within this discursive context. Inviting state officials to a performance of communal ritual reveals the concern of an Alevi leader keen to counteract a history of political violence by positioning a communal practice within the range of acceptable cultural expression. To situate Alevi ritual within the limits of legitimate difference is also to assert the community's loyalty to the regime and its commitment to the form of politics that the military and the courts have sought to regulate under the sign of "democratic order."

PLURALISM AND DISCIPLINE

In the course of this chapter, I explored the increasing prevalence among Alevis of a certain sensibility vis-à-vis ritual lament. The notion that lamentation rituals belong to the past has involved an increasing skepticism, and in some cases hostility, toward the disciplines of mourning that have traditionally guided the narration of the Karbala parables. As a social practice in its own right, the absenting of lament has found institutional supports, organized by means of a new regime of discipline. Lamentation rituals are often subjected to scrutiny by state officials, party representatives, and the news media. Some Alevi participants claim that community-specific forms of religious devotion must be curtailed in public in order to bolster the national subject against its possible fragmentation.

Efforts to publicly display Alevi ritual as an index of national unity have intensified in the past few years under the mandate of a new government project. In 2007, officials from the ruling Justice and Development Party (AKP) not only participated in an Alevi event but sponsored an official Muharram gathering. More recently, in 2011, the Directorate of Religious Affairs instructed preachers of selected mosques across the country to offer special prayers and Qur'anic recitations in honor of Husayn, and to deliver sermons discussing Karbala. Muharram gatherings throughout both metropolitan and provincial cities in Turkey continue to be attended by local officials and are increasingly covered by national media. To some extent, it is possible to interpret these events as revealing a change in the attitudes of high-level state officials, enabling Alevi rituals to be publicly recognized as legitimate rather than simply silenced. For its part, AKP has touted these events as part of a broader "democratic opening" meant to encourage pluralist political reform.[14]

Yet the disciplinary impetus of such gatherings remains potent. Time and again, reports of these events have underlined statements by speakers who stressed the unimpeachable unity of the nation. One government minister, Faruk Çelik, spoke at a Muharram gathering in Ankara: "There is no power that will disrupt this unity. . . . We will never forget Karbala, but we will also never permit the occurrence of new Karbalas. We will never give an opportunity for those who seek to ambush our unity and solidarity [birlik ve beraberliğimiz]. Whether Alevi or Sunni, we are inheritors of the same history, we are designs on the same Anatolian rug" (Zaman 2011a). Another Muharram event was sponsored in the town of Kahramanmaraş, where the local Alevi community was violently attacked in 1978. Kemal Karaküçük, the leader of a local business association, announced the intent of the gathering: "As is well known, Kahramanmaraş is a city in which our people, both Alevi and Sunni, have lived together for years. On this occasion, in the month of Muharram, we have organized a program with the aim of drawing attention to this brotherhood" (Zaman 2011c). Almost without exception, such events were described as promoting and producing the unity of the nation.

The various accounts of ritual lament that I have explored in this chapter are shaped by sensibilities that are strikingly distinctive, even incongruent: a sense of irrelevance, on the one hand, and of a potency warranting institutional monitoring, on the other. In the absence of any attempt by Alevis themselves to mobilize political activism around the performance of lament, this potency deserves to be interrogated. Why do events of Alevi lamentation trigger statements aimed at fortifying the national subject? What is the threat to which such fortifying measures are given as a response?

In the next few chapters, I track institutional investments in a certain formation of Alevi religious memory. Such investments frame and fashion Alevi pasts, by defining those pasts as signs of the nation's history. They also disqualify alternative ways of relating to the past, particularly those that imply a geography of mourning that, as indicated by Ayfer hanım at the beginning of this chapter, extends beyond the boundaries of the nation-state and encompasses regions across the Muslim world. Investigating these forces allows us to focus on social and political practices that, in fostering national commitments, eliminate alternative spatio-temporalities of collective belonging.

3 ANATOLIAN MODERN

IN OCTOBER 2004 THE PRESIDENT of the Alevi-Bektaşi Federation, Ali Doğan, released the following statement: "Alevism existed for thousands of years prior to Islam. It is outside of Islam and has its own particularities" (Zaman 2004c). Doğan's federation was an umbrella organization that represents a number of distinct Alevi civil society groups. His remarks were part of a broader campaign demanding that religious affiliation be removed from state-issued identity cards, which list both Alevis and Sunnis simply as Muslims. Efforts by some Alevi groups to change the listing from Islam to Alevism have been refused, as the state insists that it does not legally distinguish sub-groups within the Muslim community. Doğan's statement about the religious origins of Alevism was one element of a broader political strategy to attain political rights on the basis of communal identity.

Given the fact that the Federation represented a number of prominent Alevi civil society groups, Doğan's words carried significant public weight. They elicited a good deal of heated response, especially within the Alevi community itself. Hasan Meşeli, the president of a different Alevi group, known as the Hacı Bektaş-ı Veli Cultural Center, responded, "Our God is one, our Qur'an is one, our Prophet is one, and our flag is one" (Zaman 2004a). Succinctly phrased, Meşeli repudiated Doğan's claim about Alevi religious history by positioning Alevism squarely within the foundational coordinates of Islam. His comment did not specifically address the policy initiative, regarding identity cards, but it raised the political stakes much more dramatically: the flag as a symbol of the nation is juxtaposed to God, the Qur'an, and the

Prophet. Meşeli's response suggested that the national affiliation of the Alevi community was at stake in the debate over religious historical origins.

The exchange illustrates a fact noted by a number of commentators on contemporary Alevi politics: Alevis engage in public, often heated, debates about their religious identity and history, not only with state officials but amongst themselves. Their efforts to discursively objectify their traditions do not resolve disagreements but prompt more nuanced and detailed dispute (Vorhoff 1998; Massicard 2005b; Dressler 2008). More important, the dispute between Meşeli and Doğan suggests some of the anxieties that shape and animate the deliberative forum itself. Meşeli's attempt to correct Doğan's historiography is oriented toward an assertion of national unity and singularity.

The tension between collective difference from the Sunni majority, on the one hand, and a heavy-handed assertion of national loyalty, on the other, is manifest in many public expressions of Alevism. The previous chapter examined this tension in relation to Alevi attempts to ritually mourn the death of Husayn at Karbala. It is worth recalling that Alevi groups rarely use commemorations of Husayn's death to organize political activities such as rallies, demonstrations, or protests. The ethos of mourning tends not to be confrontational. Such rituals are typically small, intimate affairs, and in moments of explicit public display, organizers often feel compelled to downplay, if not discharge, the emotionally expressive dimensions of mourning. Nevertheless, Alevi organizers and participants fear that ritual enactments of lamentation may be deemed inappropriate and threatening to national harmony by politicians and state officials in attendance. The public display of Alevi difference was meant to remain commensurate with statist notions of political community. Why is it that just at the moment when certain Alevi groups are beginning to raise a challenge to entrenched nationalist discourses that claim a homogeneous body of citizens, others within the community resuscitate the emblems of state-secured unity?

The orchestration of communal difference within dominant frames of political community might be viewed as a practical concession for a persecuted minority. Given the fact that Alevis have been episodically subjected to open harassment and violence, it is not surprising that certain public representatives of Alevi communities have emphasized their loyalty to the nation. Yet this political tactic presupposes a good deal that is worth interrogating more directly, particularly the availability of a discourse that incorporates Alevism within regnant narratives of the nation. Alevi actors who, in voicing the community's identity, stress their commitment to the unity of the nation mobilize discursive practices that have a lengthy institutional history. What remains analytically pressing is an examination of the historical conditions that have made this discursive maneuver intelligible and efficacious as a political tactic in the present day.

The dilemmas of current Alevi discourses of difference, I argue, reveal some of the central contradictions of the modernist political project established in the final decades of the late Ottoman Empire and further catalyzed by the republican state in the early twentieth century. The development of a national imaginary, with its characteristic notions of fraternal solidarity and equal citizenship, was accompanied by a keen sense of the fragility of the institutional supports of that imaginary and of the threats posed to the project of politically consolidating the nation in the ruins of empire. It was in response to this sense of threat and vulnerability that nationalist ideologues turned their attention to Alevism.

Nationalist elites did not repudiate Alevis as foreigners on Turkish soil (as they did various Christian communities). On the contrary, Alevis were conceived of as integral to the nation. The governing elite viewed the community's practices as a token of the nation's past, a sign of the historical depth and perdurance of a national Turkish society. Ostensibly marking cultural difference, Alevi ritual was accepted by nationalist leaders as evidence of a historically coherent national political community. This validating impulse deserves closer investigation, inasmuch as it reveals some of the tensions and anxieties that remain at the heart of national citizenship in Turkey today.

My approach is akin to what Michel Foucault (1984) calls "effective history," an approach that interrogates the contingency and discontinuity of phenomena that lay claim to a deep and unbroken chain of historical development. An effective history is crucial to my study of pluralism because it allows me to denaturalize the notion, institutionally entrenched in the present day, that Alevi ritual offers a tangible trace of the nation's past. I seek to unearth the discursive practices that operationalized Alevism as evidence of that historical continuity. At what juncture and out of what contingencies did it become imperative to locate Alevi religiosity within the nation's historical development? What forms of political vulnerability made this operation appear necessary?

The effective history that I pursue is not, then, a social history of Alevism as it developed in the twentieth century. Instead, I interrogate the sentiments and affects that lent urgency to the category of Alevism for nationalist intellectuals. Within this history the category of Alevism served as a point of practical intervention for those witnessing the dissolution of the Ottoman political body. Discourses emerging in the late Ottoman Empire assigned to Alevism a fearsome representational burden—to stand as a sign of a viable social body that might hold together in the face of the empire's collapse. Alevism would thereby function as a suture for a modern political subject that, in the name of Ottoman citizenship, was increasingly reaching the threshold of dismemberment.

My account emphasizes the affective sensibilities—especially the anxiety and immediacy—that shaped early nationalist efforts to claim the viability of a Turkish national community. The ideologues of the time seized upon Alevism in a moment of desperation, rather than in the manner of controlled and planned reform. If, as Foucault (1984: 87) suggests, every sentiment and instinct has a history, then it is this sense of rapid and urgent seizure that continues to be felt today in the strident claims of national loyalty that police Alevi public discourse. What I pursue in this chapter is a history of the forms of sentiment, vulnerability, and volition that are constitutive of Turkey's political modernity.

HISTORIES OF VULNERABILITY

The perception that the nation's integrity is at risk may be a feature of nationalisms across the globe. If the nation is a category instantiated, performed, and reproduced in its use (cf. Brubaker 1996; Wedeen 2008), its characteristic imaginaries are neither settled in advance of their embodiment in practice nor always already efficacious in hailing their subjects. The nation, as a posited social and affective grounding of political community, remains vulnerable to the risk of failed performance. Anxieties about national vulnerability are all the more evident in a moment in which many nation-states are ceding elements of their economic and political sovereignty to global currents of capital, instruments of international law, and transnational social movements (Appadurai 2006; Özyürek 2009b). Fears of an unraveling of the social bond of the nation can be productive, energizing projects of state formation and preservation.

Such anxieties are, to be sure, variable across time and space—the institutional moorings of national imaginaries are stronger at certain moments and in certain contexts than in others. Even in contexts where imaginaries of the nation are strongly established, the perception of its vulnerability can remain powerful. Turkey, for instance, was never formally colonized. It asserted its autonomous statehood prior to many of its neighbors in the Middle East. Moreover, the nation-form is institutionally entrenched in Turkey, ballasted by the apparatuses of the military, the civil bureaucracy, and the educational system. These modern institutional apparatuses were initially established by the Ottoman Empire and were subsequently inherited by the national republican state in the aftermath of the empire's collapse. Yet the sense that the Turkish nation might be vulnerable to fragmentation has not subsided in the long history of state institutional reform. Far from resolving or completing a project of modernization, so as to render issues of national allegiance as taken-for-granted elements of political culture, questions of national loyalty, cohesiveness, and integrity have persistently reemerged as matters requiring ongoing scrutiny and confirmation.

The sense of national vulnerability developed in the violent history out of which the Turkish nation-state came into being. The final decades of the Ottoman Empire were deeply turbulent and often violent. From the Russo-Turkish War of 1876–1878 to the Balkan Wars of 1912–1913, the Ottoman Empire lost much of its territory and population. Fatma Müge Göçek (2011: 114) describes the wars as "emotional traumas" for two successive generations of Ottomans. The political tumult of the era continued through the next decade. From the Balkan Wars through World War I, and culminating in Turkey's independence struggle against incursions by European powers, which followed the demise of the empire, late Ottoman leaders and officers erected the new Turkish nation on the ruins of continuous war. The experience of the Ottoman state's dissolution, along with the sense of unceasing vulnerability and threat that accompanied it, were constitutive of the political culture of the ideologues and officials in charge of establishing the Turkish nation-state. Göçek argues that the violence of the period had a perduring impact on Turkish political life through to the present, leading to the ongoing and widely held feeling that both external powers and internal movements are attempting to undermine the nation.

In contemporary Turkey, the sense of internal vulnerability is most explicitly articulated in public discussions about the conflict between the Turkish military and Kurdish guerrilla fighters. It is voiced quite stridently in connection with debates about the Armenian genocide of the early twentieth century. Juxtaposed to these sorts of issues, displays of Alevi ritual seem rather minor, rarely eliciting the same degree of passion that excites the national public in debates about ethno-nationalist separatism or the historical memory of genocidal violence. There is, nonetheless, a concerted effort to domesticate expressions of Alevi difference within the symbolic frames of the nation—the national unity of God, Qur'an, Prophet, and flag that Hasan Meşeli evoked. If enactments of Alevi tradition do not incite militant or overt political challenges to Turkish sovereignty, then why are performances of Alevi ritual compelled to confirm the nation's unity?

There is a history to this symbolic framing, which I relate back to the emergence of the nationalizing project in the late Ottoman Empire. It was at that time that nationalist ideologues began to conceptualize Alevism as an object of knowledge, and where we can locate the emergence of a new constellation of concepts that would frame the discourse on Alevi religious history. In fleshing out various elements of this history, my aim is neither to elaborate a critique of the conceptual logic of early studies of Alevism nor to simply expose their ideological biases.[1] Rather, I want to connect the conceptual forms developed in that time period to the political exigencies and perceived vulnerabilities of the moment. The issue is how the consolidation of Alevism as an object of knowledge was motivated by these exigencies. Such political and affective motivations lie at the heart of what I call the demand for knowledge about Alevism.

OTTOMAN MODERNITY

The first systematic studies of Alevism by Ottoman intellectuals were conducted in the early twentieth century.[2] By that particular historical conjuncture the Ottoman Empire had already undergone nearly a century of structural reforms in the organization of the state. Characteristically modern forms of political authority and citizenship were at once institutionalized in the course of these reforms and also destabilized as the empire itself grew increasingly precarious through military defeat. If at the turn of the twentieth century, Ottoman citizenship and the modern political body it represented were supported by imperial institutions, their viability would be threatened by the protracted process of the empire's collapse. The study of Alevism arises at that moment, between concerted efforts at modernization and the threat of imperial extinction. It would be energized by the very dissolution of Ottoman sovereignty and the birth of the republican state that followed in its wake.

Motivated by the need to enhance the power of the empire and the efficiency of its administration, the nineteenth-century Ottoman state appealed to technologies of governance and law pioneered by western European states.[3] Ottoman reform led to a radical reorganization of the military and the bureaucracy. The restructuring of statecraft also entailed a series of decrees and ultimately laws that declared equal citizenship for all Ottoman subjects, including both Muslims and non-Muslims. The Gülhane rescript of 1839, the Reform decree of 1856, and the Constitution of 1876 progressively extended guarantees of life, property, and honor to all imperial subjects, regardless of religion or sect.[4] The 1856 decree asserted the goal of promoting "heartfelt bonds of patriotism" across communal boundaries, a goal that the modernist intelligentsia began to pursue under an inclusive banner of Ottomanism (Findley 2010: 100). More than half a century before the emergence of the republican nation-state, the Ottoman Empire had already begun to promote the language of equal citizenship.

To promote the bonds of patriotism asserted in official decrees, the Ottoman state also mobilized new forms of knowledge, again often derived from western Europe. For instance, Ottoman officials employed European methods of cartography in order to spatially represent a unified Ottoman territory. Benjamin Fortna (2002), following B. Anderson ([1983] 1991), demonstrates that these cartographic technologies were employed to produce logo-maps, that is, maps that represented Ottoman territory as an emblem of a single political community, shared across regional, ethnic, and religious differences. Moreover, the state sought to bolster the notion of Ottoman political subjectivity by launching a set of reforms aimed at drawing non-Muslims into the civil administration and government schools (Findley 2010: 102). Efforts to "vernacularize" the language of Ottoman Turkish in the newly developing media of newspapers and novels also sought to generate a sense of collective Ottoman political identity (Mardin 2006; Ertürk 2011). Commenting on the use of a journalistic Turkish vernacular in novels of the nineteenth century, Şerif Mardin (2006: 133) describes the development of a "new voice that could function as a sort of diffuse populism." This voice provided the Young Turk nationalists of the late Ottoman Empire with "a tacitly shared confirmation of the existence of an Ottoman society as a reality" (2006: 133). The project of establishing the political authority of modern citizenship as the ground of imperial rule involved extensive and simultaneous transformations in the apparatuses of law, governance, and knowledge.[5]

These efforts at concerted reform were continually pressed to the limit by a concomitant restructuring process that was by no means a product of state-led modernization. It was, rather, a result of military defeats and massive territorial excisions, which would progressively strain the project of Ottoman citizenship. Beginning in the late nineteenth century and extending through the first two decades of the twentieth, the Ottoman Empire progressively lost large portions of territory, leading up to the Empire's demise in World War I. The excision of Ottoman territory began with the Treaty of Berlin (1878), which granted Serbia, Romania, and Montenegro independence and led to the emergence of a new Bulgarian state. Bosnia and Herzegovina were occupied by Austria-Hungary, the British took control of Cyprus, and Tunisia was handed over to the French. A few years later, the British succeeded in establishing a controlling political presence in Egypt.

In a very short period of time, the Ottoman Empire had lost nearly one-third of its territory and a large percentage of its Christian population—territorial and demographic transformations that would only accelerate in the early twentieth century. Just as the Ottoman Empire was losing segments of its Christian population, it was gaining Muslim refugees from Balkan regions. One consequence of this remaking of the empire's geographic and religious landscape was that the late nineteenth-century Ottoman administration began to conceive of political citizenship in terms that suited its new demographic reality of a growing Muslim population (Salzmann 1999). The inescapable tension at the heart of modern politics between the universal (citizenship extended without restriction) and the particular (its grounding in *this* community, history, and state) was increasingly palpable and the source of tremendous volatility in the final decades of the Ottoman Empire.

These trends would only continue in the ensuing decades. The Balkan Wars (1912–1913), which led to the loss of 83 percent of the empire's remaining European territories and 69 percent of the population inhabiting the European provinces (Çağaptay 2006: 6), were particularly devastating for the Ottoman Empire. The full impact of these wars cannot be registered solely in territorial or demographic terms. Many of the empire's ruling elite hailed from regions that were lost, such as Macedonia, Albania, and Thrace, and they viewed such areas as the cultural and political core of the empire (Zürcher 2001: 114; Silverstein 2003). After the Balkan Wars, Ottoman leaders increasingly defined political identity in ethno-sectarian terms, insisting on the Turkish language as the medium of state schools, prohibiting non-Turkish languages for business correspondence, and forcing the adoption of Turkish names for Anatolian towns and residents bearing non-Turkish appellations—a set of policies sometimes referred to as "Turkification" (Ülker 2005). Such policies exacerbated the tension between the formal rights of citizenship and the ethno-religious cleavages that were increasingly shaping political identity on the ground.

The most lasting and dramatic impact of Turkification involved the movement of populations during World War I. Between 1915 and 1916, the Ottoman leadership decided to expel Armenian populations from Anatolia or simply massacre them. These relocations and killings largely eliminated an entire ethno-national population from Anatolia.[6] The Lausanne Treaty of 1923, which secured Turkey's independence as a sovereign nation-state, led to another wave of population movements: the Greek Orthodox communities in Turkey were "exchanged" by international decree with the Muslims of Greece.

The Ottoman Empire thus progressively disintegrated, and a Turkish nation-state was founded largely in what had been the imperial hinterland of Anatolia. The account that I have briefly sketched here should alert us to the fact that Anatolia was not simply now valorized where it had once been neglected. The composition of Anatolia itself had been radically transformed. Comparing Anatolia between 1913 and 1923, Zürcher (2001: 172) notes the extent of the change: "Anatolia, which had been 80 per cent Muslim before the wars, was now approximately 98 per cent Muslim. Linguistically, only two large groups were left: the Turks and the Kurds, with half a dozen smaller groups. . . . The city population had shrunk even further than the rural population." By the time of the new Turkish nation-state's formation in 1923, most political elites conflated Turkish nationality and Muslim religious identity—a conflation that remains hegemonic in Turkish political culture today (Eissenstat 2005). The remarkable social and political plurality of the Ottoman Empire in linguistic, ethnic, and religious terms had been flattened dramatically and rapidly.

From 1923 onward, under the leadership of Mustafa Kemal Atatürk, the Turkish nation-state embarked on the project of secularizing reform, both juridical-bureaucratic and in the quotidian spheres of dress, language, and sociability. The Kemalist state emphasized a radical break from the Ottoman past, and in the process it occluded from view the political and governmental rationalities that it had in fact inherited from its imperial forebear (Meeker 2002; Silverstein 2010). Given the institutionalized erasure of this indebtedness, it is worth stressing that the cultural and demographic contours of the national society, which the state claimed to represent and also sought to transform radically, were set in place during the late Ottoman period. The idea that Turkish society was largely Muslim, with the exception of small Christian and Jewish communities, which would then be recognized as minorities of suspect loyalty, was a product of the recent imperial past (Rodrigue 2013).

There is an extraordinary historical irony that has been little appreciated by commentators on contemporary Turkish politics who have focused their attention on disputes between Kemalist secularists and their Islamist opponents: Kemalist secularization was not simply imposed upon a traditional Muslim society; the very character of that society as almost exclusively Muslim was forged in the decades preceding the Kemalist period. The formation of Turkish society as Muslim, indeed the naturalization of this ethno-religious equivalence by political elites, was a historical precondition and premise of Turkish secularization.

It was at this moment of dramatic political upheaval and demographic transplantation that a new demand for knowledge about Alevis came to be articulated. Studies of Alevism were one element in a broader effort to fix a stable terrain of knowledge about an Anatolian cultural geography that had been rapidly transforming. Within the newly Muslim landscape of late Ottoman and early republican Anatolia, the status of communities such as the Alevi was a matter of intense political concern and uncertainty. Alevis were not recognizable as members of a non-Muslim religious group, which in this context was largely restricted to Jews and Christians; but nor did nationalist elites see them as unproblematically Muslim, in a context where the dominant conceptions of Islam were drawn from the Sunni majority. They were a population between the categories that defined the emergent political rationality.

AT THE LIMITS OF POLITICAL RATIONALITY

Extending back at least to the sixteenth century, the Ottoman Empire had explicitly defined itself, not merely as an Islamic state, but as one that abided by Sunni jurisprudential traditions. In the sixteenth century, this claim to Sunni Islamic authority was pitched largely in the context of conflicts with the neighboring Safavid Empire, which at that point had explicitly adopted a Shiʻi identity.

In the late nineteenth century, during the reign of Abdülhamid II (1876–1909), the Ottoman state once again made overt appeals to Sunni Islam, but it did so in a context that had witnessed the structural, modernist reforms and the rapid transformations in Ottoman territory and demography outlined above. During the fateful years preceding and following the Treaty of Berlin, when the first massive territorial losses were suffered, Abdülhamid's regime sought to assert its legitimacy and consolidate support by making overt appeals to Islam.

One result of this open embrace of Islam as the primary source of political legitimacy was that the regime felt threatened by the perceived growth of non-Sunni Muslim populations, especially the Shi'a. Selim Deringil (1990) notes that the Hamidian regime dispatched ulema (religious scholars) into Iraq, where a sizable Shi'i community had deep roots, in order to educate the population about the ills of Shi'ism. The ulema were also expected to report back to the government about communities or individuals who were fomenting rebellious sentiments. One Ottoman military officer urged the state to intervene by building schools that would promote loyalty to the empire and combat the growth of Shi'ism (Fortna 2002: 62–66). One should not conclude, however, that the Ottoman state had a single or straightforward position regarding the Shi'a. To take one example of imperial ambiguity, the Ottoman state sought to curb flagellation in rituals of mourning among the Shi'a of Iraq in the late nineteenth century, but it permitted the Iranian community of Istanbul to perform such rituals in order to demonstrate the pan-Islamic identity of the empire (Mervin 2000). The question of whether such devotional practices undermined political cohesion, which, as we saw in the previous chapter, persists as a live question in the present day, was not given a consistent answer.

Within the first decade of the twentieth century, Abdülhamid was unseated. The Committee of Union and Progress (İttihat ve Terakki Cemiyeti, İTC) took control over the Ottoman state and restored the constitution that the Hamidian regime had revoked. The İTC downplayed the earlier rhetorical appeals to the state's Islamic legitimacy, and it increasingly harnessed definitions of political sovereignty in terms of a Turkish, rather than pan-Islamic, identity. Yet as noted above, the events of the Balkan Wars and the massive scale of violence in succeeding years led İTC leaders to define Turkishness itself in terms of the Sunni Muslim majority. While Abdülhamid's rhetoric of Sunni Islamic authority was left behind, the İTC—and a decade later, the republican nation-state—nonetheless inherited the tacit convention that oriented Turkish political subjectivity toward majoritarian religious identity. One early republican politician candidly noted the seeming contradiction at the heart of the rising nation-state: while the constitution of the early republic formally granted citizenship regardless of religion or race, the deputy from Gallipoli, Celal Nuri Bey, claimed that "everybody" knew that the real citizens of Turkey were Sunni-Hanefi Muslims who spoke Turkish (Kirişci 2000: 18).[7]

Within a context that tacitly conflated political citizenship with ethno-religious identifications, Alevi communities fell within the crevices of the existing categories. They were neither manifestly non-Muslim nor evidently Sunni Muslim. Scattered across the Anatolian terrain embraced by late Otto-man and early republican elites, rural Alevi communities had long held to certain religious narratives and ritual practices that were drawn from Shi'i traditions of commemorating early Islamic martyrs, which I have called the parables of Karbala. Their situation called out for resolution: were Alevis to be recognized as members of the Turkish nation, and, if so, on what grounds?

It is worth emphasizing that there is no necessary reason why non-Sunni forms of Islamic practice could not be tolerated by early nationalist leaders, and indeed in strictly juridical terms, such practices were not proscribed. It is doubtful that İTC and early nationalist elites were strongly driven by doctrinal concerns about the religious propriety of such "unorthodox" prac-tices. Very few, if any, of these leaders were trained in religious seminaries or identified themselves as members of the ulema.[8] If early nationalist lead-ers expressed a concern about how to classify Alevi ethnicity and religiosity, such concerns were not motivated by an interest in identifying and isolating religious deviance.

In the actual course of events, Alevi practices did, in fact, raise central dilemmas for the intellectual and political leaders of the time. In the years leading up to World War I and the empire's collapse, late Ottoman elites began speaking about Alevis in an entirely new mode, mediated by a new form of knowledge. Several Ottoman elites had immersed themselves in the new Euro-pean sociology, particularly its French variants. It is well documented that major intellectuals associated with Turkish nationalist currents, such as Ziya Gökalp, were heavily indebted to the writings of Durkheim, Le Bon, Tarde, and others within this tradition (Spencer 1958; Parla 1985; Davison 1998). Rural Anatolian communities, including but not exhausted by the Alevi, became central objects of sociological examination, investigable by means of analytical concepts such as custom, belief, culture, society, and civilization. Early nationalist elites discovered a sociological, rather than heresiological, impetus to scrutinize Alevi communities.

The rise of modern sociology is crucial to understanding the concepts that allowed Alevism to become an object of concern for such elites, but it is not sufficient for understanding the demand for knowledge about these communities, to which sociology provided a possible response. The demand for this knowledge derived from the political conjuncture of the moment. Within that conjuncture, modern apparatuses of knowledge production were intimately connected to the governance of Anatolia. Such connections manifest what Zygmunt Bauman refers to as the legislative function of modernist sociology, that is, the contributions of sociology to the modern state's efforts at "moulding social reality" (1992: 10). Late Ottoman and early republican leaders were seeking to produce a cultural geography of Anatolia, even as they claimed to be merely depicting and championing it.[9]

One Turkish historian, Enver Şapolyo, notes in passing the comments of İTC and early republican leaders in which they ascribe governmental imperatives to the production of sociological knowledge. Şapolyo (1964: 2) reports the following proclamation of Talat Paşa, a leader of the İTC and later a grand vizier of the empire: "For us, Anatolia is a closed box, and I believe that it is necessary for us to first become familiar with what is inside of it, and then to provide services worthy of the nation." Responding to this call, Gökalp announced the intellectual task at hand:

> We have accomplished a political revolution. . . . But the biggest revolution is a social [içtimai] revolution. The most significant and productive revolutions in our social structure will be those that we can achieve in the field of culture. This is possible only by coming to know the social morphology and social physiology of the Turkish community. These are social institutions, which include the different religious beliefs of Anatolia and the orders, sects, and Turcoman tribes that emerged from them. (Şapolyo 1964: 2)

Anatolia was increasingly posited as a distinct social space, whose religious, historical, and cultural elements could be investigated and delineated. It is significant that the study of Anatolian society was seen by political and intellectual leaders of the time as transformative of that social space, a revolution of social institutions and culture. The project of sociological knowledge production implied a forensics of the social, charged with the task of detecting and determining the material traces of Anatolian society (its "morphology" and "physiology") by means of ethnographic and historical study.

What is perhaps only partially portrayed in the quoted statements of these leaders is the embattled political exigency of the moment. With the shedding of territories and populations in the last decade of the empire, Ottoman and early republican elites began to view Anatolia as a homeland for the Turks whose viability as such could not be taken for granted and that therefore had to be secured beyond doubt. They began to view Anatolia as "the Turk's last stand" (Zürcher 2005: 388; Reynolds 2011). It is within this crucible of events that the demand for knowledge about Anatolia's actual inhabitants arose. Given the tensions of Ottoman citizenship, the sociological study of Anatolia was guided by the perceived necessity of constructing a new Turkish nation and securing the state.

The political urgency of producing this knowledge is revealed more pro-foundly in a brief comment by Rıza Nur, a Turkish statesman who served on the delegation that concluded the Treaty of Lausanne in 1923. The treaty established the sovereignty of the Turkish nation-state in international law. It also formally set the terms of that sovereignty by defining Christians and Jews as official minorities, who were allowed certain exemptions and benefits by virtue of that status. Alevis were not so defined, but neither were they simply ignored, as if overlooked in the haste of the moment. In his memoirs published in the late 1960s—some four and a half decades after the events chronicled here—Nur (1967: 1044) reports that the Turkish delegation had to actively fight against the ascription of minority status to Alevis: "With the term 'religion,' [the European powers] were going to make two million kızılbaş, who are pure [halis] Turks, into a minority."[10] Nur's somewhat defensive astonishment reveals the characteristic category conflation described above: Alevis simply cannot be classed as a religious minority in the Turkish nation-state because they are, by his account, ethnic Turks. That Nur, a statesman, raises this question of Alevi ethno-religiosity in the context of Lausanne suggests that the problem of defining Alevism was not a purely academic matter; its resolution was an element in how the Turkish nation-state's sovereignty was established.

To contemporaries, the fact that an entirely new formulation of political sovereignty—embodied in a nation-state that would only later become hegemonic—was simultaneously being openly debated and negotiated indicated a deep indeterminacy and contingency. The outcome could hypothetically have led in a different direction—for instance, to a formal European colonization of Anatolia. At stake in discussions, studies, and policies concerned with Alevism was the viability of a new mode of sovereign power that took the recently established notion of a national society as the foundation of its legitimacy and its site of operation.

This point cannot be overstated, for without it we cannot understand the intense scrutiny almost invariably applied to efforts to define Alevism throughout the twentieth century. Whether we look back to late Ottoman writings on Alevis or to present-day statements by Turkish officials, such definitions frequently insist on the pure Turkish character of Alevi beliefs and practices. In this regard, Nur's confidence in the Turkishness of the Alevi community prefigures a good deal of late twentieth-century discourse. The incessant proclamation of Alevi Turkishness also suggests, symptomatically, a tremendous uncertainty that invited reassuring clarification and continues to provoke the production of knowledge about Alevism to this day. The political powers that determined late Ottoman and early republican sociological studies may have been forged out of a particular historical conjuncture, but the anxieties and incitements that shaped the will to knowledge about Alevism would persist in the coming decades and through to the present.

TOWARD A TOPOGRAPHY OF THE HOMELAND

Late Ottoman studies of "society" exemplify a much wider trend in both Europe and the Middle East of the time. The notion of a "social body" emerged in Britain in the second half of the nineteenth century as part of state-driven efforts to manage and govern distinct communities as a single population (Poovey 1995). Similarly, the idea of an abstract social realm that could be tangibly represented in the form of rituals, crowds, monuments, and statistics developed in Egypt only in the nineteenth century (Mitchell 1991). In both cases, what was emerging was not a new set of representations of social life, but the very idea of a social order, whose objective character was materially evidenced and could be empirically measured.[11] This notion of "society"—an abstract realm requiring representation in tangible signs—was itself an object of concerted institutional construction and regulation.

Late Ottoman and early republican studies of Alevism were guided by a new imperative to discover representations that revealed the existence of an Anatolian society. Alevi communities provided one site for late Ottoman elites to discern the ideal social reality of Anatolia. Seeking to determine the material and measurable elements of Anatolia, political leaders dispatched ethnographers to study its various religious, tribal, and ethnic groups (Dündar 2001). Baha Sait ([1918] 2000: 79), who had been sent to study the Alevis of eastern Anatolia, commented that "our Anatolia needs to be seen anew, from village to village, and its ethnography needs to be made, like a topography of the homeland [*memleketin topoğrafyası*]." The ethnographic study of Alevis was part of a broader project aimed at defining a coherent and unified social geography of Anatolia.

The call for an ethnographic topography of Anatolia had precedents. In the late nineteenth century, a number of proto-nationalist ideologues had already begun demanding more studies of Turkish folklore and language as they existed among Anatolian peasants, whose relationship to Turkish culture was purportedly less corrupt than that of the Istanbul elite (Kushner 1977: 53). In the early twentieth century, some of the Ottoman elite started to celebrate rural traditions of Anatolian "folk music," and by the beginning of the republic in the 1920s, the Turkish state's Ministry of Education was organizing field trips for the collection of Anatolian folk songs (Stokes 1992: 34). Previously isolated attempts at conceptualizing Anatolia as an autonomous social space blossomed into a program of sociological and historical research.

One consequence of this project of identifying material signs of Anatolia's social topography was that studies focused on Alevi communities would either neglect or dismiss religious traditions that extended beyond the social geography of Anatolia, such as the parables of Karbala. The result was a complicated interplay between valorizing Alevi traditions that could be historicized as particular to the Anatolian context, on the one hand, and disputing the claims of Alevis themselves concerning the moral significance of Shiʻi Islam's Twelve Imams, on the other.[12] Alevi adherence to the parables of Karbala posed a central problem for late Ottoman and early republican ethnographers, who operated under the representational imperative to identify Alevi traditions as tangible evidence of an Anatolian society.

Although Sait ([1926] 2000: 120) praised Alevis for "protecting the language, lineage, and blood of the Turks," he nonetheless offered a critical commentary on their reverence for the Twelve Imams. He targeted an Alevi tradition that follows the Shiʻi doctrine of the Twelfth Imam. According to these traditions, the Twelfth Imam never died. He went into hiding and will return as the *Mehdi*, that is, the one who will usher in the end of time and the Day of Judgment. Sait mentioned this tradition in order to undermine it. Rather than locating it within the fold of Islam, he suggested that Alevi ideas of the Mehdi resemble Jewish and Christian notions of the Messiah.[13] Crucially, he did not elaborate a theological polemic against Judaism or Christianity—for instance, by attacking the Christian conception of Jesus as a human embodiment of God. Avoiding such polemics altogether, Sait centered his concern on the historical inauthenticity of the tradition in what he understood as a Turkish-Anatolian milieux. He issued a sweeping methodological warning for students of Alevi sociology: "It is definitely not correct to connect [Anatolian Alevis] to Ali and the Imams. . . . [T]he path and ritual life of this community derives from the customs of the [Turkish] Oğuz tribe, which falls under the tent of Turkish shamanism. It is nothing else" ([1926] 2000: 121).

Sait sought to identify Alevi religiosity as the material sign of a historically perduring Turkish Anatolian society. This representational imperative led him to disarticulate Alevism from the parables of the Twelve Imams, in spite of the fact that his Alevi interlocutors claimed adherence to them. He perceived such traditions to be exogenous to the community's ethno-historical identity and contrary to the Turkish essence he sought to discern.

Yusuf Ziya Yörükan's ethnographic studies of Alevism from the early years of the republic provide further examples of the epistemological dilemmas posed by the Karbala narratives to students of the new sociology of Anatolia. Yörükan's studies were largely conducted among Tahtacıs, a community that most scholars (including Yörükan) locate within the broader rubric of Anatolian Alevism. In a series of articles published in the 1930s, he opened his account with a discussion of the Karbala parables, acknowledging that many Alevis describe their religious practices in terms of the exemplary models of the Twelve Imams. Yörükan did not attempt to explain the significance that these parables hold for existing Alevi communities; he sought to clarify the fact that these traditions do not, in fact, provide an adequate ground for understanding Anatolian Alevi customs and practices. He wanted to directly address the epistemological problems raised by the Karbala narratives to the project of studying Anatolia. His solution was to reject the relevance of the narratives altogether.

In order to set these narrative practices to the side, Yörükan claimed that many of the traditions concerning the Twelve Imams, which are shared by Alevis and Shiʻis, originated in the political history of Iran, a history he viewed as only tenuously related to Anatolian-based Alevi communities. He began by considering the fact that many Alevis revile certain figures that Sunnis revere as the first caliphs of Islam: Abu Bakr, Umar al-Khattab, and Uthman ibn Affan. Alevis share with Shiʻas elsewhere in the world the idea that such figures illegitimately usurped positions of leadership away from Ali ibn Abi Talib in the era that followed Muhammad's death. Alevis abide by a tradition that has deep roots in Shi'ism, in which they both ritually curse the three caliphs and express a love for Ali and his descendants (the Twelve Imams).[14] Yörükan (1998: 243) acknowledged that Alevis follow such traditions: "Yes, hostility toward Abu Bakr, Umar, and the Umayyad dynasty, along with a love of the Twelve Imams—which is another form of this hostility, or a more reasonable expression of it—is the most fundamental principle [umde] of Alevism." However, Yörükan was troubled by the fact that Alevis consider this principle to be a "doctrine" (akide). He refuted its alleged doctrinal status by questioning its historical origins:

> But this principle . . . is not found in any [authoritative Islamic] account about the world, the afterlife, God, or the Prophet. This [principle] is nothing other than a manifestation of a political invention, which started with the collapse of Iran in the time of Umar and can be expressed with the phrase "hostility toward Arabs." Thus, traditions [ananeler] established in the regions of Karbala and Mashhad [both Shi'i shrine cities] did not express the principles of a doctrinal system but an enmity toward Mecca and Medina (Yörükan 1998: 243–245).

To this doctrinal critique of Shi'i claims about early Islam, Yörükan added a historicist claim about the Iranian origins of the Shi'i tradition, which laid the ground for his arguments about the Anatolian culture of Alevism. His purpose was not only to clarify the true religious message from historical accretions—a typical modern reformist move—but thereby to clear a path for a more rigorous historicization of Alevism.

As with Sait, Yörükan searched for the authenticity of Alevi religiosity within the social history of Anatolia. In this regard, he did not repudiate Alevism as a false form of religion, but rather defined the criteria for deriving the historical origins of Alevi practices. According to Yörükan, Alevi invocations of the Karbala narratives had more to do with the complicated religious history of the medieval Turkish migrations from Central Asia to Anatolia than with any authoritative Islamic doctrinal tradition. In the course of that migration, Turkish Alevi groups passed through Iran, and consequently came to bear the imprint of Iranian anxieties. "But these principles belonged to Shi'ism before Alevism. They do not reveal the distinguishing attributes of Alevis. It is necessary to search in other places for the characteristics of Tahtacı-Alevi belief" (Yörükan 1998: 245).

Yörükan was suspicious of Alevi claims to derive their practices from a single, consistent religious system. He argued instead that Alevism is the product of a number of distinctive creeds, beliefs, and doctrines. "Rather than search for a system of faith [itikat]," Yörükan concluded, "I am content to relate Alevi-Tahtacı customs [adetler] as they are" (1998: 253). The distinction between "a system of faith" and "customs as they are" carries an epistemological burden: Alevi ritual can be coherently comprehended neither through a reading of scriptural and exegetical traditions nor as a practice of narrating the self in relation to moral exemplars from the Islamic past, but as a regionally and historically specific set of customs. Describing some of these customs, Yörükan mentions visitations to saints' tombs, animal sacrifices for the ill, and practices of ritual mourning that are specific to Anatolia.

Yörükan was correct that the practices associated with the Karbala narratives have a history that extends beyond the geohistorical space of Anatolia, one that encompasses—but, it must be noted, also exceeds—Iran. What made the geographically permeable history of the practice troubling to these early republican scholars was the fact that it thereby cannot easily be posited as evidence of the Turkish nation's formation within Anatolia. It fails to meet the demand for knowledge about Alevism, that is, to provide material evidence of a coherent Turkish Anatolia as a social foundation for the nation. Sait and Yörükan's studies eliminate from the archive of authorized knowledge elements of Alevi religiosity that do not conform to narratives of the nation, which at that point were only just precariously emerging.

Not all writers connected to the late Ottoman and early republican regimes found evidence of a national essence in Alevi rituals. Another nationalist researcher, Habil Adem, wrote about the importance of "civilizing" Alevis by undermining their religious traditions, which he saw as an obstacle to their assimilation to the norms of "modern" morality. This civilizing project could be achieved, according to Adem, by breaking up rural tribes and resettling them in areas that were more densely populated by Sunni Turks (Dressler 2013: 133–137).[15]

Adem's writings are a useful reminder that the selectively valorizing approaches of some nationalists never exhausted the range of positions adopted by intellectuals of the era. In their development and elaboration, Turkish nationalist ideologies have accommodated a number of different approaches to the Alevi community. However, it is also important to note that despite differences in interpretation, researchers of the time were motivated by a shared demand for knowledge about Alevi religiosity, which oriented and organized the space of debate itself and delineated the limits of possible argument. The extraordinary tension between some of these positions—between valorization and preservation, on the one hand, and assimilation and eradication, on the other—presupposed an underlying concern to secure the imaginary of a cohesive Turkish Anatolia. Nationalist writers of the time sought to resolve a problem internal to the formation of the nation-state: to provide evidence of the existence of a national society that the state could thereafter claim to represent.

THE SOVEREIGNTY OF TURKISH ANATOLIA

Many nationalist ideologues of the late Ottoman and early republican era remained uncertain about whether Alevi communities were in fact loyal to the project of nation-building. The question of loyalty was raised most acutely in relation to the influence of Protestant missionaries on Alevi communities. Commonly of American origin, the missionaries were active in eastern Anatolia during the late Ottoman Empire. They viewed Alevis as potential subjects for conversion. Some went as far as to suggest that existing Alevi beliefs, particularly concerning the purported deification of Ali, already expressed a crypto-Christian, rather than Muslim, religiosity (Karakaya-Stump 2004).

Protestant missionaries had been operating in Anatolia for decades before late Ottoman leaders "discovered" the Alevi. Late on the scene, as it were, many early Turkish nationalist ethnographers of Alevism saw missionary Christianity as a threat. The ruling İTC was worried about the missionary presence, and its efforts to produce ethnographic knowledge were shaped by a concern to investigate whether groups in Anatolia had converted to Christianity (Zürcher 2005). In the aftermath of the Balkan Wars, conversion posed a specific problem for the İTC because of the characteristic conflation of Turkish ethno-nationality with Muslim identification. The possibility that Alevis were converting to Christianity raised doubts about the community's allegiance to a nation that was de facto defined as Muslim. Nationalist depictions of Alevism, such as Sait's, guarded against missionary influences and championed, instead, the Turkish origins of Alevism's central ritual traditions. The very possibility of locating the new nation's cultural geography in Anatolia depended, in part, on this framing of Alevi religious history.

The notion that there may have been Christian influence among late Ottoman Alevi communities is not untenable, but an adequate understanding of that relationship is foreclosed by nationalist writings that conceptualized Christian influence exclusively in terms of Protestant missions. Completely ignored, if not occluded, by early Turkish writings on the Alevi is the fact that Protestant missionaries were not the only Christians present in the area. Up through the late nineteenth and early twentieth centuries, Anatolia hosted an ethnically and denominationally diverse array of Christian populations. Hans-Lukas Kieser (2004) notes that Alevi villages in eastern Anatolia were often located near Armenian Christian villages. He demonstrates that at least some eastern Alevis in the late nineteenth century were educated at the modern schools established by the Armenians. If there was a Christian influence among the Alevi populations, it was likely the result of what Kieser identifies as a significant degree of intercommunal and institutionally formalized engagement between Alevis and Armenians. The history of such encounters is extremely difficult to write, largely because the historiographical and ethnographic archives that Sait and his İTC colleagues established did not permit a cultural geography of Alevi sociality for which Turkish-Muslim Anatolia was neither the historical root nor spatial limit. Given the fact that Sait's research was conducted around the era of the Armenian relocations and massacres, it is unsurprising that he fails to acknowledge the sheer presence and possible impact of Armenians within Alevi milieux.

If nationalist ethnographers such as Sait and Yörükan often pitched their studies of Alevism in opposition to the ideas of missionaries, this claim of opposition itself papers over some important similarities between the nationalists and the missionaries, particularly concerning their commitments to historicism as a guiding framework for conceptualizing Alevism. Most Protestant missionaries defined Alevi religiosity as an accumulation of various historical religious traditions, especially those that derived from pre-Islamic origins. One missionary, Henry Perry, was disparaging in his historicism: "Their religion is a relic of paganism molded by Mohammedan tradition and custom; but to me the special interest about it arises from what I consider to be a fact that, without knowing themselves the grounds on which they stand, they are a nation of pantheists" (quoted in Türkyılmaz 2009: 261).

Perry's claim conjoins a number of elements that would be argued in equal measure by nationalists like Sait and Yörükan. First, Alevi religion is said to reveal a historical layering of various religious traditions; second, Islam is but one such tradition within this series, and by no means its deepest root; and third, Alevis themselves had little awareness of their religious history.

Nationalist writings shared with their missionary predecessors a historicist concern with locating the diverse origins of Alevi religious traditions and charting their evolving, syncretic development.[16] Each insisted that to adequately understand the Alevi past, modern forms of historical knowledge production were necessary. That Alevi traditions might have organized modalities of religious memory inaccessible to modernist forms of historical knowledge is simply excluded at the outset, regardless of whether the discourse was pejorative (as with Perry) or celebratory (as with Sait and Yörükan).

What sets nationalist discourses apart is the insistence that both the historical origins and the development of Alevi tradition represented the Turkish national character of Anatolia. Nationalist ideologues yoked a historicist imaginary to the project of asserting and establishing the nation's existence. Their efforts were motivated by a sense of urgency in defining the nation, in a moment where its geopolitical viability could not be taken for granted. The nationalist appropriation of Alevism was nothing less than a defense of the sovereignty of a Turkish national order.

CONCLUSION

Present-day debates about Alevism are often seen as disputes over representation. As exemplified in the debate between Ali Doğan and Hasan Meşeli that opened the chapter, one key question is whether to locate Alevi religiosity within or without the fold of Islam. Who, moreover, has the authority to rule on this matter—the state, public intellectuals, or Alevi organizations? These problems of representation are central to the political struggles that Alevis have faced in becoming increasingly vocal actors in Turkey's public spheres over the past few decades.

Yet analyses focused exclusively on problems of representation run the risk of eliding the institutional demand for representation as such. Out of what conjunctures and contingencies has it become not only thinkable but necessary to represent Alevism as a sociohistorical form proper to Anatolia? What perceived political vulnerabilities incite this will to knowledge about Alevism? To what anxieties is knowledge about Alevism seen to provide a formidable response?

Consider again Meşeli's striking rebuttal of Doğan's claim that Alevis should be assigned a distinct religious affiliation on national identity cards: "Our God is one, our Qur'an is one, our Prophet is one, and our flag is one." The comment reveals a central conundrum explored in this book, in which emblems of national homogeneity are mobilized within Alevi discourses that are otherwise often seen to signal a pluralization of Turkey's public sphere. Alevis today bear the burden of performing their difference in a way that secures the integrity and cohesion of the Turkish nation. I have sought to identify the historical emergence of this dynamic. The demand placed on Alevis to enact the nation's unity responds to a sense of political instability that is, in part, a product of the historical conjuncture that led to the collapse of the Ottoman Empire and the birth of the republican state.

My claim is that in the late nineteenth and early twentieth centuries a particular intelligibility came into being, framing both a new political rationality and a new form of knowledge. The category of Anatolian Alevism was invested with tremendous significance, as sign of the new nation's historical depth and as justification of the national state's territorial sovereignty over Anatolia. As a social category, it articulated with a new organization of knowledge and power. Alevism emerged as an object of knowledge—as something that could be discussed, thought, and argued over—by means of the nation's historical temporality. It was consolidated as a distinct object of thought as a way of establishing and elaborating the space-time of Turkish Anatolia.

In the final decades of the twentieth century, Alevis attained the ability to represent themselves in public forums in the name of autonomous self-expression, but they have nonetheless been pressured to narrate their history within the framework of Anatolia's social geography. The continued recurrence of tropes of national cohesion within Alevis discourses can be understood as an outcome of the demand for knowledge and the historical conjuncture from which it emerged. To extend religious identification beyond Anatolia's boundaries risks the charge that they are dividing the nation. The narrative norm that incites the representation of Alevism continues to be oriented by a modernist project of procuring evidence of the nation's consolidation in the face of stubborn heterogeneity and political violence.

It would be hasty to suggest that the conjunctures and impulses that guided late Ottoman and early republican approaches to Alevism have simply continued unchanged up to the present. What deserve greater specification are the practices that operationalize knowledge-forms about Alevism, and the agents and authorities who invoke them today. Crucial historical shifts, which I unpack in the chapters ahead, dramatically reconfigured Turkey's political and economic footing in the second half of the twentieth century. These shifts transformed the significance and salience of existing, nationalist discourses and the practices that made them available for appropriation by Alevis themselves. Two questions orient my analysis of these developments. To what extent has the space-time of the nation demarcated the limits of Alevi collective memory? How have Alevis begun to disrupt their own location and role in this dispensation of knowledge and power?

4 INCITEMENTS TO VISIBILITY

IN THE ETHNOGRAPHIC AND HISTORICAL materials examined in thus far, I have begun to analyze a constitutive tension at the heart of modern Turkish politics between a juridical dispensation of political freedom, on the one hand, and the unrelenting demands of national cohesion and singularity, on the other. The universal extension of rights to all individuals, regardless of gender, race, and religion, may be the measure of democratic citizenship, but citizenship itself remains coded within state-regulated discourses of political community. In this chapter, I explore how certain claims to equal citizenship in the name of pluralism navigate a political path by lurching between the poles of this tension.

I examine these dilemmas in relation to ongoing, often heated, public debates about the religious and political status of Alevi rituals known as the *ayin-i cem*, or *cem* for short. In recent decades, the Turkish state has insisted that such rituals constitute a treasured form of national folklore. A number of national Alevi organizations have contested this mode of legitimating Alevi ritual. They have insisted that the state classify the cem not as folklore but as a practice of worship, or *ibadet*.

Alevi organizations that seek to counter the state's categorization of communal ritual often forward a critical commentary on the majoritarian bias of the law. In asserting that their rituals must be defined as ibadet, such groups imply or directly accuse the state of privileging notions of worship derived from the Sunni majority's religious tradition. The claim is that existing law and administration violate the state's own claims to universal equality by holding the majority's ritual forms as applicable to all of Turkey's citizenry. At its most incisive, the political critique challenges the democratic legitimacy of a state that claims to represent all of its citizens in equal measure.

The politics in question, however, carries an ambivalence that becomes apparent by looking at the recent history of public performances of Alevi ritual. Public displays of communal ritual have enabled the presence of Alevi traditions in urban centers from which they had long been excluded. For many participants, public performances facilitate a pluralist politics by appropriating city spaces that, while ostensibly available to all citizens, have long been premised on the marginalization of the Alevi community. As I detail below, the social, spatial, and material form of such performances—in short, their aesthetic media—shape the community's public visibility in ways that render this visibility palatable and often pleasurable to a national audience. The practices that have enabled a pluralist challenge to the nation-state incorporate the community into the rhythms and gestures of national spectacle.

The aesthetic forms that I depict in this chapter are incited for public display by various state agencies, political parties, and news media. Alevis are institutionally encouraged to claim their difference, but they are also pressured to render this difference recognizable through forms of staging and spectatorship that validate official rubrics of national belonging. The incitement to visibility requires ethnographic unpacking in ways that reveal both the political powers that direct it and the subjectivity it fosters.

Many Alevi actors are not naive about the complicity of their public self-presentation in the machinations of statist imaginings of the nation. On the contrary, a number of my Alevi friends and interlocutors expressed unease about the way in which communal ritual has been rendered into a species of entertainment and leisure for the national viewing public. Many Alevis discern the fact that their visibility excites certain modes of affective attachment, only at the expense of others. Yet this unease is balanced by the fact that these public displays have also allowed the community to attain a stable footing in a context where they have often been vulnerable to violence. Many intellectuals, organizations, and ordinary Alevis alike readily point out the ongoing history of state-sanctioned discrimination against their community, but few are willing to directly challenge the sites and styles of performance that have sustained the community's recently achieved public visibility.

INVOCATIONS OF PLURALISM

At the heart of current policy debates concerning the governance of Alevi ritual lies the status of the cem. The cem is a central ritual practice for Turkey's Alevi community. It functions as a rite of initiation for adolescents, as a commemoration ritual for revered figures in early Islamic history, and as a site for the adjudication of social disputes among members of the community. It often includes narratives of Husayn's death, described in chapter 2, in the form of recited hymns and poetry. For several centuries, the Alevi cem was performed in gatherings explicitly closed to outsiders. Long held as a private, communal affair, the cem has gained unprecedented public exposure in the past several decades.

One of the central political demands of Alevi organizations today is that the Turkish state recognize the cem as a form of worship, or ibadet. This demand has become something of a slogan for such groups, shouted at street protests and asserted by Alevi leaders in public speeches. As it stands, the Turkish state—in particular, the Directorate of Religious Affairs—has persistently refused to grant this designation. The state's refusal has not entailed an outright repudiation of Alevi differences. Instead, the refusal to recognize the cem as a practice of worship is almost always accompanied by a clear declaration of support for the ritual. State officials celebrate Alevi ritual as a crucial element of Turkey's cultural heritage or folklore.

In a revealing interview, conducted in a journal predominantly concerned with Alevi issues, the head of the Directorate of Religious Affairs, Ali Bardakoğlu, was asked about the religious status of the *cemevi*, the site where Alevis perform the cem ritual. Bardakoğlu responded, "According to Islam, according to true knowledge of Islam, the cemevi is not a place of worship [*ibadet yeri*] and the supplications and the cem ritual that are performed in the cemevi are not a kind of worship [*ibadet*] that resembles daily worship [*namaz*] or fasting. But it is a good form of behavior [*davranış*], it is an activity that must be kept alive" (Gültekin and Işık 2005: 10). Characteristically, he expressed his approval of the cem only on the condition that it not be considered worship. The term that Bardakoğlu used, "behavior" (*davranış*), leaves the ritual status of the practice ambiguous. The interviewers continued to push Bardakoğlu on the matter, forcing him to specify further what the cem amounts to. Pressed to elaborate, he explained, "Never in our history has the cemevi been an alternative to a mosque or vice versa. They existed together, but the mosque existed as a place of worship, while cemevis were places of culture [*kültür evleri*] in which the traditions of a group within Islam flourished" (Gültekin and Işık 2005: 11).

In their insistence that the cemevi be recognized as a house of worship (*ibadethane*), many Alevi organizations have struggled against the state's designation of their rituals as culture. Recognition of Alevi practice as worship would entail certain political-economic ramifications—organizations that establish sites of worship are eligible for benefits such as free water and electricity, the allocation of building sites, and state funds.[1] Concerns for recognition in this regard have been linked to demands for a more equitable distribution of resources. The dispute over Alevi ritual has been motivated by a variety of institutional agencies, interests, and concerns.

Issues of recognition and equitable resource distribution have also been highlighted in European Union discourses on Turkish political reform. The European Commission's annual report on Turkey's EU accession status regularly includes a discussion of the Turkish state's ongoing failure to adequately recognize Alevi ritual. In its discussion of undue constraints placed on the freedom of religion, a recent report mentions that cemevis are "not recognized as places of worship and, as a result, receive no funding from authorities" (European Commission 2008:19). The concern for the European Commission is that the Turkish state systematically misrecognizes Alevi ritual and, consequently, places material constraints on its enactment.

In the course of my fieldwork, I encountered the discourse about the cem's ritual status in a number of sites—in discussions at cafes, in newspaper editorials, on Alevi web sites, and in interviews with Alevi civil society leaders. Perhaps the most surprising venue for this discourse was within a cem itself. The religious officiant conducting the ritual, known as a *dede*, reflexively commented on the status of the ritual he was leading. Within the space of the ritual, the dede's discourse was neither addressed to state officials nor attempting to contribute to public critiques of administrative classifications. The target of the dede's discourse was the form of visibility that the ritual has attained in recent years. It was an attempt to evaluate the social, aesthetic, and ethical effects of this visibility. A brief ethnographic description of the moment can help to flesh out its significance.

During my field research, I was invited to attend a number of cem ceremonies, the fact of which was itself indicative of the new publicity of Alevi practices. While in attendance, I was often able to correlate the unfolding series of ritual events with practices that I had read about in ethnographic accounts of the cem: the chanting of hymns about revered figures, a cantillation that recounts the ascension of the Prophet to heaven, the performance of religious dances, the recitation of the singularity of God (*tevhid*), and the offering of animal sacrifices.

At one cem ceremony I witnessed a moment that interrupted the formulaic steps of the ritual's typical progression. The event was hosted by the local Çorum branch of a national Alevi organization discussed in chapter 2. It took place in the organization's building—a relatively nondescript three-story building, itself located within the predominantly Alevi neighborhood of the town. The room in which the ritual was conducted was spacious, capable of holding several hundred participants. Women and men sat on separate sides of the room, leaving a narrow gap between them, which constituted the ritually demarcated center, or *meydan*. Toward the conclusion of the cem, a group of ten adolescents entered the meydan. They arrived in order to participate in the ceremony, specifically for the sake of performing the *semah*, a practice constituted by a series of prescribed rhythmical movements, usually set to the recitation of a devotional hymn, and which constitutes a part of the cem. The youth group's desire to perform a semah in the ritual context was not out of place, and indeed a version of the practice had been enacted earlier in that very cem. However, the dede was troubled by the presence of this group of youngsters and began to admonish them. "The cem is a form of worship [*ibadet*]," he declared. "This is not a stage for the performance of folklore [*folklor*]." The dede ultimately relented, allowing the group to perform the semah, but only after repeating that the performance was not a part of the act of worship for which they had congregated.

The dede's reprimand of the youth group summoned the keywords of contemporary disputes—worship and folklore—but in the context of the ritual practice itself, his criticism was directed not at state policy but at adolescents within the community. The mode of address was shaped by the social roles of the participants: the dede, on the one side, and the youth group, on the other. The reprimand carried a pedagogical, moral intonation.

No one in attendance had claimed that the cem was a piece of folklore rather than of worship, but the possibility of this interpretation haunted the scene nonetheless. In the context of ritual performance, the dede's moral rebuke targeted the aesthetics of the performance. His comments addressed what he perceived to be the social form that the youth group typified. This particular ensemble of adolescents bore the marks of many other similar groups in Turkey. They constituted what has come to be called a semah group (*semah ekibi*). These groups are recognizable by certain characteristics: participants are adolescents; they wear distinctive costumes; they rehearse their musical and dance routines in after-school programs; and they only perform certain dances such as the semah, rather than the entirety of the ritual progression that constitutes the cem.

Semah groups perform at a diverse array of venues, which include not only cem ceremonies such as the one that I attended, but summer festivals, celebrations for the opening of new businesses, and gatherings of political parties. By virtue of this wide circulation, semah groups constitute one of the primary mechanisms by which Alevi rituals have generated a public audience. Yet it was this very circulation that created tensions for the dede described above. In these sorts of settings, the semah is removed from the context of communal ritual. It is set on display for bureaucrats, industrial businessmen, and party officials as an element of national heritage and folklore.

The staging of the semah in public venues is not universally championed by Alevis; it is unsettling to many of them. A number of my Alevi interlocutors, including the dede at that particular cem event, felt uneasy about the youth groups. On the one hand, these sorts of semah groups provide an opportunity for Alevi youth to learn the traditions of their community in an urban environment that has notably lacked institutions of communal representation. Equally important, the performances of such groups have enabled Alevis to spark debates over the recognition of communal differences, debates that have been taken up in both domestic and international settings. On the other hand, the publicity of the semah, as performed by these youth groups, is contingent on being recognizable as a type of national folklore rather than as a form of communal worship. The forms of public visibility attained by Alevi organizations are hinged to the category of folklore that some of these organizations are seeking to challenge.

In claiming that the public staging of Alevi ritual is unsettling to some participants, I mean to suggest that these displays provoke troubling questions about the performative effects of the practice. The dede's comments expressed an anxiety about the ritual's public visibility, centered on the style of the semah's enactment and the sense of entertainment that it produces within a context meant for worship. The question that the dede's reprimand implicitly poses is, what sorts of subjectivity do such performances, with their particular modes of staging and spectatorship, enable? What forms of moral sensibility do they foreclose?

CITIZENSHIP, POPULATIONS, AND PLURALISM

In order to understand why Alevi actors today might seek to interrogate the conditions of their own public presence—that is, to explore its costs—it is necessary to explore the historical context in which this presence came to be legitimized. Urban Alevi organizations and a new class of public intellectuals emerged in the late 1980s and 1990s. The virtual explosion of Alevism on the national public scene was one element in a much broader political and economic liberalization. In 1980, the Turkish state adopted IMF reform packages that weakened the state's control over industry. By the 1990s, these reforms had led to the privatization of media outlets, the expansion of commercial television, the development of satellite television networks beaming in from western Europe, and later the emergence and rapid adoption of the Internet.[2] Economic privatization coupled with new communication technologies opened new paths for the development of social and political movements centered on a wide array of concerns: women's movements, environmental movements, Islamist movements, movements for Kurdish sovereignty, and of course Alevi movements.

These developments do not attest to a peaceful expansion of freedoms. At the very least, liberalization has not been experienced in identical terms by different groups. If, for instance, Islamist movements gradually developed into political parties that would, with varying degrees of success, manage to attain victories in democratic elections, Kurdish political struggles have been embroiled in violence since the early 1980s. The Kurdish guerrilla movement, Partiya Karkerên Kurdistan (PKK, Kurdish Workers' Party), has been engaged in armed struggle with the Turkish state. One result of this conflict has been the intensification of military presence and power in predominantly Kurdish cities and villages. The state has persistently closed down Kurdish political parties that seek legitimacy within democratic forums with the claim that such parties maintain ties with the PKK, which the state classes as a terrorist organization.[3]

Turkey's political-economic liberalization has impacted the development of Alevi social and political organization, but this impact has been quite distinct from that experienced by Islamist and Kurdish movements. Alevi movements have neither acquired political power as a governing party nor engaged in militant struggle. The Alevi case suggests a more ambivalent political liberalization. Since the 1980s, communal rituals have attained a degree of public legitimacy, but only by being disciplined, even at times orchestrated, by governing authorities.

What, then, was the historical motivation that led governing powers to address Alevis as objects of a disciplined liberalization? To approach this question we must first turn back to the preceding period of the 1970s, when there was rampant sectarian violence. The governmental imperative to structure Alevi public presence arose in the aftermath of those events. I argue that it was the state's inability to control the terms of sectarian interaction and dispute that led, after the military coup in 1980, to a greater investment in controlling and supervising expressions of Alevi difference.

The tensions that I describe speak to the persistence of certain ambiguities of citizenship in Turkey, which have sometimes exploded into violence and at other periods been quelled through an aggressive disciplinary discourse of national unity. Leyla Neyzi (2002: 140) argues that Turkish national identity is "Janus-faced": it is "defined in terms of a commitment to secular modernist values on the part of the citizens of Turkey," on the one hand, and yet it is understood to be organized in terms of "a single language and a single imagined ethnicity associated with a particular religious heritage," on the other. Similarly, Hamit Bozarslan (2002) maintains that at its inception, the secular Turkish nation-state presupposed Sunni Islam—the religious identification of the majority of the population—as the de facto religion of the nation. Ethnic and religious differences from the Sunni majority have had to be reconciled with the notion of a single homogeneous citizenry.

Partha Chatterjee's (2004) discussion of modern political power suggests that tensions of this kind are by no means particular to Turkey; they are inescapably at the heart of citizenship in much of the world. For Chatterjee, the tension between ethno-religious particularity and claims to universal citizenship cannot be overcome simply by encouraging a more inclusive civic nationalism or by making the spheres of public deliberation more expansive. The dilemma is that discourses of universal national citizenship and discourses that ascertain, classify, and enumerate population differences within the polity are elements of concurrent, but distinctive, modes of modern power. Drawing on Foucault (1991), Chatterjee terms the second mode of power *governmentality*. "[W]hile the political fraternity of citizens had to be constantly affirmed as one and indivisible, there was no one entity of the governed. There

was always a multiplicity of population groups that were the objects of governmentality—multiple targets with multiple characteristics, requiring multiple
techniques of administration" (Chatterjee 2004: 35–36).

Chatterjee distinguishes the concept of citizenship from the notion of
population in terms of their respective targets, mechanisms, and agencies.
Citizenship is central to the normative self-description of most modern poli-
ties: it solicits civic nationalism and fraternal participation in political deliberation. It asks of individuals that they contribute to the common good. By
contrast, the concept of population is an administrative category, amenable
to classification and enumeration. Population groups are addressed, not as a
single sovereign people, but as multiple potential electoral constituencies, as
objects of welfare assistance, as competitors in a labor market, and possibly as
targets of ethno-sectarian violence.

On this account, the conflict between nationalist imaginings of unitary
citizenship and the plurality of populations is intrinsic to politics in a modern state. The question, then, is not whether citizenship can be refashioned
in ways that more adequately represent and encompass social heterogeneity,
facilitating social reconciliation and political consensus in the aftermath of
civil strife.[4] The question, rather, is how the tension between citizenship and
population is institutionally managed, stabilized, or disrupted.

In relation to the Turkish context, there are two empirical questions I wish
to explore at this point that center on the constitutive tensions of citizenship,
and that establish the immediate historical backdrop to what will later emerge
as the period of pluralism. First, how did the expansion of governmentalizing
discourses in the 1960s and 1970s contribute to the eruption of sectarian violence? Second, what mechanisms did the state adopt in succeeding decades to
manage the tensions of citizenship and reassert control over the discourses on
population differences? I argue that the championing of folkloric presentations of Alevi ritual played an important role in this process.

VIOLENCE AND GOVERNMENTALITY

With the mass migrations of villagers to towns and cities in the 1960s and
1970s, Alevis started to establish an urban presence. They began to figure
in the calculations of urban governmentality involving the apportioning of
spaces, the sharing or partitioning of neighborhoods, the courting of electoral constituencies, and the management of labor and employment in an
increasingly unstable economic climate. It was not simply statist elites who

wielded a governmental discourse about the Alevi community—about where they lived and worked, about their political loyalties, and about their religious proclivities—but a larger number of political actors. In the second half of the twentieth century, Turkey experienced what Carter Findley (2010: 305) terms a "widening of the political spectrum," which broadened the range of actors capable of participating in political life.

In part, this widening of politics entailed the formation of new political parties. It is often claimed that Turkey endured its first test of pluralist democracy with the development of multiparty politics in the late 1940s.[5] New parties challenged the Kemalist regime of the early republic with a range of issues, from agricultural reform to the politicization of religion, that had previously been either excluded from open debate or rigidly controlled.

The establishment of new political parties was only one aspect of the expansion of politics. Particularly from the 1960s on, Turkey witnessed the emergence of multiple politicizations across a wide array of groups and actors that were not recognizable as parties in a formal sense, including new networks of religious intellectuals, politicized student groups, labor unions, and increasingly organized militia movements. These various groups often maintained informal but evident connections with official political parties. Within this heterogeneous political landscape, the state's apparatuses of knowledge production were no longer agile enough, if they ever were, to maintain strict control over the delimitation of communal differences. Various groups, autonomous of state control, began making claims about the social, religious, and political allegiances of the Alevi community. Alevis began to be targeted as a distinct urban population in ways the state was unable to manage.

From 1975 to 1980, civil violence escalated from year to year in rapid measure. Within these five years, 5,713 people were killed and 18,480 were wounded as a result of civil violence (Bozarslan 1999). Much of this violence was organized along Cold War polarizations of right- and left-wing political groups. In the provinces of central and eastern Anatolia, however, violence began to erupt along ethno-sectarian fissures, between Sunni and Alevi communities and between Turkish and Kurdish communities. The worst outbreaks of sectarian conflict between Alevis and Sunnis took place in the provinces of Kahramanmaraş, Sivas, Malatya, and Çorum. State officials were insistent that such events were the result, not of widespread communal discord, but of the provocations of extremist groups, who were stoking the flames of communal tension to further their political aims. The claim was not wholly false. The right-wing nationalist Milliyetçi Hareket Partisi (MHP, Nationalist Action Party) was electorally most successful in urban regions of Anatolia where ethno-sectarian cleavages were most pronounced—regions where the MHP proved capable of mobilizing an electorate by inciting sentiments of sectarian antagonism against Alevis (Bora and Can 1991: 70; Yavuz 2003a: 210–211). Yet the politicization of ethno-sectarian differences was by no means the product of extremist groups alone. The MHP was not operating in isolation. By the 1970s, it had established a political coalition with the center-right Adalet Partisi (AP, Justice Party) and the Islamist Milli Selamet Partisi (MSP, National Salvation Party). Moreover, the coalition of parties was linked, officially and informally, with a range of intellectuals, militia organizations, and youth groups. This somewhat unwieldy coalition of political and civil groups collectively propagated slogans that effectively consolidated a single axis of threats to the nation, by associating Alevis and Kurds with communists. In Turkish, the three groups were rhetorically united through the repetition of the consonant "K": *Kürt, Kızılbaş, Komünist.*[6]

The slogan is a deceptively simple formulation of the complex political groupings that had congealed in the 1960s and 1970s. The affiliation of Alevis with Kurds and communists is not, of course, a primordial connection, but neither was it an entirely inaccurate supposition. Many Kurdish and Alevi groups allied themselves with the Left, in part in reaction to the emergent political coalition of the AP, the MSP, and the MHP. Far from being a function of numerically small extremist groups, the politicization of sectarian and ethnic populations was a constitutive force in left-right mobilizations in the years leading up to the military coup in 1980.

The state's insistence that ethno-sectarian violence be interpreted as a political tactic by specific ideological groups begs the question of why such cleavages were available for mobilization in the first place. Emma Sinclair-Webb raises this question explicitly in her discussion of anti-Alevi violence in Kahramanmaraş in 1978:

> The question of why the MHP/Ülkücü [right-wing nationalist] militants saw the sectarian platform as a promising one on which to recruit and agitate is never asked. There was no impulse in reports or in columns to explain something like a "social background" to the events in Maraş. Apart from the names of quarters and the extracted words of witnesses, the town itself remains obscure, its communities, their respective numbers, and the

recent phenomenon of them living in the same town never mentioned. (Sinclair-Webb 2003: 229)

The logic of communities and populations—their sizes, their movements, their cleavages—is excluded from the interpretive discourse of the state and from much newspaper reporting on the events, in favor of notions of a single population, isomorphic with the nation. Yet it is clear that the logic of multiple populations was functioning on the ground: "Communalism . . . , while denied at different official public levels, seems to have been a fully operative system structuring social relations, patterns of employment, space and self-perception on all sides of the population. . . . The fallacy perpetuated in the press, by most politicians and official circles, is that of a population that prior to the events lived 'in brotherhood,' as was often stated, and where differences of sect were irrelevant" (Sinclair-Webb 2003: 229–230). The notion of national solidarity, conspicuous in references to the bonds of fraternity, was rhetorically ever present, even as the state grew increasingly incapable of governing sectarian plurality, of managing distinctions between populations, and of authorizing their legitimate manifestations.

The military coup of September 12, 1980, brought a temporary end to communal violence. The military proclaimed martial law throughout the country as a first step to quelling political unrest. Coup leaders promised a new constitution and a return to civilian government, but they also insisted that a return to the kind of political activity of the 1970s would not be acceptable. The Law to Establish a Consultative Assembly—the assembly that was selected to draft the new constitution—stated, "In view of the conditions which prevailed on 11 September 1980 and in view of the causes underlying these conditions, the purpose of the 12 September 1980 operation is not to 'return to democracy' but to re-establish a healthy and viable democratic order" (Heper 1985: 132). The military did not wish to merely reassert law and order in a situation that had deteriorated to chaos, although these were the stark terms often used to justify the intervention. Its aims were more comprehensive: to redefine what the political order itself should consist in, outlining the limits that could not be trespassed if one were to remain a legitimate political actor, and the punishments that transgressors would face.

The military regime began by banning political parties, arresting national political leaders, closing down trade unions, and dismissing thousands of elected mayors and bureaucratic functionaries—all those it held responsible for causing unrest in the 1970s. The regime then set about creating a framework for a new political order, delineating which kinds of organizations and actors would be permitted to participate in politics and through what sorts of activities. In a public address describing the new order being put into place, General Kenan Evren, head of the Armed Forces that led the coup and the military regime that followed, asserted that political parties could not claim to represent a constituency of one region, one class, or one section of people within the nation; if so, they would be "associations" rather than political parties. Conversely, Evren argued, associations would not be allowed to participate in politics, which should be the concern of political parties alone (Evren 1982: 41). The rigid administrative distinction of political parties and associations was written into law in the 1982 Constitution. Article 68 of the Constitution banned political parties from forming auxiliary branches for youth, women, and other groups. Articles 33 and 34 prohibited voluntary associations from pursuing political goals or establishing formal connections with political parties. The distinction was then reiterated in the Law on Political Parties of 1983 (Özbudun 1988: 54–55; Turan 1988).

New legislation forbade students and university staff to join political parties, and new rules penalized bureaucrats who attended public protests or participated in mass petitions (Dodd 1990: 56–57). Similarly, the Law on the Organization of Police Forces barred the police from membership in any organization other than sports clubs (Hale 1994: 251). The 1982 Constitution did not permit trade unions to "pursue a political cause, engage in political activity, receive support from political parties or give support to them," and such restrictions were extended in the Trade Unions Law of 1983, which proscribed strikes with "political objectives" (Hale 1994: 259; Margulies and Yıldızoğlu 1984: 20). This string of legislation betrayed the profound concern of the military leadership to control the conditions of political activity.[7]

Although it brought respite from violence to marginalized communities like the Alevi, military rule did not bring about a final resolution to the broader organizational tension between the fraternity of citizens and the management of populations. The return of civilian government in the 1980s and 1990s once again brought this problem to the fore, but the field of political engagement was regimented by new norms of legitimate activity.[8] Most important, state authorities did not aim to stringently extricate religion from politics; instead, they invested greater energy in defining national citizenship in terms of a particular conception of the Islamic tradition. The resulting effort, commonly referred to as the Turkish-Islamic synthesis, both presumed a Muslim identity to Turkish citizenship and interpreted Islamic traditions in ways that encouraged national allegiance. Initiated by right-wing intellectuals in the 1970s, the thesis was adopted by coup leaders and promoted by the state over the course of the next two decades, mobilizing Islamic institutions in the project of securing national identity. Receiving official sanction, the Turkish-Islamic synthesis justified the proliferation of state-run Qur'anic schools for children, the expansion of schools for training preachers, and the introduction of new courses on religion and morals in primary and secondary schools.

According to some commentators, the official promotion of the Turkish-Islamic synthesis created conditions conducive to the flourishing of (Sunni) Islamic civil society organizations and Islamic political parties in the 1980s and 1990s (Toprak 1996). However, the ideology was not promoted in order to undermine the secular-national foundations of the state, but rather to construct a conception of Islam that reinforced the affective allegiance of citizens to national fraternity and to the institutional authority of the state as its guarantor (Kaplan 2006). The conjoining of Islam and Turkish nationalism was criticized not only by Turkish secularists concerned about the rising salience of an Islamic political vocabulary but also by certain devout Muslims who identified the Muslim community in global rather than national terms.[9]

Promoting an understanding of Islam within a national ideological frame, the state appropriated the Turkish-Islamic synthesis in part to unify Muslim sects that had been politically polarized. This strategy was powerfully directed at Alevi communities. Responding to what it perceived to be the threat posed by leftist groups to the integrity of the state (Akin and Karasapan 1988), the military leadership sought to transform the widespread association of Alevis with the Left. A year and a half after the coup, the defense secretary issued a statement claiming that communists manipulated Alevis for support and in the process sparked sectarian conflict: "[C]ommunists have convinced some of our Alevi citizens that our Sunni citizens are 'right-wing backward fascists.' . . . [T]hey are trying to foment an ideological 'struggle between the left and the right,' between the two religious sects" (Kaplan 2006: 195). Not only did the defense secretary pin the blame for sectarian conflict on the Left, but repudiation of it was guided in part by an attempt to integrate Alevis into the symbolism of national fraternity. This task involved consolidating both a conception of Islam in accordance with nationalist historiography and a conception of Alevi religiosity that fell in line with the newly institutionalized Turkish-Islamic nationalism.

The path for this reinterpretation of Alevism was initially paved, not by the state, but by the right-wing political groups that, a decade prior, had instigated violence against Alevi communities. The entry of Alevis into public spaces of deliberation in the 1980s was mediated by a newly inclusive rhetoric of political parties such as the MHP. Such groups began to court the Alevi community. Tanıl Bora and Kemal Can (1991: 412) suggest that the efforts of these parties were aimed at "integrating Alevism into their ideologies and politics." Members of the MHP and intellectuals associated with it began to assert the Turkic character of Alevi religious belief, valorizing Alevism for its purported racial and cultural ties to the Turkish nation. Today representatives of political parties across the ideological spectrum appear at Alevi festivals and often sponsor public performances of Alevi rituals. This staging of national inclusion has provided a modality of legitimacy for many Alevi organizations, but a legitimacy that is underwritten by political parties that have promoted and vigilantly enforced forms of nationalism that in the recent past aggressively excluded Alevis. The legitimacy of Alevi publicity, in this sense, does not dismantle but perpetuates conceptions of national homogeneity that once violently targeted Alevis and today are more commonly marshaled for the sake of promoting anti-Kurdish sentiment.

The ideological incorporation of Alevism into narratives of the nation was rapidly taken up in official state policy. Recall that the head of the Directorate of Religious Affairs proclaimed that Alevism has contributed to the richness of Turkey's cultural history. His claim, as quoted earlier, was that Alevi ritual ought not to be labeled a form of Islamic worship. His goal in making these remarks was not shaped by the language of Islamic orthodoxy, at least in the sense that he did not condemn Alevi ritual as a form of deviance or heresy. Instead, he championed the Alevi cem as an element of the nation's heritage. His comments were not aimed at merely suppressing Alevi difference; they reveal a certain investment of power in the formation of Alevism.

At certain points in republican history, such as in the 1970s, the communal differences between Sunnis and Alevis constituted an explosive ground of political mobilization and militia attacks that the state proved incapable of managing. Following the military coup of 1980, and in the course of the succeeding political-economic liberalizations alluded to above, a new regime for managing the Janus-faced character of national identity emerged. I turn now to one key mode of management: the production and proliferation of aesthetic media that have enabled Alevi ritual performances in urban public spaces in the form of folklore.

AESTHETICS AND POLITICS

As described in the previous chapter, constitutional recognition of ethnic and religious differences has been limited to those groups recognized as minorities by the 1923 Lausanne Treaty. Alevi difference has not been an object of constitutional protection, but it has not for that reason simply been politically repressed. It has been incited for public display, particularly in the decades that followed the 1980 coup. The terms of this regulated enactment are not primarily defined by the law. Rather, Alevi difference has been regimented in the aesthetics of its institutionally orchestrated performance.

In order to unpack the politics of this aesthetic incitement, I want to return to the dede's reprimand of the dance troupe described above. The dede expressed an unease that is not adequately explained by recourse to a history of state ideologies and the late ascendancy of social movements to counteract them. As I emphasized, the dede's criticism was directed at the spatial and material forms of expression that have achieved public visibility, rather than at targets imagined as external to the community itself, such as the platforms of various political parties or the state's administrative categories. What an account of the dede's discomfort requires is an examination of the history of the aesthetic form of performance—the history of the ritual's public staging and spectacle—that is only partly coincident with the ideological and legal history often recounted in discussions of social movements that contest administrative policy.

The analysis that follows privileges the economies of sound and gesture that give material form to Alevism's public visibility. I depict the organized regime of sense experience and aesthetic expression, in which forms of visibility and spaces of public appearance are unevenly distributed across populations. Borrowing Jacques Rancière's (1999) formulation, I refer to this sensory regime as a "partition of the perceptible." The institutional authorization of certain genres of music and dance participates in this partitioning, defining the spaces allotted for performances of communal differences. The consolidation and distribution of aesthetic form has contributed to the management of population differences within statist imaginaries of national citizenship.

My interest in the aesthetics of public Alevi rituals was initially prompted by an ethnographic observation that may at first glance seem of minor importance: while the critique of state policy centers on the status of the cem ritual, Alevi anxieties about public visibility tend to focus on the performance of the semah. Historically, the semah was one element of the cem, and indeed in contemporary urban performances of the cem, the semah continues to figure as but one component of the ritual. The cem, in other words, provides an encompassing frame for the semah. Yet the youth groups that discomfited the dede rarely if ever perform the entirety of the cem. More commonly, they enact various forms of semah dances. By means of such youth groups, the semah has attained a much wider circulation than the cem itself. It is, indeed, the semah that has been crucial to the folkloric rendition of Alevi ritual, a rendition that has facilitated expressions of communal differences cast as congruent with national citizenship. I return to this point below. The historical question that I wish to pursue here is when and how the semah came to be disarticulated from the cem. How did this disarticulation reposition the aesthetics of Alevism's visibility within the apparatuses of governance? Specifically, what forms of staging did the extraction of the semah from the cem require, and what modes of participation did it entail?

In the 1970s, a full decade before Alevi religious practices became part of overt public debate, the semah had already found a public audience. At that time, it was taught at Boğaziçi University as one of the dances in the repertoire of the university's nationally renowned folklore club (Öztürkmen 2005). The semah was understood to be part of an expanding number of dances included in domestic and international folklore competitions, and performed by Alevis and non-Alevis alike. It was staged, not as a mode of communally specific worship, but as a form of national folklore. By the late 1980s, when communal identities came to the political fore, the ritual forms capable of representing Alevi identity had been in public circulation for a decade. The semah, if not the cem, was already publicly recognizable in a specific set of contexts and through a particular manner of performance.

While the state has promoted folk dancing for much of republican history, folklore clubs were granted a new legitimacy in the 1970s. Reacting against the rising numbers of overtly political youth organizations in that decade, the state authorized folklore clubs as one of the few sites of legitimate youth sociability. Whereas the state frequently banned politicized youth groups, it continued to sponsor folklore clubs and competitions (Öztürkmen 2002). The state's efforts to create a form of sociability apart from political and militant activity were not entirely successful: many folklore clubs continued to maintain associations with political organizations, and indeed the folklore club at Boğaziçi had a reputation for leftist politics in the 1970s. Yet one result of the state's legitimation tactics was that the performance of the semah as a genre of folk dance not only removed it from any necessary connection with the cem but also operated through a designation—folklore—authorized by the state and potentially recuperable by it apart from leftist politics.

Equally significant to the entry of Alevism into Turkish public life has been the role of state-run media in promoting traditional Alevi hymns as folk music. In the 1960s and 1970s, the state's Turkish Radio and Television encouraged Alevis to render elements of their spiritual repertory in a form consonant with official conceptions of a national listening audience.[10] Ritual genres like the düvaz and the mersiye, which contain explicit references to the Twelve Imams and the parables of Karbala, remained "forbidden outside the bounds of ritual" (Markoff 1986: 50).[11] Hymns that were broadcast by state radio, by contrast, were cast as folklore, removed from the ritual context of the cem, and set into new contexts of national circulation. Supported by the state and marketed as folk music, Alevi hymns acquired a public presence independently of the ritual act in which they had once been inextricably embedded.

The aesthetic history of Alevi ritual does not refer to the origins of practices such as the cem or the semah, which extend back many centuries. The institutional configurations that have shaped contemporary performance contexts emerged only in recent decades. This aesthetic history might, then, be understood in terms of what some anthropologists of Islam, following Eric Hobsbawm (1983), have called an invention of tradition. Dale Eickelman and James Piscatori (1996) reference the concept as part of their analysis of symbolic politics, which I discussed in chapter 2. In their formulation, the invention of tradition is meant to indicate the way that appeals to past authorities, such as religious figures, texts, or practices, are mobilized within contemporary institutional contexts. Symbols that ostensibly display continuity with the past are, in their local invocation, tactically positioned to achieve present-day political aims.[12] Viewing the semah as a politically positioned symbol is analytically useful but limited in this context. It highlights the institutional resources and forms of recognition that displays of the ritual potentially mobilize, but the analytical frame obscures the fact that the practice had already attained many of its characteristic modalities of public visibility in the decade that preceded the widespread rise of identity politics in Turkey. The aesthetic formation of the semah is neither historically fixed nor simply open to tactical manipulation. The mediatory forms that have rendered the semah visible, tolerable, and entertaining to public audiences are inherited, rather than invented, by contemporary Alevi actors.

Performances of the semah in the 1970s preceded the era that most social scientists recognize as the period of pluralism and identity politics in Turkey. These early efforts at staging the semah are, in a sense, discursively prehistorical—they established a social form that would serve the needs of a pluralist politics emergent only in a subsequent era. Delimited as a species of folk dancing and inserted into an available and sanctioned form of social interaction, the ritual practice that was thus consolidated carried the marks of the nation-state's authority, which would persist into the later period, creating the political ambivalences that inhere in public displays of Alevi rituals today. Attempts to invoke a pluralist politics confront their limits, not only in the obstinacy of state officials and the inadequacy of their designations, but also in the aesthetics of visibility that, in providing Alevi ritual with a public footing, has incorporated it into the dominant partition of the perceptible.

FORMS OF CIRCULATION

The encounter that I have described between the dede and the youth group took place in 2006. By that point, performances of the semah in folk-dance competitions and festivals had been in public circulation for nearly three decades. The semah-as-folk-dance represented by the youth group was easily and immediately discernible to the dede, as well as to most of the other participants in the cem. The stylistic form of the dance evoked other contexts in which the dance has been enacted. An entire chain of iteration—of actors, codings, and costumes—came into view in the performance. The semah is not only a form *in* circulation (the dance itself). It has required a distinctive form *of* circulation that shapes the channels of transmission, the various contexts of performance, and the sensibilities and expectations that attend such contexts.[13] The dance elicited for the dede a circulatory network of urban sites and performance styles.

The dede's critique of the folkloric rendition of the semah has not always been shared by Alevi leaders and organizations. In the early 1990s, many such Alevi intellectuals and groups employed rather than rebuked the folkloric modality of semah performance. At that point Alevis had only just begun to assert their cultural identity in public, and the category of folklore provided a legitimate ground for public recognition. The semah, it should be recalled, was by then recognizable as a folkloric form, made available through mass media and state sponsorship. Alevi organizations that were newly emerging taught the semah to adolescents as a way of introducing urban youth to the community's traditions. Several books written by Alevis as early contributions to the publicizing of communal identity focused on the semah, not simply as an element of the cem, but as a topic in its own right (e.g., Bozkurt 1990; Erseven 1990). Such texts treated the semah as a product of Turkish history and conceptualized it as a form of folklore. Books about the semah presupposed that the dance existed as a social form whose historical meaning could be described independently of its role in the cem.

The semah, as performed by youth groups and discussed by intellectuals, was simultaneously a sign of national folklore and an explicit demonstration of communal identity in public. Alevi groups managed to express communal distinction by employing a publicly available and sanctioned social form. In its public circulation, the semah evoked the national heritage in expressions of Alevi difference. The dance articulated a post-1980 modality of urban governmentality that confirmed reigning discourses of national citizenship.

The youth group described above imagined itself in terms of a broader communal struggle for public recognition. Several adolescents of the group explained to me that their performances are an important aspect of the "Alevi awakening" (*Alevi uyanışı*). One member said that the performance of the semah in public arenas would not have been acceptable in the past, when Alevis were more overtly persecuted, but that today it is a vehicle through which Alevis can learn about and express their identity openly. He summed up his discussion by pointedly exclaiming, "The semah allows us to announce, 'We are here!' "

This particular semah group was organized by a local neighborhood association in Çorum. The association offered *saz* and *bağlama* music instruction, drawing courses, and drama lessons, in addition to teaching the semah.[14] Students in such courses were between the ages of twelve and twenty-one. The association functioned as an after-school program, in which adolescents participated in supervised activities with other kids their age and learned about Alevi traditions at the same time. Adolescents participating in the semah group met weekly for rehearsals, learning the steps and movements of a number of different semah styles. While participants were aware that the different styles were drawn from a number of regionally distinctive traditions, taken from across central and eastern Anatolia, few were able to specify the particular origin of each style.

The semah group performed not only in cem rituals but also at a number of different locations. I observed one performance outside of a grocery store that had recently opened. The owner of the market informed me that he wanted to generate publicity for the store. He saw the semah group as providing entertainment to attract customers. The semah was employed to summon a public audience of consumers unmarked by sectarian affiliation.

The most common performance context for the youth group was the summer village festival. Alevis who migrated to the town from nearby villages often sponsored festivals, primarily as a means of drawing family and friends back for a reunion in the natal environment. Larger variants of these festivals advertised by posters on storefronts in town frequently generated an audience that included not only Alevis but Sunnis as well, an occasional politician in search of local support, and local journalists seeking to capture a photograph with a brief caption. Such festivals were usually one-day affairs. They took place in the central patch of a village or in an adjacent field. They generally sustained the ambience of a summer picnic: families grilled vegetables and meat, old friends shared news and gossip, some relaxed with beer or rakı. Often a musician was hired to provide entertainment. Semah groups were also recruited for this task.

Generally, the youth group performed twice at a festival. The two performances differed in their content: one was referred to as a *halk oyunu* (literally, folk dance) and the other as the semah. The two were distinguishable by different forms of music, instrumentation, and costumes. The instruments in the halk oyunu included the *davul* and *zurna* (respectively percussive and wind instruments), as opposed to the saz (a lute) that was used in the semah. The halk oyunu was lighthearted. Dancers played out a narrative scenario in which several boys seek the affections of a girl. Dancing was accompanied by playful shouting, and participants frequently laughed together. The semah, by contrast, presented no such narrative. The demeanor of participants was more serious. As one performer mentioned to me, "We don't talk to each other when dancing the semah—we don't even smile."

For most members of the youth group, several of whose performances I attended, the distinction between the two dances was crucial. I was often told that the differences in instrumentation, clothing, and disposition point to a distinction between folk dancing and worship (*ibadet*) that concern the contextual sensibilities appropriate to each. The davul and zurna used in the halk oyunu are commonly employed in celebrations such as weddings. Kimberly Hart (2009) reports that in certain Anatolian Sunni villages, music associated with the davul and zurna provokes controversy, and some villagers view it as leading to sinful forms of entertainment. In Alevi village festivals, the use of these instruments carries connotations of levity. The semah, by contrast, is accompanied by religious hymns (*nefes* and *deyiş*). When I asked several of the performers about the difference between the two dances, they all explained that the semah is a form of worship, which needs to be performed with a gravity that is absent in the halk oyunu.

However important the distinction between the two dances, a number of performers claimed that such festivals are for entertainment (*eğlence*) and are therefore not conducive to acts of worship. One of the participants warned me against misconstruing the semah, which he insisted was in fact part of an act of worship, in terms of the sensibilities fostered in the setting of the festival. Participants, in this sense, sought to distinguish the essence of the ritual from the contexts in which they had come to perform it.

Such festivals hold both a promise and a danger. They offer a site for the reproduction of Alevi traditions and enable the public display of communal rituals. As Mark Soileau (2005) argues, festivals are among the most vibrant and widespread sites where narratives of Alevi communal history are consolidated and transmitted to younger generations. However, they also embed the community's ritual traditions within an aesthetics of visibility that most observers and participants find difficult to reconcile with the postures and dispositions that they recognize as specific to worship. The categories of folklore and worship are not simply competing discursive descriptions of Alevi ritual practices. They articulate with new institutional and social contexts, as well as the forms of sociability and engagement those contexts enable. The claim that the semah and the cem are practices of worship rather than forms of folklore or recreation increasingly contradicts the aesthetic conditions of their contexts of performance.

The dede's critique of the Alevi youth groups that I depicted above was not idiosyncratic: a number of Alevis whom I came to know in the course of my fieldwork expressed a concern about the mode of semah performance exemplified by youth dance troupes. Specifically, my interlocutors were not persuaded by the youth group's efforts to tease out a distinction between the semah, as a practice of worship, and the festival in which it is performed, as a context of recreation. Ercan, an elementary school teacher, criticized these youth groups, arguing that the semah should not be performed outside of the cem. Offering me an example, he described being in a bar in a small town on the Aegean coast when a popularized rendition of an Alevi hymn was played. A number of individuals spontaneously began to dance the semah. Ercan is by no means religiously devout. Most commonly he identifies as a socialist with only a halfhearted belief in God. He was nonetheless taken aback by the spectacle. He concluded with some indignation, "The semah is a part of worship [ibadet'in bir parçası] and not a form of entertainment." Although the semah he witnessed on this occasion was not performed by a youth group, he saw in its enactment a similar dilemma: the semah, conceived as a social form unto itself, has attained a circulation through contexts of leisure and entertainment, which would not otherwise sustain a practice of worship. Indeed, the semah is visible in sites such as bars where performances of the cem would be incongruous and inappropriate.

Yet the newfound visibility is not without its ambiguities. Ercan concluded by qualifying his criticism. He claimed that semah performances fulfill an important role in introducing Alevi rituals to a public audience that would otherwise have no exposure to the communal form. The semah enables a form of public recognition.

This ambivalent critique registers an uncertainty about the value of public visibility and the regnant partition of the perceptible that organizes its aesthetic form. In this regard, the significance of the semah's public visibility is far more undecided for Alevis than is the political import ascribed to the visibility of veiling by many women associated with Sunni Islamic revivalism in Turkey. A number of recent accounts of Islamic movements have emphasized the political consequences of religious movements acquiring public visibility. Nilüfer Göle argues that "Islamic public visibility presents a critique of a secular version of the public sphere" (2002: 188). Alev Çınar similarly assesses the politics of donning the headscarf in Turkish public spaces: "The headscarf has given an undeniable visibility and presence to Islam in the secular public sphere. It was the wearing of the headscarf in a particular manner that came to be recognized as the mark of an Islamist ideology, and its appearance not just anyplace, but on the university campus—a monumental space of modernity and secularism—made it an issue of public controversy" (2005: 84). Veiling has gained "public visibility in ways that escape and undermine existing categories," thereby "subverting the authority and control of the secular public gaze" (Çınar 2005: 47). Wearing a headscarf is not only a sign of gendered Muslim piety; the style ("wearing a headscarf in a particular manner") and site (donning it on the university campus) of the performance are relatively stable indexes of a transgression of secularist norms. By attaining public visibility, veiling has acquired a political signification.

In contrast to the political aesthetics of the veil, the visibility of the semah has not overtly instigated a political challenge to state-enforced categories of the nation. Alevis like Ercan and the dede with whom I began are far from assured about the political significance of the semah's visibility. Alevi ritual performances have served simultaneously as a mode of representing a marginalized identity in urban spaces long dominated by the majority and as a medium for managing and domesticating the strains of modern Turkish citizenship.

RE-MEDIATING ALEVI VISIBILITY

The ambiguities attached to Alevism's public visibility are most apparent in the ordering and organization of cem ceremonies in urban settings. As indicated earlier, it is the cem, rather than the semah, that is at the heart of public debates about whether Alevi ritual constitutes a form of worship and ought to be recognized by the state as such. How, then, has the newfound visibility of the semah, along with the sensibilities it evokes and articulates, impacted the politics of pluralism centered on the classification of the cem?

As Alevi organizations emerged in major metropolitan centers and in the provinces of central and eastern Anatolia in the 1990s, they sought to provide local Alevi communities with spaces for communal ritual expression that had previously only been available in rural settings. They created urban spaces for Alevis to participate in cem rituals. Although the sites created for the performance of the cem were designed in relation to ideas of its historical practice, several novel features imposed by the urban space have affected the development of the ritual. First, in rural settings, the cem was often not only a form of worship but also a context for adjudicating and reconciling disputes between villagers. The urban cem, by contrast, is open not only to those belonging to a single face-to-face interactive community but also to Alevis of wide-ranging origin—from different villages, towns, and provinces. The new cem is ordered in relation to a distinctly urban stranger sociability.[15]

Second, the site of the cem, or the cemevi, is no longer simply any large, open space, as it was in rural areas. Rather, it is created in relationship to a specific institutional status. The emergence of Alevism as a "public religion" has taken place within the institutional context of Turkey's post-1980 political economy. Alevis were not the only community to seek public recognition in this period; a large number of other groups did so too, including women's groups, business groups, environmentalists, groups that represent migrants, Islamic organizations, and so forth. Such groups have organized under the rubric of civil society, which has involved taking on a particular status and conforming to its regulations.[16] For instance, Alevi institutions and the cemevis they support are classed as foundations and are not eligible for the tax exemptions granted to mosques, which are governed by a distinct ministry of state. This particular material concern is, however, but one materialization of a broader issue: contemporary cemevis are not simply new spaces for hosting essentially the same ritual; rather, the ritual itself is being constituted through new modes of institutional engagement.

Third, whereas access to rural cems was often restricted to members of the proximate village community, the urban cem has a public presence. Foreign researchers, curious Sunnis, and occasional journalists are common and by now expected spectators at such events. The urban cem operates not only according to the ritual functions sought out by local Alevis but also for the sake of representing Alevism on a public stage, serving to dispel disparaging myths about the community.

With the cem reframed in contexts of stranger sociability, modern institutionality, and urban publicity, the aesthetics of public performance of the semah became especially significant. The semah often figures prominently, featuring not merely as one element in the ritual's progression but also often as a public form inserted into an intimate communal event. The semah is frequently the portion of the ritual photographed by journalists and mentioned in news reports. Re-embedded in the cem, from which it had been extracted, the new aesthetics of the semah has affected the legibility of Alevi religion in public discourse and the visibility of Alevi ritual in urban space.

There is a growing body of ethnographic research that depicts the way in which the newly circulating semah is re-embedded within the cem. Writing about Alevis in Germany, Ruth Mandel (2008: 286) notes that they commonly and publicly stage the cem as a "folklorized performance." While not detailing the contexts of the semah's circulation, Mandel hints at its effect on the ethos of the cem. She notes that Alevi youth today "have learned the semah not from watching their grandmother in a small clandestine cemevi in an Anatolian village but instead at folkdance classes. . . . No longer the exclusive domain of esoteric secrecy, the new cems have joined company with other publicly staged performances that might take place on a proscenium stage for a ticket-buying audience" (Mandel 2008: 286). Learned in a folkdance class, the semah defines the appropriate context and audience for the cem as a staged performance.

Martin Sökefeld's research among German Alevis reveals a similar dilemma. He cites an Alevi interlocutor's complaint about the folkloriza-tion of the cem, in which the semah is singled out as a major source of the problem: "Cem is a spiritual practice; it is not a cultural event. . . . We have to return from this folklorization to the fundament of cem, to what cem actually is. Unfortunately it has become a habit to dance semah like folklore at weddings. This is not good for semah and cem. Weddings and cultural shows are one thing but cem is something else" (Sökefeld 2008: 158). The question of why the semah is being danced "like folklore at weddings" is not posed, but the effect of its re-embedding within the cem is acutely registered and bemoaned.

Alevi organizations in the early 1990s drew upon the form of the semah that had been rendered recognizable since the 1970s. Reporting on ethno-graphic research in 1994 among Alevis in Hatay, Martin Stokes indicates the re-embedding of the semah within the cem:

> The cem that I observed was dominated by semah and by deyiş. The former is a dance, and the latter songs from a spiritual repertory. . . . As opposed to a communal ritual in which everybody takes place, the dance movements of the semah were carried out by a group of young men and women. There was a certain emphasis upon uniformity: the young people were, in effect, rehearsing the dance as a performance to be observed by others. Who these others were to be was not entirely clear, either to me, or to those who were attending, with me, for the first time. "Is this folklore (*folklor*) or a real cem? I mean can anybody join in as the mood takes them?" I heard one elderly visiting dede ask the musician. (Stokes 1996: 196–197)

The semah plays a crucial role in this cem. The movements of the dance, the age restrictions on participants, and the rehearsed quality of the performance serve as aesthetic cues of the semah's social genre, carrying the traces of its circulation. For the elderly visiting dede, these aesthetic cues recalled what was by then a twenty-year-old mode of folk dancing, triggering a set of associations and contexts that shape the ethos of the cem as a whole.

I earlier argued that contemporary performances of the semah are mediated by specific styles of performance and practices of staging, spectacle, and display associated with entertainment and leisure. I now suggest that the semah has come to serve as a vector of mediation in its own right. Separated from the cem, which once encompassed and ordered it, the semah began to circulate on its own, only to return and infiltrate the cem from without. The semah, in effect, now re-mediates the cem.

In the cem that I observed in 2006, the dede posed the problem of folklore in an assertive, critical tone rather than in the form of a question, as in Stokes's depiction. His reprimand was sharp. In the days following that cem, I visited with a number of elderly individuals who had attended the ritual, asking them what they thought of the dede's admonishment of the semah group. With little hesitation, several unequivocally agreed with the dede. One woman offered the following explanation: "The youth group arrived late. So they didn't participate in the whole cem. They only came to the cem in order to perform a folklore dance." Another man concurred that the adolescents did not sit in the cem, and as a result did not have the proper concentration that would have come from participating in the entire length of the ritual. He concluded that the group did not perform the semah as a form of worship.

Some of these criticisms point to correctable contingencies in the youth group's behavior, such as late arrival and the failure to participate in other segments of the ritual. Yet the ascription of folklore to the group's performance also suggests recognition of a more systemic problem with the form of their dance. The men and women attending the cem discerned in the youth group's performance the modes of public visibility that have authorized a rendition of Alevi ritual as a type of folk dancing. Several characteristics of the youth group's dance marked it as such, features that were most apparent when contrasted with a version of the semah that had been performed earlier that night. The earlier semah was performed by several elderly men and women, each wearing their quotidian clothing rather than costumes. Their semah took place within the unfolding progression of the cem. By contrast, the youth group did not include anyone above the age of twenty-one, they wore specially designed outfits that distinguished them from the rest of the individuals in attendance, and their performance occurred at the conclusion of the ritual rather than within it. Each of these elements served to create a staging effect that distinguished performer from onlooker in terms of participant and spectator. For the duration of the youth group's performance, attendees in the cem found themselves cast as audience members viewing a show—a performance similar to what they might view in a summer festival or at a publicity event for a grocery store—rather than participating in a communal act of worship.

The sense that one is viewing a show and being entertained recalled the other contexts of the youth group's circulation. It created a disjuncture between the ethos of recreation conjured by those contexts and the solemn concentration of worship that participants in the cem sought to establish. This mode of performing the semah is not easy to construe in abstraction from the festivals in which it is most often enacted. Entering the context of the cem, the youth group was criticized by many attendees for bringing the sensibilities of the festival into an arena of worship. Their performance carried the risk of recontextualizing the practice of the cem itself through the aesthetics of the semah's public visibility.

The urban cem reveals the difficulties faced by contemporary Alevi communities in seeking to invoke a politics of pluralism. Efforts to organize the ritual in urban spaces are often motivated by a concern to offer communal representation in a milieu that has been historically hostile to its ritual forms. Performances of urban cems are, in this sense, assertions of communal distinction, in contrast to the unmarked yet institutionally supported modes of majoritarian religious worship. The element of the cem that has most successfully traversed public space in Turkey is the semah. Yet its success in achieving public recognition is inextricably tied to an aesthetic history in which it came to be delimited as a piece of folk dancing and later embedded in various contexts of recreation and leisure. Alevi groups struggling to create spaces of communal worship not only discover opportunities but also encounter their limits in those practices that have achieved public visibility. The social form that has most prominently facilitated the development of Alevism into a public religion simultaneously invokes an aesthetics of visibility that many Alevi actors and organizations, in the name of pluralism, seek to contest.

A POLITICS OF BECOMING

Over the past few decades, Turkey has witnessed a political and economic liberalization that, as with many other parts of the post-Cold War world, appears to threaten nationalist ideologies of homogeneous citizenship. Of the numerous examples that manifest this trend within Turkey, the emergence of

Alevi movements presents both an exemplification and a limiting case. Newly established publishing houses, intellectuals, organizations, and ritual performances in public sites have remade the urban landscape in ways that pose challenges to the state's efforts at controlling religious practice. In this chapter I have depicted the aesthetic forms that have permitted Alevis to occupy and appropriate public spaces in urban settings from which they had long been excluded and even violently prevented from entering. The proliferation of Alevi public engagements has compelled journalists, Sunni Islamic intellectuals, and state officials alike to reconsider the legitimacy of the plural religious allegiances of the nation's citizenry.

Far from leading to an unambiguous loosening of nationalist ideologies of citizenship, however, such performances are promoted by political parties and state officials committed to long-standing narratives of the nation. The aesthetic forms of performance—the ethos of its contexts of performance, the styles of enactment, the costumes and adornments expected from performers, and the staging effects such performances produce—regiment Alevi publicity in ways that further entrench the framing of Alevism as an element of the nation's folkloric heritage. Enactments of Alevism that express newfound minority liberties are deeply imbricated in strategies of governmentality that discipline differences of population within the frameworks of national belonging. To think about pluralism along these lines requires an understanding of the expansion of minority freedoms as constituted by, rather than as strictly countering, the disciplinary modalities of political authority.

William Connolly offers a conceptualization of pluralism that begins to account for the tensions elaborated here. Pluralism, for Connolly, is only in part a matter of political debate between groups and communities whose representative forms, political demands, and social indexes are relatively established and widely recognizable. It also entails what he terms a politics of becoming, centered on movements that have not yet breached the threshold of recognizability, after which they might be ascribed the status of community. This dimension of pluralism "addresses the constitutive tension between already existing diversity and the politics of becoming by which new constituencies struggle to modify the register of legitimate diversity" (Connolly 2005: 68). Connolly's formulation allows us to conceptualize the political work involved in legitimating social difference, along with the difficulties encountered by certain groups who are not yet locatable within that legitimated space.

For any constituency engaged in a politics of becoming, the pragmatics of this sort of engagement present serious dilemmas. The register of legitimate diversity regiments the mechanics of practical engagement—its technologies, speech genres, and aesthetic media—that are available for political action. The semah, as one such mechanism, is among the most widely recognizable mediatory forms that enable Alevis to participate in public spaces long premised on their exclusion. The widespread circulation of the semah has undoubtedly modified the register of legitimate diversity, but that register continues to regulate the spaces in which the ritual can appear and the aesthetics of its performance. The struggle to modify legitimate diversity runs the risk of further stabilizing the organized partition of the perceptible and its disciplinary technologies.

One result of the liberalizing transformations of the past few decades is that Alevis are relatively free to express their communal identity in public forums. However, they are not free to refuse the form of public circulation that has been made available to them, at least not without severely placing at risk the tentative footing the community has attained in urban Turkey in recent decades. For a community that has struggled, and to some extent continues to struggle, against sectarian discrimination and violence, the costs of this wager are not easily borne.

5 PEDAGOGIES OF HISTORY

> *The activity that produces meaning and establishes an*
> *intelligibility of the past is also the symptom of an activity*
> *endured.*
>
> —*Michel de Certeau,* The Writing of History

UNTIL THE SECOND HALF OF the twentieth century, Alevis themselves played very little role in the modernist construction of Anatolian Alevism. In the first decades of the century, late Ottoman intellectuals attuned to the currents of modern sociology began to define Alevism as a representation of Turkish Anatolia's past (see chapter 3). At that point, most Alevi communities continued to reside in rural settlements, largely outside of the urban centers where the new sociology and its institutional supports were being established. Key shifts in Turkey's political economy after World War II propelled Alevis into urban environments and institutions of higher education, and ultimately facilitated an increasing Alevi presence in public spheres where their religious identity was being debated.

From the 1960s onward, the state initiated an explicit shift from a largely agrarian economy to planned industrialization, protecting domestic industries by exacting high tariffs on imports. Industrialization was accompanied by an accelerating process of urbanization. Approximately 214,000 people migrated from villages to cities between 1945 and 1950. The number more than quadrupled between 1950 and 1955, leading to village-to-city migrations of 904,000 individuals. Almost twice that many would migrate over the succeeding five years (Akşit 1998).

Alevi communities were influenced by these changes in typical ways. They attended modern schools beyond the elementary level and entered the industrial capitalist workforce, primarily as wage laborers or on the lower rungs of the state bureaucracy. The Alevi intellectual Fuat Bozkurt describes the structural positioning of Alevi migrants as follows: "[Alevis] settled at the edges of cities in unkempt houses. Most of them earned their livelihood by struggling as doormen, guards, unskilled laborers, and petty bureaucrats" (2000: 73).[1] A number of consequences followed from these structural shifts: A large segment of the Alevi population gained access to public schooling, leading to growing rates of literacy; traditional liturgical texts, previously accessible only to spiritual leaders, were translated into the modern linguistic standard and more widely distributed; and city-based Alevis developed civil society organizations to provide social and political support to new migrants (Küçük 2003; Massicard 2005a).

From the late 1980s onward, Alevis began to appropriate the media of the mass public—its genres, discourses, and performance contexts—in order to depict the history of their traditions, whether for the sake of educating youth within the community, dispelling disparaging myths held by members of the Sunni majority, or lobbying for changes in state policy. Alevis came to wield modernist genres established in late Ottoman and early republican times, such as social history. These genres provided Alevis with a form of discourse that facilitated their participation in Turkey's public spheres. This history follows a broader trend found in many parts of the Muslim world, where the onset of mass education and the expansion of communication technologies have led to new forms of civic consciousness and political awareness (J. Anderson 2003; Eickelman and Piscatori 1996; Hefner 2001; Roy 2004; Salvatore 1997; Starrett 1998).

In this chapter, I explore how the forms of public engagement enabled by modernist genres of expression, like history writing, are themselves politically authorized. What disciplinary impetus obliges Alevis to organize their cultural memory in accordance with the norms of historicism? I am working from the assumption that the act of historicizing a religious tradition is a social practice, what de Certeau (1988) refers to as a historiographical procedure or operation. De Certeau emphasizes the institutional conditions and practices that render the act of historicization socially relevant and efficacious in the present day. Tracing the social purchase of historicism across a series of practices, I discuss the use of religious and political icons in contexts of public performance, the writing of social histories, and the organization of public ritual commemorations. The sites, actors, and authorities that shape these practices are varied rather than singular; they are, at times, contradictory rather than consistent; and no single political apparatus coordinates their diverse enactments. I seek, in other words, to explore the practice of historicization amid its dispersal across manifold scenes and activities. I analyze these various practices together because it is through their instantiations that we can explore the dense social normativity that produces a historically reflexive Alevi subject and the institutional pressures that compel its emergence.

ICONOGRAPHIC DISPENSATIONS

Zehra teyze was an Alevi woman in her mid-fifties when I met her. I introduced her in chapter 2 as an individual who viewed ritual lament as part of her biographical past and the village life of her youth, but which she had long since left behind. I return to her now in order to explore the social significance of another semiotic absence, this time concerning the image of Ali ibn Abi Talib, the cousin and son in law of the Prophet Muhammad.

At the time of my fieldwork, Zehra teyze lived in a lower-middle-class neighborhood in Çorum with her husband and two of her three children. Most of my conversations with Zehra teyze and her family circled around her youngest son's inability to get a job and his subsequent dissatisfaction with Turkey's system of educating and employing its citizens. None of Zehra's family was particularly engaged in contemporary Alevi political action, nor were they active participants in the sorts of religious activities organized by urban Alevi groups, so it was only on occasion that our discussions veered toward topics that seemed, at the time, to be tied to my explicit research objectives. Yet the relative silence on such topics was neither incidental nor peculiar, and it would take me some time to realize that it was just this silence with regard to their religious participation that warranted my attention. The ethnographic significance of this silence hit home for me when Zehra teyze informed me that she owned several images of Ali ibn Abi Talib, but kept them buried in a cardboard box in her closet.

As noted earlier, Ali is a figure honored by most Muslims as one of Muhammad's closest companions. Alevis in Turkey share with many Shi'i Muslims elsewhere a particular reverence for Ali and a line of eleven of his male descendants, referring to this lineage as the Twelve Imams. Shi'i communities in many regions of the world, such as Iran and India, have long produced images of the Twelve Imams, incorporating them into public, domestic, and ritual contexts.[2]

Why, then, had Zehra teyze consigned the image of Ali to a box? She explained her discretion by relating a story that took place several decades earlier when the family lived in a different Anatolian province, whose inhabitants are predominantly Sunni rather than Alevi. At that point, Zehra teyze had displayed one modestly sized image of Ali in their living room. Soon after they had first moved into their apartment, several neighbors, all Sunni in religious orientation, paid a visit to welcome her, but they were visibly discomfited by the image of Ali. The image was not one that would be commonly found in Sunni households, in part due to a religious proscription on depicting the likeness of Muhammad and his companions. It is common, however, to find images of Ali in Alevi and Shi'i communities. Zehra teyze indicated that in a Turkish context, the portrait of Ali could easily be interpreted as a sign that her family was Alevi. In the context of the 1970s, when sectarian tensions were mounting into episodes of violence, such signs could condense a tremendous amount of social and psychic energy. Zehra teyze explained that she felt pressured to take the image down. She felt a certain anxiety about the public visibility of the icon, an anxiety that has persisted up to the present, despite the fact that her family now lives in a predominantly Alevi neighborhood.

By the time of my conversation with Zehra teyze, several decades had passed since the day she felt compelled to remove the image of Ali. Since that time, Alevi communities have begun to elaborate an entirely new cultural iconography, characterized by a distinctly public circulation. The familiar image of Ali has not been thrown out, but rather has become a key emblem of Alevi identity within this newly public iconography. From street protests to summer festivals, it is increasingly common to see the image of Ali displayed openly. The mobilization of such images addresses a public audience, at once national and global, consisting of journalists, political officials, foreign anthropologists, and observers from the European Union. It was during this span of time that Alevis began to experience a dramatic growth in the number of organizations and intellectuals capable of publicly representing the community. One result was that the image of Ali acquired legitimate footing in public space.

What I wish to explore is the newfound legitimacy of Ali's portrait in Turkey's public spaces without, however, ignoring Zehra teyze's ongoing anxiety about displaying it in her own home. The legitimacy of displaying Ali's image is contingent on certain conventions of portrayal and arrangement—what we might call an iconographic dispensation that governs how the portrait is publicly presented. Zehra teyze's reluctance to take her portraits of Ali out of the closet does not simply reflect an outdated anxiety in an era of pluralist tolerance; it reveals, rather, her awareness of the institutional scrutiny that accompanies Ali's public portrayal, along with the boundaries and limits that tacitly regiment that presentation.

In this iconographic dispensation, Ali's image rarely stands alone. It is almost always juxtaposed to images of two additional figures: Mustafa Kemal Atatürk, the leader of the nationalist forces that created the Turkish republican state in the 1920s, and Hacı Bektaş-ı Veli, a medieval Anatolian saint. The conjunction of images cuts across a variety of historical moments, creating a linear series only through some rather unwieldy narrative jumps, moving from early Islam (with the image of Ali) to medieval Anatolia (represented by Hacı Bektaş) and up to the modern, secular Turkish Republic (iconized by Atatürk). The juxtaposition of these three icons has become so common a feature of Alevi public events that it tends not to be commented upon or questioned, either by participants or by outside observers.[3] For the sake of analysis, it is worth denaturalizing this presentation of Alevi identity and decomposing the interrelation of its component parts.

The insertion of Atatürk into this sequence of images may strike an outside observer as unexpected. The act of publicly displaying the portrait of Ali, after all, is one manner in which Alevis are publicly asserting their particular identity. Yet the public presence of Ali, as an emblem of that particularity, is anchored in this iconography by the paradigmatic icon of the modernist nation-state—a state that, as discussed in earlier parts of this book, stipulated terms of citizenly belonging that often rendered Alevis vulnerable to nationalist suspicion and aggression.[4] The image of Atatürk is by no means unique to this context. It is ubiquitous across the country. The state mandates that all government offices prominently display a photograph of his bust, and city centers frequently contain statues in his honor. Yael Navaro-Yashin (2002) has aptly referred to this iconic ubiquity as a "cult of Atatürk," which has been promoted by the state and therefore predominates across Turkey.

One explanation of the use of Atatürk's portrait in Alevi settings is that many Alevi communities not only supported Mustafa Kemal as a political leader but "mythologized" him, comparing him to and even identifying him with figures from religious history, such as Ali and Hacı Bektaş (Kehl-Bodrogi 2003). However, this argument begs a number of historical questions about how a religious tradition that is centuries-old came to accommodate a modern political figure. Which Alevi groups made this accommodation possible, and, equally important, who opposed it? What institutional powers allowed for opposition to be overcome? If there was no opposition to the religious incorporation of Atatürk, a claim that would assume considerable homogeneity among an internally differentiated community, then what accounts for the ease and rapidity of this transformation? Most important, the claim that certain Alevis have felt an intimate, perhaps even religious, connection to Atatürk does not in itself explain why this connection is expressed in the form of specific visual icons, familiar from spaces dominated by state authority, such as public schools and government offices. Alevi portrayals of Atatürk's image reveal a fealty not simply to his political vision or his mythological aura but to the practice of portrayal itself. The iconographic practice carries strongly statist resonances. It is one manner of inscribing Alevi publicity within the cultural politics of the Turkish state.

The tension in this iconography—that it at once emblematizes Alevi difference and mobilizes the statist symbolics of the nation—echoes the dilemmas of modern political authority examined in previous chapters. It derives from the efforts of late Ottoman intellectuals and governing authorities to generate knowledge of Anatolia's variegated cultural geography but to grasp it within the terms of a unilinear historical evolution; that is to say, to identify traces of cultural plurality as elements of the Turkish nation's developmental trajectory. Yet in the iconographic dispensation that I am discussing here, the social actors deploying these signs are not primarily state officiants. Alevis themselves—individuals participating in street marches and organizations that sponsor public events—mobilize the iconography. In contrast to the late Ottoman and early republican periods, contemporary Turkish cities host large populations of Alevis capable of addressing the national public. The fact that the representational and iconographic modes of Alevi public address extend the forms of political authority established in earlier periods deserves greater attention. What institutional impetus encourages the continued salience of the republican state's cultural politics at a time when Alevis have become political agents in their own right?

NATIONALISM AND RELIGION

A key historical turning point in the development of Alevi publicity was the military-led coup d'état in 1980. The military's response to the escalation of political violence in the 1970s was, initially, the imposition of martial law, and later, with the return to civilian governance in the 1980s, a cultural politics that invested heavily in the symbolics of national citizenship. As discussed in the previous chapter, the politics in question is often glossed as the Turkish-

Islamic synthesis, which not only defines Turkish citizenship in terms of a Muslim identity, but also promotes understandings of Islam in terms of Turkish national history. This synthesis was motived by several aims: its advocates sought to delegitimate leftist political groups (Akin and Karasapan 1988), but it was also meant to underwrite a conception of citizenship that incorporates all Muslims into the polity, regardless of sect. Crucially, this latter aim was not pursued by tenaciously removing any sign of religion from the political domain (a strategy that might be expected from an aggressively secularist state), but by attempting to define a common national religiosity.

The thirteenth-century Anatolian saint Hacı Bektaş provided symbolic leverage for this project. According to most accounts, Hacı Bektaş was born in Khorasan in Central Asia and subsequently migrated to Anatolia, where he is said to have become famous for performing miracles and to have rapidly generated a popular following. He is taken by many Alevis to be something akin to a patron saint. Phrases ascribed to him are often invoked by Alevis today in the form of moral guidance. Rituals associated with the eponymous Bektaşi Sufi brotherhood, such as the *ayin-i cem*, are performed by many Alevi groups as central rites of the community. His image is often displayed prominently at public Alevi events.[5]

After 1980, intellectuals on the right, some of whom were associated with the right-wing Nationalist Action Party (Milliyetçi Hareket Partisi, MHP), which had sponsored violent attacks on Alevis in the 1970s, began to embrace Hacı Bektaş and the Bektaşi brotherhood. They promulgated the view that both the saint and the Sufi order were important elements in the Turkish nation's historical development. Some such authors saw the Bektaşi brotherhood as a distinctly Turkic institution, and by emphasizing the link between Bektaşis and Alevis, stressed the Turkic character of the latter (Bora and Can 1991: 414). Over the course of the past two decades, this ethno-national framing of Alevism has been advocated with increasing frequency by state officials. Today it is common to find representatives of most mainstream political parties appearing at Alevi public events, often proclaiming that Hacı Bektaş brought enlightenment to ignorant villagers of Anatolia, furthering the moral progress of the nation in its long historical march.

I do not mean to argue that the figure of Hacı Bektaş has been completely co-opted by right-wing nationalists. There are undoubtedly various ways in which Alevis commemorate the life of the medieval saint, many of which escape nationalist framings. I simply suggest that the act of displaying an image of Hacı Bektaş at Alevi public events in the 1990s and 2000s did not represent a liberated subaltern Alevi voice presenting itself to a majority-dominated public unprepared for its emergence. The ground of public legitimacy for the medieval saint's portrayal was already laid by the very groups that, in prior decades, led militant campaigns against Alevis. Add to this the fact that the saint's portrait is commonly held alongside that of Atatürk, and the ideological purchase of this iconographic dispensation comes into view more clearly. The practice of displaying such images may have opened up a footing for Alevis in a national public from which they had long been marginalized, but it did so in a space of legitimacy already pried open by nationalist political authorities. An organized partition of the perceptible, to return to Rancière's phrase, authorized the conditions of public visibility for this iconography.

TIME AND THE NATION

There is, then, an undeniable ideological power to this iconography, a power that explains why Zehra teyze might continue to feel uncertain about taking the image of Ali out of the closet where it has long laid hidden. The public legitimacy of the portrait has only been attained by juxtaposing it alongside icons invested with the authority of the nation-state and the officially sanctioned national past. There is a relatively circumscribed range of possibilities for portraying the icon of Ali when one is limited to the authorized narratives of the nation. One might prop up the image of Ali incorrectly, in ways that do not rehearse the history of the nation. Zehra teyze's hesitancy responds to the diffusely applied, if sharply felt, field of power that choreographs the portrayal of the icon.

In part, the ideological investment in this iconography can be identified in the sequencing of its symbols, allowing us to imagine alternative historical narratives based on different combinations of icons. Indeed, some Alevi groups opt for alternative symbolism. Alevis with a strong connection to leftist politics often deploy the image of Pir Sultan Abdal, a sixteenth-century rebel bard killed by Ottoman authorities. The image of Pir Sultan with arms raised in defiance of political authority carries a political charge that state-supported images of Hacı Bektaş and Atatürk are meant to mollify in the name of national unity.

Without discounting the differences in political sensibility associated with these rival images, I maintain that the ideological investments in this iconography are not simply a product of the narrative produced by one or another combination of symbols. What warrants interrogation as an ideological effect is a more basic presumption of modern Alevi sociopolitics, namely, that the Alevi past ought to be read as a historical narrative at all. What conceptions of social belonging and political authority are bundled into this historicist assumption?

In posing this question, I want to throw into question the apparent self-evidence of the act of historicizing Alevi religiosity. As de Certeau insists, the act of historicization is a social and political operation, always bound to local institutions (see also Malkki 1995; Trouillot 1995; Palmié 2013). Despite modernist claims to its universal relevance—as a rational method for understanding the origins and development of any social phenomena—the institutionalized act of historicization must first identify and construct, within the local context, objects capable of being subjected to that operation. Alevism has to be formed as an object available for historicization, and in that formation a certain organization of political authority finds expression.

Benedict Anderson's ([1983] 1991) interrogation of nationalism provides an important reference point for conceptualizing the forms of political authority at work in historicist objectification. Anderson argues that the nation is best conceived of as a cultural artifact. It presupposes often implicit understandings of space and time that distinguish it from earlier cultural-political systems, such as those that prevailed in Latin Christendom, the medieval Muslim world, or China's Middle Kingdom. Anderson proposes that in contrast to these older cultural-political dispensations, the nation became thinkable only by means of a new apprehension of time as measured by clock and calendar. The new apprehension of time enabled a distinctive imagining of political collectivity. In a striking passage, Anderson maintains that a new notion of a social body, locatable through its movements in historical time, is the linchpin of the imaginary of the nation: "The idea of a sociological organism moving calendrically through homogeneous, empty time is a precise analogue of the idea of the nation, which also is conceived as a solid community moving steadily down (or up) history" (Anderson 1991: 26). It is not simply that the discourse of nationalist ideologues posits or fabricates certain falsifiable interpretations of history, something that a more robust and less biased historiography could correct. In the first instance, the discourse of the nation operates a distinctive social ontology, projecting a social body with historical depth.

As numerous scholars following Anderson have indicated, this projection cannot be taken for granted, even today, when the nation-form exhibits hegemonic pretensions. It has to be continually enacted, entrenching its inter-pellative mechanisms or confronting alternatives to its imaginary (see, e.g., Bhabha 1994; Duara 1995; Wedeen 2008). The ongoing projection of the nation's social ontology represents a political practice in its own right, one that is concerned less with authorizing one or another interpretation of history than with locating society in a historical time line as such. It is the imagin-ing of a sociological organism capable of trolling across calendrical time that makes the act of historicization both intelligible and politically necessary.

The iconographic dispensation found in many Alevi communities today is one element in a broader array of practices that convey a characteristically modern, historicist sensibility. Looking across such practices, it becomes apparent that there is a concerted effort to locate the Alevi religious past within a historical timeline. What I wish to emphasize is that the act of his-toricizing the Alevi past is no meager feat. It requires a complex procedure of establishing the social ontology of the nation—its imagining of a sociological organism with historical depth—as the ground for understanding the Alevi past and present. The homogeneous, empty time of the nation is not simply the given ground of contemporary Alevi self-understanding; it has to be con-tinually invoked and reproduced in practice. The form of power I describe is that which enables the historicization of Alevi pasts and institutes its social ontology as the condition of intelligibility for Alevi religiosity today.

In order to understand how this historicizing procedure functions, as well as problems raised in its functioning, I turn my attention to a set of practices concerned with the writing of Alevi histories. It is in such writings that ques-tions concerning the historicization of Alevi religious pasts are given explicit elaboration, and where difficulties in establishing the social ontology of the nation begin to come into view.

GENRES OF REFLEXIVITY

Sibel and Ercan were in their forties, and like Zehra teyze, mentioned earlier, they lived in a modest apartment in the lower-middle-class Alevi neighbor-hood in Çorum. They had three kids, one of whom was in high school at the time of my fieldwork, while the other two were beginning preschool. Ercan, described in previous chapters, was a teacher in a local elementary school, and Sibel had spent the previous few years at home, raising her two youngest children. I frequently dropped by their home in the evenings, where we would share some tea or beer and watch a soccer match or a television serial. Sibel and

Ercan were the sort of friends ethnographers hope to find—always available to help interpret my ethnographic observations, but at the same time offering a comfortable respite from the vigilance and rigor of constant participant observation.

One evening, Ercan turned from the television and broke into an elaborate disquisition on Alevism and leftist politics. Like many Alevis of his generation, Ercan was a self-identified socialist. "We need, of course, to raise our kids to be socialists," he began. "But we also have to teach them about Alevi culture." I prodded him to elaborate, and without much hesitation he continued, "Many Alevi youth don't really know much about the meaning of Alevi practices like the *semah* and the *cem*."[6] Gesturing with his arms and hands in poses that resembled the semah, Ercan explained that each motion symbolizes a deeper meaning. Most Alevi youth, he claimed, are not aware of these meanings. He explained that he had acquired a partial understanding only because he read a book on the subject. He added that his cousin, an Alevi intellectual who had written a number of books on Alevi rituals such as the semah, was much more knowledgeable on these matters.

What was striking about these remarks was not so much the fact that Alevi youth, and to some extent Ercan himself, were said to be ignorant, but the criteria by which that ignorance was measured. Ercan seemed to adopt something of a symbolic hermeneutics as a frame for understanding Alevi ritual. A proper understanding of Alevi ritual required the ability to decode and read the meanings represented by the movements and gestures of the practice. For Ercan, the natural site for learning the symbolics of the semah was in the writings of contemporary Alevi intellectuals.

Some months later, Sibel echoed these sentiments, mentioning her own ignorance on matters of Alevi ritual. She had asked me how my research was progressing and with some embarrassment apologized for not being more helpful to me. "My father raised us in Sunni culture. We fasted during Ramadan, we performed *mevlit* rituals.[7] I didn't grow up going to cems or dancing the semah. So, I don't know much about Alevi culture." As if to clarify further she added, "I haven't read much about Alevism."

Although married, Ercan and Sibel self-identified with very different backgrounds. Ercan, the socialist, had little truck with Sunni Islam, often viewing revivalist currents within it as fanatical and politically threatening to Alevis like himself. Sibel, by contrast, felt at home in what she termed the "Sunni culture" of her youth. They formulated their ignorance of Alevi ritual in somewhat different terms: for Ercan, it was a matter of deepening an understanding of ritual symbolism; for Sibel, ignorance was the product of a lack of exposure to such practices. What they shared, however, was a sense that reading books on Alevism was one important way of redressing their ignorance.

The notion that one's ignorance of Alevi ritual is indexed by a lack of reading deserves greater elaboration, because what is glossed in the most general terms as "reading" implies a specific set of assumptions about the texts at hand and the authority they command. When Ercan and Sibel spoke about the importance of reading as a necessary task of acquiring knowledge about Alevism, not just any sort of textuality was being commended. What they were referencing was a genre of discourse invested with the authority to set the criteria of accurate knowledge (social history), presuming a certain kind of writer and audience (a modern intellectual and a national public), and positing a distinctive social ontology (the sociological organism of modern historicism). This assemblage of elements is formative of a key practice of historicization in contemporary Alevi communities.

In speaking of social history as a genre, I mean to indicate that it is defined by certain recognizable patterns, concerning its narrative styles, its sites of production, and its criteria of evaluation. As Mikhail Bakhtin (1981, 1986) emphasized, such patterns are only relatively stable, always manifesting signs of their location within broader historical dynamics. Genres are embedded within particular material practices and interactive contexts, and they carry traces of the institutional and ideological forms from which they historically derive.

Social history was bound to the state's nationalist project from early on. It extends back to the late Ottoman Empire and early Turkish Republic, when nationalist ideologues dispatched ethnographers to central and eastern Anatolia to study Alevi communities. Almost invariably, such studies identified Alevi rituals as tokens of the Turkish nation's authentic past. Social history, as a globally pervasive mode of modernist writing, articulated with a particular historical moment and ideological project within Turkey, especially in its application to Alevi religiosity.

It is out of this same history that the idea of Alevi ignorance, articulated in particular ways by Ercan and Sibel, developed as a politically effective trope, one that was connected to the social ontology of modern historicism. The early republican ethnographers examined in chapter 3, such as Baha Sait and Yusuf Ziya Yörükan, insisted that Alevis misunderstood the historical derivation of their own traditions. Recall, for instance, Yörükan's efforts to debunk Alevi claims to scriptural authenticity. Rather than searching for Alevi traditions within authoritative interpretations of the Qur'an or of hadith compilations, he submitted that one must seek the origins of the community's traditions in the history of Anatolia. Sait equally insisted that the historical roots of Alevism must not be sought by examining the lives and deeds of Ali ibn Abi Talib and his descendants—the Twelve Imams whom Alevi communities hold at the center of many of their devotional rites. Rather, Sait maintained, Alevism was a product of Turkish history, originally developed through the guiding influence of Central Asian shamanism. For both Yörükan and Sait, the ignorance of Alevi communities represented a lack of historical knowledge. The efforts of nationalist intellectuals to locate Alevism in historical time not only supplied knowledge that Alevis themselves supposedly lacked; in that process of historicization these intellectuals also threw into relief the social body of the nation and its historical development.

It was only in the second half of the twentieth century, and more particularly from the late 1980s on, that Alevis themselves began to narrate the community's past and present by means of the genre of social history. Alevi efforts to historicize their religious traditions are often pitched as a response to the perceived ignorance, not only of the Sunni majority but of Alevis themselves, to the history and meaning of the community's practices. Unlike some of the early republican intellectuals like Yörükan, the historicization of Alevism conducted by Alevi intellectuals is not meant to clarify the true sources of Islam from historical and cultural remnants. But what remains pertinent today, as it was in the first decades of the republic, is the notion that the modern discourse of social history offers the promise of an objective understanding of Alevi religiosity.

The work of Alevis themselves to textually historicize their community's past has attracted the attention of a number of scholars in recent years. Markus Dressler refers to the upsurge in written narratives as the "increasing scriptural fixation of the predominantly oral tradition" (2008: 301). David Shankland similarly argues that the unprecedented scale of textual production reveals "the express process of codification of [the Alevi community's] previously diverse largely unrecorded culture within the modern city setting" (2003: 13). In these accounts, the project of entextualized historiography itself appears to mark a historical transition for the community. The written form of the discourse is contrasted with the oral character of traditional Alevi societies. The emphasis on the oral-written divide focuses on the sheer impact of literate textuality. What tends to fall out of view in this approach are the political disputes that emerge over the genres mediating this writing, which are invested with the capacity to produce authoritative knowledge (Tambar 2012).

The Alevi appropriation of the genre of social history is marked by a deep political ambiguity. On the one hand, it is through the writing of social histories that Alevi intellectuals have begun to construct a public voice for the community for the first time in republican history. This constructive project can only be transformative of a national public that had hitherto been predicated on the absence of Alevis from its spheres of deliberation. On the other hand, the genre itself carries with it a number of assumptions put into place by the early modernist project, concerning the social space and historical time of the national political body. The Alevi effort to historicize the community's past has entailed a calibration of cultural memory in accordance with the dictates of national historicism. Investigating the Alevi appropriation of this genre allows a glimpse into one site where Alevis are struggling to negotiate the institutional demands of national allegiance while concerned to assert communal difference in the name of pluralist politics.

The texts at hand are composed by a new class of Alevi public intellectuals, who either were born in urban settings or migrated there as children. Most of these writers attended public schools, and many hold higher degrees from Turkish universities. These intellectuals frequently participate in political debates about the state's classification of the community and its rituals, appearing in a wide range of state-run and private media, including television programs, newspaper editorials, published books, and Internet forums and blogs. Indeed, part of what defines these actors as *public* intellectuals is their capacity to mobilize genres of writing and speech that are capable of summoning and addressing a national audience in various mediatized modalities.

The rise of Alevi public intellectuals represents one strand of a broader trend in Turkey. The past few decades have also seen the emergence of a new class of public intellectuals within Turkey's Sunni majority, educated through the state's public school system and capable of mobilizing the same array of new media forms (Meeker 1994b). Yet certain historical and discursive features distinguish intellectual production among Alevis from that among Sunnis. As mentioned earlier, Alevi intellectual production developed in the aftermath of sectarian violence directed against the community, most dramatically in the late 1970s and most recently in the early 1990s. Alevi expressions of communal tradition have had to contend with accusations of disloyalty to the nation that have been backed with threats and acts of violence. The experience of political vulnerability has led many Alevis to conform to, rather than openly transgress, state-sustained norms of public expression.

The sensed vulnerability to communal violence has influenced the kind of discourse Alevi intellectuals have produced, in contrast to their Sunni counterparts. As Brian Silverstein (2005, 2010) shows, Turkish Sunni intellectuals have investigated the conditions of their engagement with the Islamic tradition in a number of ways. They specify those conditions as contextually shaped by late Ottoman and early republican modernization efforts, but they supply grounds for justifying the continued relevance of traditional Islamic genres. Some Sunni intellectuals inveigh against the Kemalist project of state-led modernization and the modes of knowledge production it derived from western Europe.[8] Alevi intellectuals, by contrast, have frequently embraced Kemalist modernization in explicit ideological terms, and they have tended not to claim the validity of Islamic knowledge forms overtly. They have generally employed state-authorized modernist genres, particularly that of social history.

Two crucial presumptions underlie this genre. First, Anatolia is taken as the social space within which Alevi religiosity was established and developed. Anatolia is neither an arbitrary nor an ideologically neutral selection: it has grounded most of Turkey's national historiography since the republic's inception (Copeaux 1997). It has come to be accepted by most commentators as the geographical space that nourished the emergence and growth of both the nation and the Alevi community. This emplacement of Alevi religious tradition within Anatolia also bears the marks of the more recently developed Turkish-Islamic synthesis mentioned earlier. Writings on Alevi history rarely provide overt citations of the thesis, but the discursive ground of this literature exemplifies many of its characteristic elements. The notion of an Islamic tradition, whose geography of adherents exists in excess of any given sovereign national territory, has little role in these discourses on Alevi religion.[9]

Second, the discourse emplots Alevi religious history across the course of Turkic migrations from Central Asia into Anatolia, revealing an evolution of communal traditions under the rule of various Turkic dynasties, through the Ottoman Empire, and down to the republic. The empty, homogeneous, and chronological time characteristic of nationalist historiography throughout much of the world is taken as the temporal ground on which the past of Alevi religion is conceived and authenticated.

These two assumptions provide a spatio-temporal frame for nearly all writing on Alevism today. They are powerfully instituted, anchored at once by the particular ideologies of Turkish nationalism that developed in the course of the twentieth century and by modernist epistemologies that have gained global purchase in that same period of time. However, it is crucial to recognize that the authority of the genre, both locally and globally, has not precluded attempts by Alevis to invoke accounts of the martyrdom of the Twelve Imams, which are not easily accommodated by the genre's structuring principles. There is a running tension in many Alevi writings between loyalty to the modes of historicism mandated by the discourse of nationalism, on the one hand, and invocations of discursive traditions of piety and martyrdom that violate the conventions of social history, on the other.

The work of Cemal Şener exemplifies this tension. Şener was a prominent Alevi intellectual and an author of many books on the subject. Like many other Alevi intellectuals (e.g., Bozkurt 1990; Öz 2001), he insisted on distinguishing Alevism from Shi'ism, rooting this distinction in the fact that unique aspects of Alevi religiosity derive from Anatolian history. In one of his earliest texts, Şener (1989) recounts the community's history through medieval and modern Anatolia, the experience of which is said to shape Alevism's characteristic religious forms.

The genre of social history allows Şener to forward a commentary on Alevi identity that is intelligible as a modern discourse. It is only to the extent that it is intelligible within such modern discursive conditions that it can participate in the broader mobilization of a pluralist politics, alongside the exhibition of Alevi icons in public demonstrations described above. In both street action and written texts, Alevis are asserting the community's presence in the physical and discursive spaces associated with the national public in Turkey from which they were long excluded. In the case of Alevi writings, the genre of social history enables this presence.

Yet Şener's text also approaches the genre's limits. It reveals a profound ambiguity concerning the historicism that otherwise renders his text potent and effective within the national public. Given the spatial and temporal orientations of the genre—orientations that Alevi intellectuals generally abide by—it is crucial to note that Şener opens his narrative with a discussion of the Arabian peninsula in the seventh century, that is, with an account of early

Islamic history. Claiming that Alevism has a 1,300 year history, Şener (1989: 8) draws the reader back to the origins of Islam. Despite general adherence to the genre of social history, he nonetheless begins his narrative with an account of the life of the Prophet and his kin. Highlighting in particular the significance of the Prophet's cousin, Ali, and the death of Husayn, Şener's discourse rehearses an account of early Islamic history, whose major pivot is the battle of Karbala. The narrative is not one that Şener himself has invented; it has been sustained by Shiʻi hadith compilations and elaborated by Shiʻi scholars for centuries.

He discusses, for instance, episodes in the life of the Prophet where Muhammad is said to have appointed Ali as his successor (Şener 1989: 21). Şener goes further, describing how efforts by Muhammad to write his last testament, just prior to his death, were resisted by Umar ibn al-Khattab, a figure honored in the Sunni tradition (22–24). Both of these points are guided by traditions of interpretive commentary that depend upon Shiʻi compilations of hadith reports. Among the other important events mentioned by Şener are those involving Umar's use of violence in coercing members of the Muslim community to recognize Abu Bakr's claim to the caliphate (29) and the dispute between Fatima and Abu Bakr over the inheritance of the Fadak land (27–28). Both of these topics have been subject to extensive debate among scholars across the Muslim world. As before, Şener's understandings fall within Shiʻi interpretations of these events. Şener himself never acknowledges his dependence on Shiʻi traditions of commentary, and indeed in the most explicit terms he repudiates any equation of Alevism with Shiʻism. In fact, the larger aim of the work is to provide a history of Alevism in Anatolia. But the genre of a different scene of communication—one constituted through centuries of Shiʻi doctrinal elaboration—shadows his prologue.

Even as it works within the principles of public address established by the genre of social history, the text labors upon the limits of those principles. Şener is not unique in opening his social history with an account of the morally exemplary life of Ali and his descendants; this effort to work within and against the existing genre is found in the work of many contemporary Alevi intellectuals.[10] Following Michael Warner (2002: 146), it would be plausible to suggest that this body of work enacts the "poetic or creative function of public address." It helps to fashion new conditions of discursive intelligibility, not by claiming a position apart from the institutionally regnant genre of social history, but immanent in its employment.

The conditions for this creative engagement, however, are by no means settled by the rhetorical structure of the texts alone. The institutional authority of the genre of social history is revealed in critiques of Alevi writings. An assessment of the texts' creative effectivity requires an examination of how they have been received. Some prominent interlocutors have assumed an antagonistic stance toward texts like Şener's that seek to compose a modern historiographical account of Alevi tradition but begin the narrative with a reflection on the martyrdom of the Twelve Imams. Ahmet Yaşar Ocak—a professional historian with an academic appointment—offers a trenchant critique of such accounts. It is worth briefly examining the target of this critique, as it bears directly on the ambiguity of historicism in contemporary Alevi discourses.

Ocak's approach to the study of Alevism is of major import in Turkey today because it operates at two levels, offering both an analysis of Anatolian religious history and elaborating a critique of the historiography of that history as it emerged in the Turkish Republic. He has, for instance, been a major critic of the nationalist ambitions of early republican scholarship, and in one collection of essays, he frames his own contribution as a correction to the historiographical distortions introduced by early nationalist ideologues (Ocak 2004). Ocak's work has not, however, elaborated a critique of the genre of social history itself. It remains within the terms of that genre, and it is from that stance that he has also pursued a critique of the writings of contemporary Alevi intellectuals.

Specifically Ocak draws out the consequences of beginning a historical account of Alevism with the early Muslim community.

> Most Alevi researchers and Alevis themselves identify the beginnings of Alevism with the era of the Caliphate struggles between Ali and Muawiya.[11] What appears correct about this at first sight is the personage of Ali, who is the subject of primary belief in Alevism. The basic logic of this approach is as follows: Alevism formed in the environment of Ali, and Alevism places him at the center of its theology. . . . However, this starting point is valid for Shi'ism. (Ocak 2004: 259)

From the perspective of a professional historian like Ocak, "the historical starting place of Alevism is not in the Arab lands, where the disputes over the Caliphate took place, but in the lands of Anatolia" (2004: 259–260). To identify the origins of Alevism with the Caliphate struggles of early Islam is to extend communal religious history beyond the geohistorical boundaries of the Turkic migrations into Anatolia. For Ocak, the narrative move introduces "theology" into what should otherwise function as a strictly historical account.

Ocak's criticism addresses the conditions of intelligibility of Şener's invocation of the narratives of early Islamic history and the martyrdom of the Twelve Imams. Insisting upon a scrupulously historicist framing, Ocak seeks to display the ambiguity and untenability of such references within a text that otherwise purports to offer a social history of Anatolian Alevism. He invites us to question the validity of these invocations of early Islam in relation to the genre that provides the text with the context of its engagement. The critique has been backed by some Alevis themselves, who have explicitly sought to chart Alevi history in the chronological progression of Turkic migrations from Central Asia to Anatolia, avoiding in the process a narrative form that would begin with the martyrs of early Islam (e.g., Birdoğan 1990).

The criticisms faced by texts such as Şener's reveal the manner in which the genre that guides the practice of historicism in Turkey is constitutive of the possibilities and limits of Alevi public reflexivity. Şener's text struggles to voice, within a genre hostile to its expression, accounts of early Islam that have long been sustained within Alevi communities in the form of narrated tales, ritual lament, recited hymns, and devotional poetry. The form of discourse that sustains Şener's text as a circulable contribution to public debate is simultaneously what places at risk the intelligibility of the parables of Karbala that open his narrative.

When turning from the iconographic dispensation to the writings of Alevi intellectuals, important similarities and differences come into view. In both cases, Alevism is presented in the form of a historical narrative that tends to conform to the mandates of national historiography. Yet in contrast to the iconographic dispensation, these writings have opened up an explicit debate over the status of early Islamic narratives within an account of Alevi social history. Whereas the image of Ali seems to have acquired a relatively stable footing in Alevi public protests and gatherings, efforts by Alevi intellectuals to relate the parables of his life and deeds are criticized as inadequate to the form of knowledge they seek to produce. That the historicizing of Alevism has tolerated the icon of Ali in one domain but hindered its entry in another suggests a social landscape that remains labile and not ruled by a single governing principle. Despite the deep institutional entrenchment of modern historicism in Turkey, questions about how the Alevi past ought to be represented, by which political agencies, and by means of what forms of knowledge all remain unsettled in the last instance, disturbed rather than confirmed by Alevi efforts to visualize and discourse about their past.

SUBJECTS OF HISTORICISM

Alevi public discourses are pedagogical. Writers and organizations in the community are often motivated by the aim of teaching other Alevis (especially youth), as noted by Ercan above. They also aim to teach non-Alevis about the community's traditions. As one Alevi organizer explained to me, "we can dispel false rumors about our community that continue to spread among Sunnis." Instruction, whether to Alevi youth or to the Sunni majority, is often cast by Alevis as a matter of disseminating accurate knowledge.

In addition to this notion of instruction through dissemination, there is a second mode of pedagogy operative in Alevi public discourses. Sites of communal publicity can become occasions for teaching members of the community how to historicize their past. Ocak's commentary on Alevi intellectuals is offered in a pedagogical spirit, with the aim of correcting what he perceives as the narrative flaws and incongruences of their writings. Here, instruction operates at a metadiscursive level, directed not at the dissemination of knowledge but at molding and disciplining the form of that knowledge.

These two modes of pedagogy are not necessarily temporally distinct, and in fact efforts to disseminate knowledge about Alevi history often offer metadiscursive remarks on the form of the narrative. One prominent Alevi intellectual, Nejat Birdoğan (1990), opens his lengthy social history of Alevism with a comment on a metadiscursive problem that faces a writer of Alevi history: where and when to begin the narrative. Echoing the controversies mentioned above concerning the status of early Islam in Alevi historiography, Birdoğan insists that an account of the community's past ought not to begin from the life of Ali. He proceeds then to trace the historical roots of Anatolian Alevi religiosity back to the Turkic tribes of Central Asia.

The metadiscursive mode of pedagogy is not restricted to concerns about narrative form. The very notion that Alevis ought to conceptualize their religiosity in the form of a historical narrative presumes a distanced, observational stance that is worth interrogating as a sociocultural effect of this pedagogy. What sorts of pedagogical practices fashion a subject capable of recognizing, reading, and valuing the historicization of the Alevi past? What political interests and anxieties motivate the act of teaching Alevis to view early Muslim exemplars with a historian's gaze? The object of this pedagogy is a form of consciousness and a set of affective sensibilities. The aim is to guide how Alevis listen to and engage narratives of their community's past. The process of subject-formation is not easily examined by analyzing disputes among intellectuals such as Şener, Birdoğan, and Ocak. Such disputes tend to presuppose as a condition of their intelligibility a modern historical consciousness, whose scene of formation lies elsewhere.

In the broadest sense, a historical consciousness is fostered by Turkey's public school curriculum. Over the course of the twentieth century, mass education has made more Turkish citizens not only literate, but more specifically, fluent in the genre of historical writing. It is in the classroom where narratives of the Turkish nation are taught and students are tested for their knowledge.[12] However, the school curriculum has long been silent when it comes to the Alevi past. Questions about whether and how Alevism should be depicted in school textbooks on religion continue to be hotly debated in Turkey. The state has tended to see its role in religious education as one of providing basic knowledge about Islam to which any Muslim could assent. As such, it refuses to distinguish among particular denominations of Islam within its educational materials. Some Alevi groups and individuals have challenged the presumption that the state's understanding of Islam's fundamental elements is neutral with respect to sect. Launching legal campaigns to exempt Alevi students from mandatory courses on religion and morality, a number of Alevi organizations argue that the materials used in public school courses on religion presume Sunni Islam as their de facto basis. One result of state policy is that the classroom is not a principal site where historicist sensibilities toward the Alevi past are being cultivated.[13]

The sites where such sensibilities are produced are ones organized by Alevi groups themselves. As mentioned above, massive migrations of Alevis from rural areas to urban settings began in the 1960s and accelerated in the 1980s. While the first few decades of this process witnessed the initial development of civil society organizations claiming to support and represent newly urbanizing Alevis, the number of such groups proliferated in the 1990s. Since the mid to late 1990s, Alevi organizations have sought to create contexts of ritual performance in city centers and provincial towns, where the sorts of religiohistorical narratives elaborated in published texts such as Şener's and Ocak's were collectively orchestrated, voiced, and heard by urban constituencies. The contexts constructed by Alevi organizations are pedagogical spaces in both modalities. They are sites where Alevi groups attempt to educate urban Alevis and the broader public about the community's religiosity. They are also sites to discipline the form of narrative about the community's religious past and the form of subjectivity involved in listening to such narratives.

I want to focus on one particular event that occurred several weeks after Ashura, the day commemorating the death of Husayn, just outside of Çorum in a small town of the neighboring province of Amasya. This particular event was organized as a *Şükrancılık cemi*, a gathering to give thanks to God for allowing one of Husayn's sons, Zayn al-Abidin, to survive the battle of Karbala. The event included several speeches, delivered by government officials, civil society leaders, and an academic, as well as a staged ritual performance. It was organized by the Alevi group described in the previous chapter, the local branch of a national organization.

In its enactment, the event exemplified a tension found in many public performances of Alevi ritual between communal autonomy and state surveillance. Alevi groups who organize community events are formally independent of state institutional control. They are not, for instance, administered by the state's Directorate of Religious Affairs. Yet the ostensible autonomy of such Alevi groups is balanced by pressures felt by some Alevi organizers to demonstrate to state officials, political parties, and the news media their community's inclusion within authoritative narratives of the nation's history.

The tension between autonomy and state scrutiny creates an ambiguity in many public displays of Alevi ritual between, on the one hand, an effort to enact in an urban setting a traditional commemoration of the lives and deaths of early Muslim martyrs and, on the other hand, an effort to display for public consumption what Alevi tradition once looked like in rural Anatolia. One of the organizers in charge of leading the Şükrancılık cemi was Bayram, the director of the Alevi organization whom I introduced in chapter 2. He repeatedly informed the audience that the ritual being staged was merely a "representation" (*temsil*) of how the traditional practice was once performed. As the ritual was enacted, various individuals provided mutually discrepant answers to the question of what kind of event was transpiring: a ritual remembrance of Zayn al-Abidin's survival of the battle of Karbala, or a remembrance of ritual traditions derived from Turkish Anatolia's medieval and early modern past.

One particular moment of the event stands out as significant to the discussion at hand: a speech delivered by an academic, whom I shall refer to as Süleyman. As a professor of religious history, Süleyman has written a number of books on Sufi communities in Anatolian history. I should emphasize that he is not a preacher, and he was not delivering a sermon at this gathering. Moreover, he did not present himself as a participant in an emotional commemoration of Zayn al-Abidin's survival—what would traditionally be referred to as a *majlis* gathering—but instead as a professor offering a public lecture. I was somewhat surprised when, at the beginning of his speech, Süleyman recited the following hadith report ascribed to the Prophet, which is commonly heard in Alevi circles: "I entrust you with two weighty things: the Qur'an and the people of my house [*Ahl al-Bayt*]."

The hadith account is well known and contentious in the Muslim world. It is one of the statements in which Muhammad is seen to indicate the authority of Ali and his descendants as political and religious leaders for the Muslim community—a claim embraced by Shiʻi Muslims.[14] The hadith passage provides scriptural warrant for a range of practices, such as rituals for the remembrance of Ali and his descendants, including the commemoration of Zayn al-Abidin's survival that was at the center of this particular Alevi event. Many Sunni Muslims do not accept the authority of such practices and the hadiths on which they are based.

Standing before a lectern, Süleyman faced an audience of several hundred people sitting in tightly packed rows on plastic folding chairs. Like many such urban Alevi events, the space was not reserved solely for these sorts of rituals; it was a banquet hall, more commonly used for wedding parties (*düğün salonu*). Behind the stage, Alevi organizers had hung posters of Ali, Hacı Bektaş-ı Veli, and Mustafa Kemal Atatürk. Even before Süleyman spoke, the reigning iconographic dispensation established a visual and narrative context for his discourse. The image of Ali was already located in a narrative portraying the nation's progressive development.

The mixed-sex audience he addressed at this event spanned a great variety of ages: babies, adolescents, the middle aged, and the elderly. Seating was not segregated by either sex or age. However, several local dignitaries were seated in the front row—the mayor of the town that hosted the event, the state-appointed director of religious affairs for the province (*müftü*), and representatives of several political parties.

The presence of state officials and party representatives was not unexpected. As indicated in previous chapters, these sorts of individuals have become common attendees at urban Alevi events. Their presence did, however, cause some consternation to the Alevi organizers of the event. I had a sense of this concern because, prior to the event, I shared a meal with several of the organizers. The group included two Alevi *dedes* (religious leaders), several Alevi civil society activists, Bayram, and Süleyman. The conversation focused heavily on how the Şükrancılık cemi should be staged, such that it would not offend the various populations present. Organizers were clearly concerned about cues that might conjure up the history of sectarian fracture between Alevis and the Sunni majority. One of the dedes pointedly asked Süleyman what he would speak about. Without waiting long for a response, the dede insisted that Süleyman not make too many references to Qur'anic passages and hadith accounts, as this might render conspicuous sectarian differences that ought not to be made blatant in this context. The dede's remarks evidenced an anxiety about how a contentious hadith account would be received by a mixed audience.

In his speech, Süleyman did of course mention the key hadith account. He proceeded to describe Muhammad's love for Husayn and the valor Husayn exhibited in his life, culminating in his courage and death at Karbala. In referencing this narrative of early Islamic history, Süleyman was not seeking to antagonize audience members hailing from Sunni backgrounds. On the contrary, he was attempting to provide a publicly palatable account of Alevi Islamic traditions. He pursued this end by situating the account of the Islamic past within a reflexive practice organized by the genre of Anatolian social history. Jumping quickly from the battle of Karbala to a discussion of Anatolia's medieval history, Süleyman made biographical references to a number of Anatolian saints, such as Hacı Bektaş-ı Veli, Mevlana, and Yunus Emre. None of this was entirely surprising to me, given that Süleyman's scholarly expertise lies precisely in the religious history shaped by these figures.

Süleyman's narration functioned pedagogically. His speech was offered in the spirit of informing the audience about the history of Alevi religiosity. The significance of his narration, however, was defined not only by the ideas he conveyed; his discourse also mediated how audience members related to the narrative. Süleyman's account functioned as an attempt to regiment the corporeal and affective practices that audience members brought to bear upon the narrative of early Islamic history. In order to provide a sense of the regimenting work of Süleyman's discourse, I want to turn back to a key moment of his narrative, when he mentioned Husayn's death.

As Süleyman described Husayn's martyrdom at the hands of the tyrannical ruler, Yazid, a few audience members called out curses upon his killers. The act of cursing was not wholly unexpected: curses upon Husayn's oppressors constitute regular components of traditional ritual acts of mourning, often accompanied by weeping.[15] Positioning the audience members within a lengthy historical practice, the act of cursing brought into view the possibility that the practical context of Süleyman's hadith utterance was not simply a historian's public lecture, stripped of devotional emotions, but an event of ritual mourning.

These two metapragmatic framings—academic lecture and devotional mourning—could, of course, co-exist, orienting the event in one manner or the other for various participants. In its occurrence, however, the cursing left but a thin echo. Few participants joined in, and no one that I could see began to weep. For his part, Süleyman refused to be provoked by the cursing and did not embellish his account of Husayn's death in ways that might have encouraged further curses or acts of weeping. His tone of voice undisturbed, he continued his lecture with the moderated formality of an experienced academic, alluding to the Muslim saints of medieval Anatolia.

The saints are not archaic. As I have emphasized throughout, across republican history they have been recuperated by nationalist leaders and academics alike as forebears of the Turkish nation (see also Soileau 2006). In the unfolding context of the event, the invocation of these figures was efficacious: in conjunction with the posters on stage and the anxiety induced by the presence of state officials in the audience, the reference to Anatolian saints helped to regiment what might otherwise have been an occasion to weep for fallen martyrs of early Islamic history as an event to recollect the history of Turkish Anatolia. These various elements established conditions of cogency that rendered Süleyman's utterance legible as social history and concomitantly placed at risk the intelligibility of the act of cursing as an appropriate and recognizable mode of responding to the narrative. Süleyman did not perceive the calling of curses as an alternative orientation to the narrative, one that would demand critical riposte; rather he treated the curses as a noisy disruption, best left unacknowledged. The objects of pedagogy in contemporary Alevi performance contexts are not only the key narratives of Alevi religion but the affective modalities of responding (or not responding) to narrative cues.

This pedagogy of history is not, then, simply a method of more accurately, more objectively, or more rationally understanding the significance of a religious figure. Historical discourses are invoked in public events as a situated practice, hinged to state institutions that establish the conditions and limits of religious difference. The Şükrancılık cemi event revealed the way in which modern historicism acts as a disciplinary force in Alevi milieux, shaping but also constraining the formation of collective religious memory.

THE CRITIQUE OF HISTORICISM

Earlier I argued that many Alevis in contemporary Turkey report a disinterest in the disciplines of mourning. This disinterest does not mean that the parables of Karbala have been wholly excised from Alevi contexts. These religious narratives continue to be invoked by Alevis in new contexts of public performance and in new formats of discursive production: in the writings of Alevi intellectuals, in events hosted by urban Alevi organizations, in television programs and on Internet sites promoted by various Alevi groups in both Turkey and Europe. As the narrative is loosened from practices of lamentation, it is being affixed to new contexts of enunciation, articulated by new modes of self-relation and self-expression, and defined by a new regime of representation. The reorganization of the narrative in these practices and contexts of engagement provides a vehicle for Alevi participation in public and political debates in Turkey. It also yields new mechanisms and sites for the state to demand from its Alevi citizens allegiance to its norms of national cohesion.

The act of historicizing the Alevi past, I have argued, carries this ambiguity and raises in a particularly acute manner the paradoxical nature of pluralism in Turkey today. Public representations of Alevism challenge the long-standing statist image of a homogeneous national body, but the practices of representation are organized by the space-time of historicism over which the nation-state itself presides. What persists across the varied instantiations of this historicism—in the iconographic dispensation, the writing of Alevi social histories, and public enunciations of Alevi religious narratives—is the formation of Alevism as a token of the nation's past. The homogeneous, empty time of the nation inscribes itself as a condition for the intelligibility of Alevi religiosity. If the historicizing of Alevi pasts is one manner of demanding public recognition for a marginalized community, it is also a mode of rendering the community recognizable to governing authorities in terms controlled by the latter. The various practices of historicization being developed today are instrumentalized as technologies of governance, material holds that can be grasped within existing institutional apparatuses.

To say this need not imply a single agent of governance. The mobilization of these technologies of governance draws together a wide range of actors—state officials, journalists, political party representatives, academics, and some Alevi organizers. It involves different forms of activity—the establishment of iconographic conventions, the production of historical knowledge and the historiographical debates to which they are given, and the organization of Alevi public events. Nor need we assume that this governing activity is exhaustively effective or given to a singular effect—whether the images of early Muslim exemplars and the parables of their lives ought to enter into these sites of public display is not settled; it is perceived to be more troubling in certain domains than in others. The historicization of Alevism is moored by various sites of enactment that are by no means calibrated under a single organizational mandate. The rendering of Alevism into an object available for historicization is a process that is ongoing.

Alevi organizations are not unaware of the fact that their own activities may be complicit with statist imaginings of political community. They engage in heated internal disputes about the extent to which their own sponsorship entrenches or combats the state's governing imperatives. Recall from the second chapter that Bayram, the director of the Çorum branch of a major Alevi organization, was anxious to display national harmony in Alevi events that were to be monitored by state officials and photographed by local journalists. Bayram's persistent concern about displaying national harmony often conflicted with the commitment of the Ankara-based leaders of the organization to a confrontational politics with state authorities. While the events sponsored by provincial branches are meant to reflect the stances of the national organization, it is not uncommon for divergences to emerge between organizers in Ankara and provincial directors. A few years after I left the field, Bayram was removed from his office. According to Bayram, organizers in Ankara were upset that he had invited the *müftü* of the province (the state-appointed head of religious affairs) to Alevi gatherings, along with other state officials and political party representatives. They were concerned that extending invitations to such figures did not simply promote national unity, as Bayram had claimed, but furthered the assimilation of Alevis to state-enforced norms.

An even more striking series of events, which took place between November and December 2011, suggests that in some quarters the political authority of historicism is beginning to be queried. The events in question did not concern Çorum but the eastern province of Tunceli, which is largely inhabited by Alevi Kurds and lies in the heart of a territory once referred to as Dersim. The region is mountainous and hard to access. It was notoriously difficult for the Ottoman state and then the Turkish republican state to control. In the name of Turkification—a policy bent on homogenizing Anatolia's ethnically and religiously diverse population—the republican state extensively bombed the region between 1937 and 1938. Tens of thousands of local inhabitants were killed or forcibly evacuated. The Dersim events constituted one of the early republican state's most repressive military attacks.[16] In November 2011, Hüseyin Aygün, the parliamentary representative of Tunceli and a member of the major opposition party, the Republican People's Party (CHP), publicly remarked on the violent political history that shaped Alevi experiences of Turkey's past. He commented on the dissonance between official state narratives of what transpired in Dersim and what actually took place, claiming that the events had escalated to the point of genocide.

Aygün continued his remarks with a stunning assessment of his own party's involvement. The CHP was the party of Atatürk. By and large, it was the only political party that existed for the first decades of the republic.[17] Aygün asserted that the CHP must and, indeed, is beginning to "face up to its own history" (Zaman 2011b). Almost immediately, various members of the CHP called for Aygün's expulsion from the party. Faced with a crisis within the CHP, the leader of the party, Kemal Kılıçdaroğlu—himself of Tunceli origin—called for party leaders to stop discussing the matter publicly. The issue of Dersim did not, however, go away. Seizing the political moment, Recep Tayyip Erdoğan, Turkey's prime minister and chairman of the ruling AKP, went before parliament and offered a public apology on behalf of the state for the Dersim massacres. Erdoğan referred to the massacres as "the most tragic incident of our near past" (*Hürriyet Daily News* 2011).

Much could be made about the politics of this historical apology. A taboo subject had been officially broached, a historical silence finally broken. Along the way, Erdoğan managed to score tactical political points by exploiting tensions within a rival party. What interests me, however, is not the politics of the apology itself, but the difficulties faced by many Alevis in forming a critical response. Alevis have often been staunchly opposed to the AKP and have long been supporters of the CHP. Here, the AKP had seized the moral high ground, apologizing for violence against an Alevi community, and the CHP appeared completely fractured in its willingness even to acknowledge the scale of the repression. The chain of events led certain Alevi groups and intellectuals explicitly to question the support that the community has offered to the party. Even more powerfully, some Alevis began critically to question their support of the founding narratives of Turkey's political modernity, especially with regard to the process of nationalization. If nation-building was premised on the violent repression of certain Alevi communities, was it still valid to maintain that Alevis were foundational elements of the Turkish nation?

One Alevi intellectual from Tunceli, Cafer Solgun, raised the question directly. Solgun, who published a book on the events of Dersim, was interviewed after Erdoğan's apology. After discussing the events that took place in Dersim in the 1930s and then offering his opinion on the politics of the apology, Solgun turned his critical gaze inward, toward the Alevi community's relationship to Atatürk and the Kemalist project of nation-building: "In order to avoid death, in order to stay alive, in order to protect their children, our elders thought that there was only one available path, and they named their children, that is they named us, Kemal and İsmet." The names in question refer to leaders of the early republican state, Mustafa Kemal Atatürk and İsmet İnönü. Solgun continued that now that the events of Dersim were coming to light and entering into explicit public discussion, it would no longer be possible for Alevis, or anyone else, to hold on to the myth that Atatürk was unaware of what had happened in Dersim; evidence suggests that he ratified the operations. Prodded to respond to the fact that Atatürk's picture is often hung next to that of Ali in Alevi cemevis, Solgun answered decisively, "Atatürk's portrait will definitely be removed" (Taraf 2011).

Solgun's critique resonated with a comment made by Aygün, the CHP parliamentarian whose public statements first initiated the controversy about the Dersim events. In those remarks, Aygün did not restrict himself to criticism of the early republican state and the commanding role of the CHP in those events. He also indicated the outlines of a critique of the Alevi practice of displaying the photograph of Atatürk: "In all of the policies pursued during the period, Atatürk was the head of state. However, in order to separate Mustafa Kemal from [the political activities] of the period, in order to not allow a shadow to fall upon his identity as 'the great leader,' Alevis hung his photograph next to Ali. They made themselves believe that he was unaware of the massacres" (Zaman 2011b). Solgun and Aygün's efforts were directed at dislodging Alevism from the dominating iconic trope of Turkish political modernity.

The deployment of the image of Atatürk in Alevi events, I have argued, is a key element in a distinctly historicist practice, one that positions Alevi religiosity as a sign of the nation's historical past. The image is displayed in public events behind speakers who overtly locate Alevism within the authorized narratives of Turkish nationalism. The icon of Atatürk is an anchoring sign within a narrative that the nation-state credits as official history. Querying the validity of that image in Alevi contexts enables a kind of political criticism that is not only directed outward at institutions that constrained, repressed, or otherwise maligned Alevis in the past, but immanently implicates certain Alevi social practices in tactics of state control. Solgun and Aygün's critical targets were precisely those practices by which Alevis have inscribed themselves into statist narratives of Turkish modernity in the course of the twentieth century: practices of naming and practices of iconographic display.[18] They sought to question the legitimated modes of Alevi collective belonging.

Efforts to interrogate the authority of this iconographic dispensation are troubling, even outrageous, to many in Turkey today: in the weeks following the interview in which Solgun claimed that Atatürk's picture would be removed, he received a number of death threats (*Demokrat Haber* 2012). The new line of Alevi critique is scandalous to some because it dissects the discursive and aesthetic forms of political community engendered by historicism, only to implicate those forms in practices of state repression and governmental control. It interrogates the forms of violence that have sustained the field of politics in which Alevis are today being offered a location. Alevi critics who are questioning the costs of abiding by the given conditions of public engagement are left in a vulnerable position, compounded by the fact that their community is already marginalized in Turkey. Their line of critical inquiry stands in reference to a field of politics they refuse to accept, but they do not possess the authority to reconfigure that field in ways that would stabilize their position.

Some Alevi intellectuals and leaders who supported Solgun have softened, if not blunted, the purchase of his critique. They justified the excision of Atatürk's image from the ritual space by claiming that he was a political rather than religious leader.[19] Solgun himself relied on this argument to argue for the removal of the image from sites of ritual performance. This line of support legitimizes the call for removing Atatürk's portrait, but it does so at the risk of abandoning the stronger political critique of Atatürk's actions in the historical repression of Alevi communities. Removing Atatürk's photograph from ritual halls because he was a political figure defers the question of the nature of his political leadership, of the violence he ratified, and of the oppression he monitored. The argument elides Solgun's more unsettling assertion that Atatürk's role in the mass killing and exiling of Alevis ought to be interrogated in its own right, and that above all, Alevis themselves ought to interrogate how their own public presence has been sustained only by expressing loyalty and commitment to a regime that exacted extraordinary political violence against them.

In the following chapter, I examine another Alevi community that has begun to scrutinize the limits of historicism. The group in question has been less overtly political in its aims—it has not launched an extensive critique of early republican political violence. Yet in another respect it has more radically challenged the authority of historicism, repudiating the forms of visibility and the genres of vocality that have allocated to Alevis a legitimate space in public life. The activities of this group allow us to explore the sorts of practices that foster a critique of the regnant modes of historical consciousness and the risks entailed in such a project.

6 THE MORALITY OF MOURNING

IN JANUARY 2006, I JOINED a small group of Alevis, listening to an emotional account of the virtuous life and tragic death of Husayn, the grandson of the Prophet Muhammad. As noted earlier, rituals of lamentation in honor of Husayn are held every year during the first ten days of the Islamic month of Muharram by Alevis and Shi'i Muslims around the world. These ten days mark the time period that Husayn and his small band of followers spent in the desert of Karbala, Iraq in 680 CE, battling the tyrant Yazid.

The group of Alevis performing the ritual commemorations referred to itself not as a political organization or a social movement, but as a *cemaat* (Arabic: *jamā'a*), that is, as a congregation of pious individuals. Its efforts are directed not toward explicit political ends, such as forming political parties or lobbying for changes in state policies, but rather at creating contexts for the cultivation of devotional emotions, including those produced in the practice of ritual mourning. The room in which I observed the cemaat enacting rituals of lamentation was draped in black cloth, punctuated with a number of signs, one of which read, "Every place is Karbala, every day is Ashura." The phrase expresses the promise of believers not only to preserve Husayn's memory but also to seize upon that memory at any and every opportunity. One Alevi participant explained the intent of this statement to me in the following manner: "I often think about Husayn, and not just during Muharram. At any time of the year, I might think about Husayn, and when I do, I begin to cry."

The emphasis placed by the cemaat on devotional mourning strikes a dissonant chord with the forms of institutionalized historicism detailed in the preceding chapters. Over the past few decades, in just those years often seen as revealing a pluralization of the public sphere, Alevis have been urged to historicize their religious memory within state-authorized narratives of the nation. The concerted effort to discipline Alevi memory has led to the widespread claim that Alevism constitutes a token of the Turkish nation's cultural and folkloric heritage, and to the concomitant erasure of alternative formulations of the Alevi past that do not conform to national historicism, particularly those centered on the commemoration of early Muslim exemplars.

This chapter focuses on the practices of the cemaat in order to explore one effort at cultivating affective sensibilities that the reigning disciplines of historicism have sought to transform. The cemaat appeals to practices, institutional forms, and discourses derived from Twelver Shi'ism, which is the most prominent branch of Shi'ism found throughout the world, including for instance in Iran, Lebanon, Iraq, Azerbaijan, Pakistan, and India. The cemaat first began to congregate in the late 1980s. It organizes practices of daily worship (*namaz*) in a mosque that it erected in Çorum—the only mosque in town that is not directly run by the state. The preachers at the mosque were trained, not in religious schools and institutes in Turkey, where instruction takes place primarily in terms of state-approved renditions of Sunni Islam, but in Shi'i religious seminaries in Iran. Unlike in state mosques, where preachers are trained and supervised by the Turkish state, sermons in the cemaat's mosque are not vetted by state officials. They frequently invoke references to the lives and deaths of the Twelve Imams and the parables of Karbala.

The cemaat's practices of mourning foster devotional subjectivities that are more commonly perceived in Turkey to be anachronistic in the modern world (see chapter 2). It promotes a form of religious practice that for many Alevis today appears to be retrograde, dislocated from contemporary social and political demands. Precisely because of this disjunctive relationship to reigning conceptions of what constitutes contemporary relevance, certain members of the cemaat have begun to reflect on the disciplinary powers invested in this understanding of the present, opening up a space to consider the limits of historicist imaginings of collective belonging and the forms of subjectivity such imaginings authorize as progressive. Calling into question the historicist temporality that has shaped the modern discourse of Alevism, the cemaat's discursive and ritual practices entail a disarticulation of communal religiosity from the epistemological coordinates of the nation-state and the forms of knowledge it deploys.

Such a project has not unfolded easily. Most Alevi organizations do not view the cemaat's efforts with sympathy, and they have generally refrained from seeing it as contributing to a critical or resistant pluralist politics. If anything, many Alevi groups have strongly repudiated the cemaat for uncritically embracing Shiʿism, an embrace that potentially elides what is unique to Alevism's religiosity and erodes its authentic historical identity. These critiques are not misplaced in at least one crucial sense: the cemaat does, indeed, reject the historicism that governs the discourse on Alevism, refusing to privilege the locality of Anatolia in their conception of the community's religion.

My aim in this chapter is not to salvage the cemaat from its critics by, for instance, recuperating its agency as politically critical in its own right. I do not wish to assimilate the cemaat's project to the existing terms of pluralist critique, because its provocation lies in the extent to which it calls those very terms into question. To be sure, the cemaat's response to the denunciations it has faced has entailed a measure of counter-critique, but its riposte has been most trenchant in challenging the validity of the deliberative field within which public criticism can take place and in questioning the forms of affective sensibility entrenched by spaces of public participation. The cemaat's primary ambitions are to cultivate affective sensibilities toward the early Islamic past that the disciplines of historicism have disabled.

I begin this chapter by examining the hostile critiques that the cemaat's project elicits. These various critiques symptomatically indicate the forms of knowledge that the cemaat is putting into question. I then move to consider the discursive and affective practices where the cemaat is, in fact, struggling to reorder the formation of Alevi subjectivity. If the linear historical time of the nation has become a privileged measure of modern politics, then from what position, and by means of what discursive and affective resources, might one take the measure of historical time?

THE PROVOCATION OF THE CEMAAT

The cemaat's efforts represent a tenuous experiment at the limits of institutionally authorized forms of subjectivity. The sheer number of individuals who regularly attend the mosque for Friday prayers is precariously low—approximately eighty to ninety local Alevis.[1] Members range in age, from young adults to the elderly, and they are almost exclusively men.[2] Most are originally from Çorum or neighboring villages, and many of them have been industrial laborers, as is frequently the case among Alevis who participated in processes of urbanization from the 1960s on.

Despite the relatively small number of participants in the cemaat, the group has provoked considerable controversy. Given its provincial location and its devotional, rather than statist, ambitions, it is somewhat surprising to note the variety and tenor of the cemaat's critics. The criticisms to which it is subject are by no means united, either in their sociological profile or in the agencies that express them. Its critics are drawn from across state institutions and civil society organizations, including government officials, academics, journalists, public intellectuals, and ordinary individuals both within and outside of the Alevi community.

Some criticisms take the form of historiographical argument. Ercan, the Alevi schoolteacher mentioned earlier, offered a cogent formulation of this critique, arguing that the cemaat's appropriation of Shi'ism was not completely misguided but historically too limited: "Sure, Ali and Husayn are important in Alevism. The name of Ali is where the word Alevism comes from, after all. But those aren't the only significant figures. There's also Hacı Bektaş, Pir Sultan Abdal, and other figures who were important in Anatolia. You can't just take Ali and Husayn and throw away these other people."

Ercan's assessment relied heavily on the historicist framework that has become prominent in Turkey. It acknowledged the significance of early Islam in Alevi religious narratives, but it ultimately recentered Alevi religiosity within the projected space-time of medieval and early modern Anatolia. Ercan suggested that an adequate understanding of Alevism requires a knowledge of Anatolia's religious history.

I encountered more politically polemic variants of this historicist critique, particularly among intellectuals and academics. One Çorum-based academic offered the following argument as a way of discrediting the cemaat: "Historically speaking, Alevis in Anatolia have never embraced the Shi'ism of Iran." As a result, he concluded, the cemaat has failed to garner a wide following, and its membership has dwindled since its inception. The nature of the criticism was familiar. We saw a very similar discourse in chapter 3: early republican ethnographers of Alevism sought to distinguish the Anatolian-Turkic roots of the community's religiosity from the Shi'i tradition, often claiming the latter to be derived from Iran's religious history. The historicism of such arguments is bolstered by a national political geography that isolates Alevi religiosity from elements that might extend beyond the Turkish nation's imagined geohistory.

Other critics, such as the Alevi public intellectual Baki Öz (2001: 167–216), insist that projects attempting to link Alevism to Shi'ism are not only historically inauthentic but ideologically motivated. Such critics make explicit the problems raised by Shi'ism's political geography. I frequently came across this critique in the course of my fieldwork. Indeed, when I first began this research project, I consulted with a number of Turkish academics and was often reproached for selecting a Shi'i cemaat as a site for the study of Alevism. One sociologist with an academic appointment in Ankara responded to my discussion of this group by saying of the cemaat: "It sounds like they are engaged in politics and nothing else," implying that the ethical impetus of many of the cemaat's activities was merely a screen for other political ends. Just what these purported ends might be was whispered in conspiratorial tones rather than supported with evidence. A local Alevi affiliated with a rival Alevi organization in Çorum offered a similar, if more direct, condemnation of the cemaat: "They are tied to Iran. They get money from the Iranian state, and they spread its ideology." According to the prominent Alevi writer Fuat Bozkurt (1998), linking Alevism to Iranian Shi'ism is "irresponsible" and contributes to the "erosion" of Anatolian Alevi identity.

These critiques are not entirely misplaced: to the extent that the cemaat's preachers were trained in Iranian religious seminaries and have ongoing relationships of friendship and mentorship with teachers and students associated with those schools, the congregation is indeed connected to social and religious life in Iran. The criticisms to which the cemaat has been subject, however, are intoned with a sense of political threat that is far in excess of what these connections actually entail. The cemaat is not attempting to export Iran's revolution in Turkey, nor is it organizing a party-based political movement in order to remake the Turkish state in Iran's image. Its links to Iran are manifested much more directly in terms of the forms of devotional religiosity it seeks to foster among Alevis.

Local government officials have not remained neutral in these controversies. They have made public statements that suggest a link between the cemaat and the Iranian state, a linkage that is then used to question the national loyalty of the cemaat's members. Consider, for example, the remarks of the müftü of the province of Çorum—the bureaucrat in charge of religious affairs for the province—concerning the cemaat's preacher. The statement was given in an interview soon after the mosque had opened for prayer.

In my opinion, the [Alevi] community does not approve of the mosque. Despite the fact that it drew their interest in its first days, that interest has declined. I think the citizens [*vatandaş*] felt something. Why has a mullah come from Iran to lead prayers? Like an Iranian mullah, he wears the cloak [*cübbe*] of Khomeini. Citizens are uncomfortable with that. Before everything else, Alevi citizens love their country [*memleket*], they love the principles of Atatürk. What do they care about Iran? (*Nokta Dergisi* 1990: 21)

The rhetorical moves of the critique are revealing. The müftü begins by asserting that the Alevi community does not like the cemaat's mosque and then shifts his political register to a statement about what might provoke a negative feeling in a citizen. Shuttling back and forth between the particularity of Alevi collectivity and the purported universality of citizenly belonging, he juxtaposes Khomeini to Atatürk as objects of political commitment. The müftü leads us to the conclusion that the cemaat's religious orientation is not only misguided but runs counter to the political loyalties required of Turkish citizenship. Negative appraisals by a government official heighten the political stakes of the critique of the cemaat. Such evaluations carry the possibility of state action, and indeed on several occasions the state has threatened to remove the cemaat's preacher from his post and replace him with a state-trained imam.

These variously situated discourses about the cemaat present a heterogeneous landscape of criticisms. The cemaat is simultaneously framed as inauthentic by historiographical argumentation, unjustifiable by modern evidentiary protocols of knowledge production, provincial by sociological and statistical proof, and possibly threatening to the indivisibility and unity of the Turkish nation. This broad assemblage of institutional power and knowledge represents the variegated but concerted disciplinary impetus that calibrates existing discourses on Alevism and casts the cemaat's appeal to Shi'i traditions of devotional religiosity as alternately inauthentic or politically disruptive. For many of the cemaat's active participants, the project is not simply to persuade other Alevis and non-Alevis that the community's religious identity derives from Shi'ism, but to query the disciplinary assemblage that has framed the problem of Alevi religious identity within the historicist narratives of the nation.

AGAINST HISTORICIST REASON

Several members of the cemaat have written books, newspaper articles, and entries on Internet forums that make the case for a Shi'i understanding of

Alevism. This form of printed, textual argumentation is not the only or even primary mode of agency found in the cemaat, but it does represent the most explicit confrontation with historicism. The confrontation derives from the fact that the subject position of the writer as public intellectual, the genre available to that subject, and the readership of the text are all coordinated by institutionalized historicist knowledge forms. To contest historicism from this location requires that the writer adopt its discursive practice only to dismantle it. The challenge is to undermine it from within.

I focus here on one particular intellectual associated with the cemaat, Teoman Şahin. Şahin is one of the founding members of the cemaat and its most prominent public representative. The son of a local politician, he grew up in the town of Çorum, attended public schools, and ultimately scored high enough on national exams to attend law school in Ankara. In the mid-1980s, Şahin returned to Çorum and began working in a law practice that he runs today. In his political and economic profile, he resembles the sorts of public intellectuals that have emerged in both Sunni and Alevi communities over the past few decades. He mobilizes the education acquired in modern secular schools for the sake of addressing arguments about religious identity. Şahin refers to himself as an intellectual (aydın), and with good reason: his office is lined with bookshelves, encasing large volumes of Turkish republican jurisprudence and hundreds of texts about Alevism and Islam. He has taken very seriously the eruption of public discourse on Alevi religious tradition. His own writings represent a metadiscursive project that aims to query and subvert some of the framing conditions of contemporary Alevi discourse.

The title of his 1995 book Alevilere Söylenen Yalanlar (Lies That Are Told to Alevis) gives a sense of the polemical nature of Şahin's intellectual project. His concrete aim is to investigate the historical roots of the connection, often presumed today, between Alevism and the Bektaşi Sufi order. Şahin argues that this relationship is neither natural nor obvious, but is the product of an uncertain, politically motivated, and institutionally contentious history.

The text employs the conventions of modernist social history. Throughout the book, he cites the work of professional historians and also makes reference to archival sources. In addition to its practices of citation and reference, the text also proceeds in terms of a chronological narrative, focused particularly on medieval Anatolia, the emergence and development of the Ottoman state, and the rise of the early Turkish Republic. Şahin seeks to persuade on the basis of historiographical reason that Bektaşi Sufism only came to be represented as a foundation of Alevism through various political machinations. Bektaşism, he maintains, provided a mechanism for the Ottoman and then republican state to politically control Alevi populations.

Şahin's effort to unstitch the conceptual bond between Alevism and Bektaşism is a contribution to the ongoing historiographical debates about Alevi identity. There are few Alevi writers today who take such a hostile stand against the historical connection between the two. Şahin's stance is controversial in part because the Alevi-Bektaşi connection is familiar and commonplace in Turkey today, such that some Alevi organizations adopt the phrase "Alevi-Bektaşi" or the eponym of Hacı Bektaş in their organizational names.

Yet if Şahin's text is controversial, its provocation cannot be understood only in terms of its historiographical argument. More important, it disrupts the historicism that provides the relatively stable ground for public discourses on Alevism today. Şahin indicates this ambition early in his text:

> In recent times oppressors who fear the revelation of truth in the topic of Alevism have put forward a poison called Anatolian Alevism. In our understanding the foundations of Islam rest on the Qur'an and the family of the Prophet. Being Alevi is established on these foundations. It means to be a partisan of Ali, to be a partisan of the Prophet, and to remain fully within the limits that God has ordained. Alevism is a divine path, starting with Ali and continuing with the Twelve Imams. The character of a divine path is such that the principles and the sources of this path must be derived from God. In short, the principles of Alevism have been established by God. These principles have been presented to humanity by the Prophet. The task of protecting and enabling these principles has been given to our Twelve Imams. . . . Principles connected to Alevism, for this reason, are not bound to a time and place. . . . If a society wants to be Alevi, or in other words Muslim, it must abandon and eliminate cultural elements that are contrary to Alevism. (Şahin 1995: 19–20)

At first sight, the passage appears to represent a typical example of modern Islamic revivalism, found across the Muslim world at various points in the twentieth century. Revivalist writings often privilege the purity of the scriptural text over and against any form of historically specific, local expression. As numerous scholars have insisted, these writings do not reveal an effort at returning to a premodern form of religiosity; they are modern both in the social formation of such authors, who are often trained in modern schools rather than religious seminaries, and in terms of the critical accounts of modern state institutions and government policies commonly found in such writings (e.g., Lapidus 1997; Lawrence 1998; Euben 1999).

Understanding Şahin as a participant in the broader currents of Islamic revivalism in this way would not be wrong. Referring to Anatolian Alevism as a poison, Şahin rejects the geohistorical delimitation of Alevi religiosity. His appeal to the Qur'an, the Prophet, and the Twelve Imams as the only foundation of Alevism is a clear reference to the orthodox Shi'i tradition he advocates. Yet locating Şahin within revivalist currents ought to serve as an opening for analysis rather than its conclusion. It is worth noting that Şahin's claim to the universality of his religious message does not simply repudiate local knowledge. His claim crucially rests on a hadith account, which is widely known within the Alevi community, that defines Islam in terms of the two foundations of the Qur'an and the family of the Prophet.[3] He is appealing to a certain dimension of local historical experience.

Şahin, then, is not repudiating locality in the abstract. The locality that he is interrogating—Anatolia—is not merely an empirical positivity, but an intensely valorized and institutionalized category in republican Turkey. Its invocation has, over the past century, taken the form of a particular social and political practice: contextualizing Alevism within the historicist narratives of the nation. When Şahin refers to the concept of Anatolian Alevism as a *poison*, he is without question trying to provoke his audience, but his rhetoric is also positioned against the pervasive tendency to assume that Alevism requires historicization within Turkish Anatolia. It is worth qualifying the claim about Şahin's revivalism: He is not merely repudiating local cultural particularity in the name of a transcendent religiosity. Rather, he appeals to a certain form of local knowledge against the dominant narrative of locality, whose frame is Anatolia's geography and history.

Finding the occasion to discuss his book, I asked Şahin about his attack on the idea of Anatolian Alevism. He explained his intent succinctly: "Too many people writing about Alevism start from this idea of Anatolian Alevism. But to start from here is like building a house with rotted foundations." His intervention aims to strike at the foundations of the existing discursive field.

It is hard to ignore Şahin's choice of words such as "poison" and "rotted foundations." The terms indicate not just a source-criticism of prevailing writings on Alevism, concerned with the quantity, sufficiency, or reliability of the materials used to support one or another thesis on Alevi history. His word choice indicates a concern about the effects of historicism that are as much about affective consequences as they are about adequate evidence. They suggest an ethical impetus to his meta-discursive critique.

This ethical impetus is apparent in the inversion Şahin seeks to effect. Within the reigning historicist discourses on Alevism, the moral parables of early Islamic history are often seen to distort the narrative account of an Anatolia-based community's socio-religious history (see chapter 5). Şahin suggests the opposite: the history of Anatolia corrupts a moral account of Alevism. Rather than allowing social history to frame the significance of Islamic source materials for the Alevi community, as has been the case since the early twentieth-century discourses of intellectuals in the late Ottoman Empire, Şahin seeks to frame and evaluate the validity of social historical narratives of Anatolia in terms of an interpretation of the Qur'an and the sayings and deeds of the Prophet and his family.

In presenting his argument, Şahin does not avoid the language of historicism but argues through it. He labors at length on the empirical problems of rooting an account of Alevism in Anatolia's cultural history, arguing, for instance, that the Ottoman Empire and then the republican state contributed to the domination of Alevi communities by pressuring them to assimilate to statist conceptions of religious tradition. In Şahin's account, Anatolia's cultural history beleaguers, rather than enlivens, Alevi religiosity. He disputes the association between Alevism and Anatolian history by pointing to its contingent and deeply ideological formation.

Şahin's text reads like a prolegomenon to a project that is far larger than it can, in itself, performatively enact. He is calling for the establishment of new terms of debate and a new mode of reflexivity; in other words, he is attempting to instigate the formation of what some scholars have called a counterpublic, opposed to the orienting norms of existing public debate (Warner 2002; Hirschkind 2006). Yet this counterpublic does not exist among Alevis today, and his text alone cannot summon it into being. Symptomatic of this is the fact that Şahin calls for a new framing of Alevism within the limits of the Qur'an and the traditions of the Prophet and his kin but does not offer an extended commentary on these sources. This latter project is not only beyond the scope of his book, but is outside the field of discourse on Alevi tradition within which the book functions as a subversive text. Indeed, Şahin's work is intelligible as a subversive text within this debate only to the extent that it abides by the reigning historicist conditions of reflexivity. Extended scriptural commentary would fail to address a public Alevi readership as it currently exists. It would also require a form of education in traditional methods of Islamic argument that Şahin lacks. The reflexive discourse he seeks to subvert is one that, as a Turkish public intellectual, he is capable of speaking within. This situation lends his text a transgressive tone: he makes use of the space of public discourse opened to Alevis in recent years, and yet he does so for the sake of undercutting the very conditions of formation for the reading public capable of understanding his text.

FORMS OF KNOWLEDGE

Şahin's interrogation of historicism represents one modality of action for the cemaat, but this sort of critical endeavor is neither the most exemplary of cemaat activities nor the most important for many of its members. Few cemaat participants write articles, editorial missives, or books about Alevi religious history. More important, very few even read such texts, despite their rapid proliferation in recent decades. The issue is not primarily about the level of literacy or knowledge within the cemaat, but about the form of literate knowledge that is valued by its members. I found that some people were highly motivated to read about their religion, but the texts to be studied were not drawn from the publications of Alevi public intellectuals about Anatolian Alevi identity.

An ethnographic misunderstanding clarified this for me. Mehmet, a college student in his early twenties, performed daily prayers at the cemaat's mosque when he was home for the holidays. His father was one of the preachers at the mosque. Mehmet was interested in pursuing a career in computer technologies. He was keen to learn English, and I was happy to engage him in conversational practice. During his summer break, I met with him frequently at his family's home and at a local park.

On one occasion, I mentioned to him that I had been to Şahin's office and had noticed the many books lining his shelves. I asked Mehmet whether he also read books about Alevism. His immediate response was, "No, I'm not interested in those debates about Alevism," but he quickly broke off. Reflecting on my question, he backed up and started over: "Wait, if by Alevism you mean books about Ali, then yes, I try to read books that discuss Ali's life, what he did, and what he said." Mehmet's confusion with my question was not simply a matter of the polysemic nature of the term "Alevism" (which has multiple meanings and is open to multiple interpretations). Rather, he had noticed that my query broached two different subjects: debates among Alevi intellectuals about the community's historical identity, and the life, deeds, and parables of early Muslim martyrs such as Ali ibn Abi Talib. Mehmet sought to distinguish these subjects as entirely different fields of discourse.

I had a similar interaction with another member of the cemaat, Levent, a man in his late twenties at the time. He had struggled to find a stable job. When I knew him, he had taken a job as a security guard for several months and then later worked as a laborer in a local brick factory. On this occasion, I had invited him to my apartment for tea, where he noticed that I had a number of books that were written by Alevi public intellectuals about the community's social and religious history. Seeking to redirect my interest in Alevism, Levent suggested that "instead of reading all those books about Anatolian Alevism," I should focus my attention on a famous compilation of sermons said to be delivered by Ali, known as *Nahj al-Balagha*. He then lent me his copy of one edition of the text. As with Mehmet, Levent wanted to distinguish between two fields of discourse and the framing of Alevism established within each.

In light of Şahin's attack on historicism, we might discern in both Mehmet and Levent's attitudes a skepticism regarding the validity of the growing domain of discourse on Alevi history in contemporary Turkey. Neither valued the discursive space that enabled public debates about Alevi religiosity. More generally, I rarely found cemaat members engaging in such debates about Alevi religious identity, not even for the sake of asserting the truth of their claim that Alevi religiosity ought to be defined in terms of Shi'ism. If cemaat members like Mehmet and Levent elected not to read about or even debate the community's historical identity, their attitudes should not be interpreted as the result of willful ignorance, but as an effort to clear a space for a different form of knowledge.

AFFECTIVE CAPACITIES

The term "knowledge" might be misleading, if it is taken to imply a primarily cognitive understanding of concepts and reasoning. The form of reasoning and the kind of knowledge that are of central concern to the cemaat center on the task of intensifying certain emotional capacities.

I noticed a concerted effort on the part of cemaat members to cultivate an emotional responsiveness to religious narratives. For instance, many members of the cemaat talked about having love for Ali, or *Ali sevgisi*. The phrase is not peculiar; it is invoked in many Alevi milieux, well beyond the bounds of this particular cemaat. Within the cemaat, individuals employed the phrase in order to launch into a discussion of what that love entailed—for example, performing regular prayers diligently or concertedly trying to remember Ali in one's daily life as a moral measure of one's own activity. Very commonly, cemaat members would complain to me that many Alevis talk about having love for Ali without exerting themselves in ways that would properly manifest this love.

In addition to describing *Ali sevgisi*, individuals in the cemaat were also strongly concerned about developing the ability to weep when listening to accounts of the narratives of Karbala. As related in the anecdote at the start of this chapter, members of the cemaat sought to mourn Husayn's death anywhere, at any time. The ability to weep on cue was regarded as a sign that one had attained a high degree of piety (*takva derecesi*).

The capacity to feel love for Ali or to mourn for Husayn represent central elements of what might be glossed as a culturally or historically specific repertoire of emotion. Recent anthropological scholarship has developed extensive analytical tools for understanding emotion in its historical variability. The emphasis on variability has allowed analysts to examine the role of emotion in articulating social relationships and in the achievement of practical ends, as well as the transformations of those relationships and ends over time (Lutz 1988; Wilce 2009). Clarifying this analytical frame, Lila Abu-Lughod and Catherine Lutz (1990) distinguish between emotional discourses and discourses on emotion. Emotional discourses are culturally specific forms of affective expression, such as ritual lamentations for Husayn. Discourses on emotion, in contrast, refer to the ways that actors talk about emotions—for instance, valorizing ritual lament as motivating new virtues of civic activism, as in Lebanon (Deeb 2006), or denigrating it as backward or out of date, as has become common in many Alevi settings.

These analytical approaches raise crucial questions concerning the historical and pragmatic form of emotion. But how should we conceptualize a situation where a community is not only trying to transform a discourse on emotion—resignifying a practice that is commonly deemed retrograde—but where its members aim to render themselves more sensitive to its emotionality? The issue is not simply one of learning to read contextual cues for affective content, but of becoming increasingly responsive to its triggers. What social labor is necessary to make oneself or another susceptible to the affective cues of the martyrdom narrative?

Talal Asad's (1993) discussion of ritual emotion broaches a similar set of questions. Discussing ritual traditions of medieval Christianity, Asad describes the efforts of monastic communities to shed "tears of desire for heaven"—a desire that these communities could not presuppose but needed to cultivate. "In this way," Asad writes, "emotions . . . could be progressively organized by increasingly apt performance of conventional behavior" (1993: 64). At stake in such Christian communities is not the symbolic meaning or social function of the tears but the ability to weep, which has to be engendered across distinctive events over time. Similarly, Saba Mahmood (2005: 128–131) describes the manner in which members of a Muslim piety movement in Egypt participate in projects of disciplined self-cultivation, including developing the capacity to weep in the act of ritual worship. For members of this movement, Mahmood explains, the capacity to weep cannot be taken for granted; it has to be fostered across enactments of ritual worship. In this model of piety, the iteration of ritual practice is seen to have a cumulative character, progressively enabling the development of a pious self, capable of emotional expression. The social actors in both Asad and Mahmood's discussions are augmenting the ability to weep. They are intensifying their susceptibility to the affective charge of a narrative, what Brian Massumi (2002) describes as the capacity to affect and to be affected.

If the cemaat's members are seeking to open up a space of knowledge foreclosed by regnant forms of historicism in Turkey, this knowledge centers on the lives and deaths of figures like Ali and Husayn. It is a knowledge that implies emotional dispositions and affective capacities. In this, it is no different from the historicist modalities of knowledge that are institutionally empowered in Turkey today. Yet the form of emotionality and subjectivity endorsed by historicism has tended to preclude and at times silence the modalities of devotional engagement that often anchor ritual commemorations of the Karbala narrative. What I wish to explore in greater depth is how the cemaat has sought to intensify affective susceptibilities to the moral parables depicted in these narratives.

SPATIAL ORIENTATIONS

To cultivate the ability to be affected by the narratives of Karbala requires ongoing exertion and effort. In order to pursue this end, the cemaat has needed to make specific material investments that enable particular genres of utterance, such as the forms of preaching, exhortation, and recitation associated with lamentation. To begin with, the cemaat had to construct a space for ritual lament. In the late 1980s, the cemaat began to construct a mosque in Çorum. As is common in Turkey, the building was funded by private donations, both from local Alevis and from remittances received from those working abroad in Europe and in the Middle East.

Unlike most of Turkey's mosques, the cemaat's mosque is independent of the state. It is the only mosque in Çorum—and one of few nationwide—to issue a Shiʻi call to prayer, one that includes the name of Ali ibn Abi Talib.[4] Worship in the cemaat's mosque is Shiʻi in form, and it holds rituals of mourning for the Twelve Imams, which is not done in any other mosque in Çorum. The mosque creates a physical space for the cemaat to pursue the practice of Shiʻi traditions of Islam, which are not represented by the state.

The mosque is not, however, merely a material edifice. It is a received social form, bundled with various historically derived sensibilities. For residents of the neighborhood, the mosque as a social institution carries associations and political histories that cannot easily be cast aside. Very few Alevi groups in Turkey organize rituals in mosques, often associating them with the authority of the state and the religious practices of the Sunni majority. Cemal Şener, an Alevi intellectual discussed in the previous chapter, elaborates a sentiment widespread among Alevis: "[M]ost of the threats that Anatolian Alevis have [historically] faced have originated in mosques. Mosques are accepted [by Alevis] as a center of conservatism, fanaticism, and hostility toward Alevis" (Şener 1989: 97). Şener notes the fact that various episodes of violence to which Alevi communities have been subjected have been incited by militant organizations that sought to use mosques as sites for mobilizing supporters. He adds: "For Alevis, a Shiʻism that arose and developed within the mosque appears to be a phenomenon close to Sunnism" (Şener 1989: 97). Even though the cemaat is organizationally autonomous of the state, for many Alevis the institution of the mosque carries the marks of a violent past.

I heard similar sentiments in the course of my fieldwork. Abbas, a forty-year-old Alevi man who frequently attended Friday prayers with the cemaat, explained how other Alevis in town viewed his group's mosque: "A certain Alevi spirit [ruh] is offended by the building of a mosque. The state has built mosques in Alevi villages and neighborhoods, and Alevis are offended by this because violence committed against Alevis originated in those mosques." Abbas echoed Şener's comments in acknowledging the historical use of mosques as sites from which to launch violent campaigns against Alevis. If

Alevis view the cemaat's mosque with some suspicion, it is because the institutional form itself evokes a history of sectarian discord. The cemaat faces a challenge that is confronted by many emergent movements: the practices it fosters must be generated out of received social forms, whose conditions of intelligibility it has yet to transform. The mosque is one such form.

The emergent character of the cemaat is, however, also enabling. Within the mosque, practices of lamentation are not performed through traditional Alevi instrumentation and song. Many Alevi organizations that seek to host ritual lamentations within urban cemevis employ forms of music and dance that have come to be mediated in the past few decades through an aesthetics of folklore. As described in chapter 4, there is a key tension for such groups between the ethos of leisure and entertainment sustained by those aesthetic media and the gravity of worship they seek to foster in the cemevi. The cemaat, in contrast, locates Alevi rituals of mourning in a sensory ecology organized in accordance with the spatial and social forms of a mosque: participants sit in prayer rows, and the individual narrating the tale also serves as the congregation's prayer leader and preacher. In building a mosque and performing rituals within it, the cemaat creates a context of ritual weeping that is not mediated by the ethos of recreation and leisure associated with folklore. The context allows the cemaat, in effect, to sidestep the mediations of folklore that beleaguer the efforts of many other Alevi organizations to create spaces for religious practice.

The mosque is an important element in the cemaat's project of cultivating passionate engagements with the Karbala narrative, but its sheer presence cannot guarantee the incitement of such emotions. I want to turn, now, to some of the ways in which members of the cemaat seek to exploit the potentialities of the mosque and, thereby, to refashion their collective memory in relation to the early Islamic past. To do so, I look at three ritual performances conducted by the cemaat.

The first event took place during the month of Muharram, the paradigmatic time of ritual lamentation, when most members of the cemaat expected to weep and did so with little hesitation. During Muharram, the affects of mourning were profusely enacted. In the second event, which occurred several months after Muharram during a commemoration of the birth of Fatima, the Prophet's daughter, members of the cemaat struggled to weep and were uncertain about whether the event-space was appropriate for the expression of mourning. The final event took place during Ramadan, the month in which

Ali was martyred. In this event, members of the cemaat manifested preliminary signs of mourning—by placing their heads in their hands, for instance—
but the intensity of the moment quickly gave way, impeding any expressions
of weeping. My description of the last two events reveals the challenges faced
by the cemaat in motivating a scene of weeping. Although members of the
cemaat seek to cultivate among themselves the susceptibility to an emotion
that is otherwise absent in the urban setting, they do not always succeed.

MORALITY AND THE *MECLİS*

Shi'i commemorations of the Karbala narrative take place in *meclis* (Arabic:
majlis) gatherings. Such gatherings create contexts in which listeners can
weep to emotional narrations. The meclis is not necessarily attached to any
particular physical location: across spaces and times, Shi'i communities have
organized such gatherings in mosques, in public squares, or in private homes.
The meclis is a ritual event-space, in which the narrative text of the Karbala
paradigm is articulated with an affect-laden ritual narration. The cemaat's
meclis gatherings take place almost exclusively in its mosque.

Despite the relative autonomy of the mosque from state supervision, the
cemaat has faced difficulties in provoking event-spaces of mourning. In
contrast to many other Shi'i communities around the world, which enact
events of ritual weeping throughout the year, the cemaat concentrates its
mourning rituals largely within the relatively short period of ten days during Muharram. While there are efforts by the cemaat at other points in the
year to commemorate early Islamic history, such commemorative events
are attended by far fewer participants and are organized and announced
with less formality. There is, in other words, a disparity between the
cemaat's broader intention to foster ritual weeping at any point in time,
and its actual ability to convoke event-spaces in which that weeping can
be induced.

The difficulties faced by the cemaat in staging meclis gatherings before or
after Muharram are not merely a function of organizational limitations, such
as limited resources for creating posters and announcing events in the neighborhood or the state's legal restrictions on ritual expression. Such constraints,
which to varying degrees are indeed present, might be addressed by means
that are external to the ritual itself—for instance, by finding new sources of
funding or by pursuing legal action against the state. Yet such ritual-external
means would not account for the challenges I witnessed during my research

that are faced by cemaat members themselves to weep for exemplary moral personae.

During the time of my fieldwork, the cemaat hosted rituals for the first ten days of the month of Muharram, in which the struggles and the martyrdom of Husayn were discussed in depth. In the cemaat's mosque, there was a gradual escalation in the intensity of activities during the ten days of meclis gatherings. The preacher of the mosque devoted approximately thirty minutes prior to the afternoon prayer to recounting tales from the Karbala narrative. Participants were mostly elderly and middle-aged men, and occasionally children—often the former's grandchildren. Several young men were also present. As these sessions were held in the middle of the day, attendance was restricted to those who were either unemployed or retired. Only rarely could someone leave work in order to participate.

The narrations performed in the mosque were emotional. Audience members responded to the preacher's discourse by weeping and cursing. Participants viewed the expression of emotion in the ritual as achieving a moral aim. At the first meclis session during Muharram 2006, the preacher began by linking the emotional character of the event to a moral pedagogy: "Muharram is a month of sadness [hüzün], a month of sorrow [keder], a month of pain [dert], but it is also a month in which to learn some lessons." The meclis gatherings aligned the emotions of mourning with moral lessons derived from the exemplary life of Husayn.[5]

The connection drawn by cemaat members between morality and mourning is well established in the Shiʻi tradition. In his study of Shiʻi piety, Mahmoud Ayoub (1978) argues that the martyrdom of Husayn has been regarded as morally redemptive in two ways. First, the content of the narrative conveys a moral lesson. Husayn's death highlighted for his contemporaries, as for future generations, the difference between divine truth and falsehood. His death established an ideal to which all Muslims must continue to struggle. Second, the events of Karbala are imagined to be redemptive through the participation of believers in the present day in the sorrows of Husayn and his companions. Describing Shiʻi traditions that mention the sorrow of the Twelve Imams and their followers, Ayoub writes, "sorrow and weeping for the martyrdom of Imam Husayn and the suffering of the Holy Family became a source of salvation for those who chose to participate in this unending flow of tears" (1978: 147). In Ayoub's account, the narrative content of Husayn's struggle is but one part of the morality of the tale. The weeping of believers in the present is itself a moral act, contributing to the practitioners' efforts to achieve salvation.[6]

Consistent with Ayoub's description, leaders of the cemaat encouraged the expression of mourning during Muharram. Ritual commemoration across these days tended not to be of the variety and symbolic pomp found in other parts of the Shi'i world. For instance, the cemaat did not sponsor theatrical representations of the battle of Karbala, as is common in Iran (Chelkowski 1979). Nor did it lead public processions on neighborhood streets in honor of Husayn, as is found in the Shi'i neighborhoods of Beirut (Deeb 2006). The cemaat's most public gesture involved placing certain adornments on the outside of the mosque, such as black flags hanging from the dome and signs draped across the front that included quotations attributed to Husayn. Commemorations at the mosque leading up to the tenth of Muharram were far more subdued than in many other countries. Nonetheless, believers at the mosque participated in prescribed acts of weeping everyday for the first week and a half of the month.

Participants arrived prior to prayer time in order to hear the mosque's preacher speak about the events of Karbala. Taking cues from their contextual surround, participants adopted a demeanor similar to that which they would evince in listening to a sermon.[7] The preacher opened each session with salutations to the Prophet and to those of his kin that the Shi'a revere as the Twelve Imams. Delivered in Arabic, this brief recitation called the meclis into being. Informal chatting ceased and people aligned themselves into prayer rows, adopting a quiet and attentive comportment.

The meclis gatherings reproduced a relatively stable rhetorical structure. In the first half, the preacher offered justifications of the gathering, often describing the sayings and deeds of exemplary figures from early Islamic history that assert the moral purpose of weeping for Husayn. Such invocations produced a reflexive discourse on the purpose and legitimacy of the gathering itself. In the second half of the meclis, the preacher related tales from the Karbala narrative, inducing fits of weeping in the audience.

The preacher opened the first session by emphasizing the moral value of attending the meclis: "May God be satisfied with your coming here today, remembering the name of Husayn, and grieving [hüzünlenmeniz] the events of Karbala." Participation in the meclis has its own value, irreducible to the import of learning about what happened at Karbala. Indeed, most participants knew many of the details of the battle, having heard such narratives on ritual occasions throughout their lives. Few if any participants were unfamiliar with the substantive content of the moral lessons to be drawn from such narratives. Rather than remain content with the knowledge of the narratives as acquired through previous ritual participation, attendees continued to return year upon year to the meclis of Muharram.

Specifying the value of attending the meclis, the preacher referred to a story about Imam Sadiq, the sixth of the Twelve Imams and great-grandson of Husayn, in which the Imam relates the importance of weeping for his ancestor:

> One year, during Muharram, Imam Sadiq asked a poet if he knew any poems about Husayn. When the poet began to recite the requested pieces, Imam Sadiq began to weep. His weeping was so loud that people passing by took notice of it. Imam Sadiq then told the poet that whoever recites a poem about Husayn, or recites a *mersiye* [dirge], or explains the events, will go to heaven if at least fifty people around him cry as a result. A little while later, Imam Sadiq said that only forty people need to cry for that reciter to go to heaven. Then he brought the number down to one. Only one person needs to cry. Finally, Imam Sadiq said that if a single person, sitting by himself, thinks about Karbala, remembers Husayn, or remembers Ashura [the day of Husayn's death], if that person cries, he will go to heaven.

The story endows the act of weeping with soteriological value. The significance of attending the meclis is that it provides a site in which to cry for Husayn. Weeping reflects the emotional relationship that one should maintain with the Karbala narrative.

Invoking this passage from the life of Imam Sadiq, the preacher commented on the importance of remembering Husayn's struggle through the act of weeping. The meclis is not only a context for narrating the battle of Karbala; it also contains within it a metanarrative about how one should hear the narrative and respond to its affective cues. The metanarrative elaborated in the first half of the meclis develops ideas about the proper comportment of the self in relation to that narrative. The narrative and metanarrative represent the two sides of what Ayoub calls the "redemptive" character of Husayn's death, each contributing to the morality of mourning during Muharram.

As the first day's meclis progressed, the preacher transitioned from a discourse on the virtues of weeping to an emotional discussion of Karbala. He marked this transition with the statement, "I am now going to relate the calamity [*musibet*] of Karbala. May our hearts be set ablaze [*yüreklerimiz yansın, ciğerlerimiz tutuşsun*]."[8]

While the content of the narrative is crucial to the task of stirring the passions of the audience, the preacher was aware that how he presents this content is equally important. The speech genre he employed when he intended to induce weeping was the *mersiye* (Arabic: *marthiya*), which refers to an emotional rendering of the events of Karbala.

"On the way to the mosque today," the preacher began, "I was trying to think about whose story to tell. If people are to grieve [*kederlenseler*], who among the oppressed [*mazlum*] of Karbala should I describe? And then it struck me. I should tell you about Ruqaya, the four-year-old daughter of Husayn." On the name, Ruqaya, the preacher's voice began to tremble. He proceeded to list the many deaths the young girl had to witness in Karbala—the death of her older brother, Ali Akbar, the death of her valiant uncle, Abbas, and the death of her father, Husayn. With his voice shaking, he explained how she was taken prisoner. Held in chains, she was forced to march from Karbala to Yazid's palace, along with the other survivors. Finally, the preacher described how she ceaselessly called for her father as she lay in Yazid's prison. Zaynab, Husayn's sister, was unable to comfort Ruqaya. Eventually, she died of sorrow. By this point, the preacher had broken down into tears. His words became difficult to follow.

In the midst of the mersiye, members of the audience regularly commented on the narrative, occasionally calling out curses when the names of certain individuals were mentioned or their wicked deeds related. The preacher explained how upon hearing Ruqaya continually calling for her father, Yazid sent down Husayn's head, which had been chopped off of his body at Karbala. The sound of weeping in the audience quickly and briefly transformed into curses: *Lanet olsun!* (May Yazid be damned). The curses did not figure as interruptions, as might the ringing of a cell phone. They did not break the emotional force of the preacher's speech, nor were they unexpected. In contrast to the cursing that was effectively silenced in the Şukrancılık cemi discussed in the previous chapter, the damning of Yazid functioned as an expected part of this discursive moment. Cursing the enemies of the Twelve Imams has long been part of the repertoire of Alevi mourning during Muharram and is a practice authorized by the Shiʿi doctrine of *teberra* (Arabic: *tabarraʾ*).[9] Curses damning Yazid were one of the ways that members of the audience followed a prescribed form of participating in the mersiye.

The weeping of the preacher and the curses called out by members of the audience interfered with the strictly denotational content of the narrative being related. It was hard to hear the words of the preacher when he began to sob. His hands covered his face, he sniffled between and over words, and his voice trembled. The curses of participants were not whispered but yelled. They were often much more clearly uttered than the narrative voiced by the weeping preacher. This sort of denotational interference, akin to what Steven Feld (1990b: 242) describes as "the sonic features of the crying voice," was not external to the event of narration but a central part of it. It contributed to the material economy of mourning through which participants morally engaged the narrative.

The cemaat's meclis gatherings during Muharram facilitated narrations of the battle of Karbala guided by the experience of weeping and cursing. Such gatherings established a ritualized articulation of the narrative text with an emotional narration, calibrated in part through an explicit discourse on the significance of weeping. Cursing, crying, and covering one's face contributed to the authorized mode of narrating the battle of Karbala in the Muharram meclis.

However, it proved more challenging to establish events of mourning outside of the restricted temporal frame of Muharram. In the second event that I shall describe, one involving commemorations of Fatima's birth, the narration of early Islamic history did not immediately or uniformly prompt bouts of weeping in members of the audience. Despite the fact that members of the cemaat commonly said that a true believer feels sorrow whenever he thinks of Husayn, regardless of the day or the time, as an empirical matter, members of the cemaat did not regularly shed tears of lament before or after the month of Muharram. The project of cultivating devotional emotions requires that the cemaat's members summon the event-space of the meclis in periods in which it otherwise seems out of place.

ENGENDERING CONTEXTS

Fatima was the daughter of the Prophet and the wife of Ali. She is honored by all Muslims but is given special reverence by the Shiʿa. Given particular significance is the relationship she maintained with her father, or what Louis Massignon (1969: 587), in his discussion of devotion to Fatima, calls a "spiritual connection." Fatima is said to have been so devoted to her father that within months of his being slain, she died of grief. During this final period of her life, Shi'i sources claim that she vigorously argued for Ali's claim to the caliphate and was consequently abused by his political opponents, Abu Bakr and Umar. For the Shi'a, Fatima's devotion to her father and her suffering after his death are intimately connected. Together they form a critical moment in the Karbala narrative, which will ultimately lead to the martyrdom of Fatima's son, Husayn.

Despite the fact that Alevis have historically revered Fatima as an individual who had been granted divine pardon from sin, very few Alevi individuals in contemporary urban Turkey engage in ritual commemorations of her birth. Most Alevis that I knew were unaware of when the date of her birth had arrived that year.

Across a two-week span, one of the cemaat's preachers narrated the life and death of Fatima at the mosque. He spoke of these narrations not as meclis gatherings but as lessons (*dersler*). As mentioned previously, the lessons were informally convened, and there were significantly smaller numbers of participants. The preacher explained to me the purpose of these narrations, saying that he wanted to "convey information to the cemaat about one of Islam's most virtuous individuals." He did not classify his narrations as mersiye, such as are performed during the Muharram meclis in an effort at inducing weeping. The preacher's assertion that he was merely conveying information (*tebliğ etme*; Arabic: *tablīgh*) suggested a speech genre distinct from that of the mersiye, one that is ostensibly about transmitting the content of the narrative. One consequence of this orientation toward speech genres was that the first week and a half of lessons did not involve acts of weeping.

As became apparent in the course of these lessons, however, the distinction between the genres of the mersiye and the tebliğ was not rigid, and ultimately it was blurred. In the final three lessons, the narrations grew increasingly emotional, not only expressed with the aim of clear denotation but intoned with the passions prescribed by Shi'i traditions. During these final lessons, in contrast to those that preceded them, the preacher and several in his audience broke down into tears. The intelligibility of the narration, as contextually given by the event-space of a lesson, gave way to a scene charged with the emotions of a meclis. How were these affective sensibilities summoned and incited?

The final set of lessons witnessed a narrative shift, in which the preacher focused on the hardships endured by Fatima toward the end of her life. The preacher focused, in particular, on the manner in which land left by the

Prophet to Fatima was usurped after the Prophet's death. He also described in detail how Fatima was physically assaulted, leading her to a miscarriage. Yet this narrative shift was not the only significant change: the mode of the preacher's exposition and the style of participation of certain audience members also realigned. As the preacher described the manner in which Fatima was assaulted, an elderly member of the audience shouted out a curse upon the aggressor. As in the meclis gatherings during Muharram, the act of cursing interrupted the referential flow of the preacher's rhetoric, even as it contributed to the ethos of mourning in accordance with the Shi'i doctrine of teberra. The shouting of curses helped to create a meclis-like environment within the context of the lessons. The tebliğ began to recall the affective force of the mersiye.

In contrast to the Muharram commemorations, however, not all of the participants in these lessons were committed to an ethos that would sacrifice communicative clarity for emotional intensity. If many participants called out curses at meclis gatherings, most members of the audience at these lessons refrained from such response-talk. As the elderly man continued cursing over the preacher's speech, another participant called for members of the audience to remain silent. The clamor interrupted his ability to hear and understand the content of the preacher's narrative.

At issue in this reprimand was whether such curses were contributing to or interrupting the coherence of the communicative moment as a whole. In this case, the judgment depended on the conflicting speech genres that participants attributed to the preacher's discourse. The lessons about Fatima were not characterized as meclis events, and the genre of the narration was not classed as a mersiye. As a symptom of this ambiguity, participants held differing expectations about the "ethics of listening" appropriate to the event (Hirschkind 2006). While some participants sought to forge an emotional relationship to the narrative characterized by cursing and weeping, others wanted to listen silently to a historical account of Fatima's life. What was being negotiated in the narration was the nature of its moral authority: did the act of mourning disrupt the narrative account of Fatima's life or was it the ultimate goal of the gathering?

The preacher helped resolve this ambiguity. Following the acts of cursing, the preacher began to weep as he narrated the final days of Fatima's life. As in the meclis gatherings during Muharram, the preacher's weeping obscured the denotational clarity of his own discourse. The trembling of his voice and the raising of his hand up to his face made it difficult to hear the words of his narrative, but these acts did not impede the capacity of many participants to follow. Weeping may have broken up the flow of referential speech, but it was communicative all the same. The noise of the preacher's weeping, like the cursing that preceded it, further established the ethos of a meclis amid the lessons. Before long, others in the audience began to hold their heads in their hands or to cry.

Taken in isolation, the emotions provoked by these lessons may have been anomalous within a Turkish context, in which Fatima's birth and death are not often the object of ritual commemoration. Yet seen as one moment in a series of ritual excitations within the cemaat, the tears shed for Fatima recalled the acts of weeping performed for Husayn several months earlier. The interplay of discourse, cursing, and weeping established a discernible communicative pattern, iconic of the meclis gatherings. A lesson that began as a biographical account of Fatima's life was effectively transformed into an event of devotional mourning.

MORAL LIMITS

From the Muharram meclis to the lessons on Fatima, we see some of the challenges involved in coordinating the articulation of what Bakhtin called "the event that is narrated in the work and the event of narration itself" (1981: 255). If cemaat participants entered the mosque during Muharram prepared for the emotional demands of a meclis event, the expectations attendant on the latter could not be presupposed in the lessons on Fatima. Such expectations were established in the act of narration itself. Weeping for Husayn and Fatima may be prescribed by doctrine, but its ritual performance has to be cultivated within its iterations in actual events.

That ritual emotion needs to be cultivated across performances is not unique to the cemaat. One scholar of Shi'ism, Syed Akbar Hyder, describes attending meclis events as a child in India, emphasizing the emotional limits of moral immaturity: "At times when we tried our very best to cry, our theatrical sobs gave way to gales of laughter, much to our elders' dismay. That sorrow comes with age is self-evident to young Shi'as" (Hyder 2006: 50). Through a process of moral maturation, acquired by ongoing participation in such events across one's life, Shi'i individuals attain the capacity to respond mournfully to the Karbala narrative.

The cultivation of ritual weeping seems paradoxical. On the one hand, weeping is spontaneous and dependent on the emotive capacities of the

individual. Not everyone is equally capable of weeping for exemplary figures. On the other hand, weeping is formally prescribed. When entering the
mosque in order to attend a meclis session, people expect that, as in years
past, they will hear narratives meant to induce tears. As one Indian Shiʿi
critical of certain mourning rituals in his community is reported as saying,
"*Matam* [mourning] is supposed to be a spontaneous show of grief; how can
you schedule it? . . . How can you schedule your grief if it's real?" (quoted in
Pinault 1992:148).

The scheduling of a "spontaneous show of grief" is paradoxical, I suggest,
only if the scheduled event is abstracted from the series of iterations across
which its affects acquire momentum and impetus.[10] Discussing traditions of
weeping within Sunni Islam, Saba Mahmood (2001) characterizes the cultivation of the capacity to experience spontaneous emotion within a formal
ritual progression as "rehearsed spontaneity." The phrase refers to the process
by which a susceptibility to emotive response is developed through repeated
practice. The fostering of this susceptibility is a moral task. In the Shiʿi tradition, ritual weeping contributes to the realization of a soteriological aim. The
incapacity to cry marks a moral limit.

Efforts by the cemaat to cultivate pious sensibilities are not restricted to
the mosque. One of the ways that the cemaat's preacher seeks to indirectly
spread knowledge about figures such as Fatima to the wider Alevi community
is by utilizing the kinship connections of mosque participants. Both in his
lessons and in his Friday sermon that same week, he told participants that
they should distribute candies or small gifts to friends and family members
on Fatima's birthday. Recipients of the gift might then be motivated to inquire
about, and subsequently remember, the significance of the day.

Fatima's birthday came and went. The lessons came to an end. Curious
as to the extent to which members of the cemaat followed the preacher's
instructions about distributing gifts, I asked various members of the cemaat
where they had handed out the candy. To my surprise, not a single person
had distributed gifts or otherwise disseminated knowledge about Fatima's life.
I noticed the same pattern when, several weeks after Fatima's birthday, the
birthday of Fatima's husband, Ali, arrived and passed. Encouraged to distribute sweets to mark the occasion, members of the cemaat again failed to follow
their instructions.

When I asked a number of cemaat members why they had not com-
plied with the preacher's instruction, many interlocutors quietly ignored

my question or changed the topic. Sensing the discomfort prompted by my query, one member offered a forthright response: "Our people don't like hearing about religious things. If we started talking to our relatives about Fatima, they wouldn't consider it to be pleasant [hoş]." This rather blunt statement need not be taken at face value—there are, of course, many Alevis who do not dismiss religion out of hand. The comment does, however, index the fact that Alevi organizations rarely transgress state-sanctioned norms of sociability by narrating emotional tales about early Islamic martyrs, especially after Muharram. As a result only a small number of Alevis regularly participate in practices of listening to such narratives, in which they might develop the capacity to weep. To the extent that it occurs, the distribution of candy to those outside of the cemaat is not an activity shaped by the practices and expectations appropriate to meclis event-spaces, in which the normative task of moral cultivation is regimented. Such encounters transpire outside of the chain of iteration that the cemaat forges within the mosque itself. The forms of disciplinary practice cultivated in narrative iterations within the mosque tend not to shape informal conversations emergent in encounters between neighbors and kin outside of it.

The limits of moral discipline do not, however, lie only at the boundary of the cemaat; they exist within it as well. As mentioned earlier, Alevis in Turkey, including those at the cemaat's mosque, rarely convene meclis gatherings after the annual mourning rituals during Muharram. This temporal circumscription contrasts with expectations elsewhere in the Shi'i world, where commemorations of the life and death of the Twelve Imams take place throughout the year. "This is clearest in the month of Ramadan, which in contrast with the Sunni calendar has [in Shi'i contexts] become a memorial for Ali," Michael Fischer writes (1980: 172). Ali, the husband of Fatima and father of Husayn, was killed during Ramadan. As a result, the final ten days of Ramadan "are dedicated to the memory of Ali and [are celebrated] for the gift of revelation of the Qur'an" (Fischer 1980: 173). In Iran, Ali's death is commemorated as a public holiday (Momen 1985). For Iranian Shi'is, the end of Ramadan joins sorrow at the death of Ali with a celebration of Qur'anic revelation.

Ali's death is an important moment in the Karbala narrative. In addition to Ali's martyrdom, it marks the end of his command of the Muslim community and the onset of Muawiya's ascent to the caliphate, which culminates in the killing of Ali's son Hasan and precipitates the martyrdom of Husayn at Karbala.

With regard to the mourning of Ali's death, Ramadan in Turkey bears little resemblance to the situation in Iran. Even within Alevi neighborhoods, such as the one in which the cemaat's mosque is located, there are almost no efforts to memorialize Ali's life and death. The ethos is decidedly festive, even for those who are not fasting, and lacks traces of lament. In the face of the prevalent norms of sociability, the cemaat's mosque is one of the few organizational sites concerned with informing Alevis of Ali's death. The day of Ali's death happened to fall on a Friday during Ramadan that year, and the mosque's preacher used the occasion to deliver a sermon about his martyrdom. He related familiar aspects of the Karbala narrative, explaining how Abu Bakr prevented Ali's wife, Fatima, from inheriting land left to her by the Prophet. He further described how Umar threatened to set Ali's house on fire when the latter refused to acknowledge Abu Bakr's claim to the caliphate. Both of these stories contributed to the narrative lessons on Fatima discussed earlier. They are crucial pieces of a repertoire of tales widely known by Alevis in Turkey, which are sometimes described in the texts produced by public intellectuals as part of the new corpus of communal historiography produced in the past few decades. Despite the widespread textual circulation of the narrative, however, most Alevis do not expect to participate in rituals of lamentation for Ali's death.

The accounts offered by the cemaat's preacher, on the other hand, functioned to invoke the narrative of Karbala, as well as the genres appropriate to its narration. Responding to the emerging signs of the narrative's unfolding, several audience members called out curses on Umar. Elements of the genre of the mersiye, known to participants through their formal presentation in the context of a meclis, began to enter the sermon (*hutbe*). Just as the preacher's tebliğ about Fatima acquired emotional momentum in the degree that it resembled a mersiye, his sermon began to evoke a context of mourning.

The intensity of the moment, however, collapsed quickly. Unlike the meclis sessions or the lessons on Fatima, the sermon did not lead to bouts of weeping, although the preacher's voice quivered at points, prompting some listeners to place their heads in their hands. Such signs of mourning arose out of participants' recognition of the intergeneric indexicality that conjured the conventions of the mersiye in the midst of a sermon, yet these signs did not crescendo into a ritual of weeping. The preacher and his audience regained their composure, and the narration concluded without the redemptive tears understood to mark the moral experience of its reception.

The relatively limited degree of weeping and cursing reveals the extent to which the cemaat's members continue to be shaped by the reigning social ethos in Turkey, despite their claim to mourn at any time and place. Aware of this situation, the preacher of the mosque suggested to me one way of interpreting the Ramadan event: "In these sorts of affairs, we Alevis are like schoolchildren or novices, still in the process of learning about Islam." In referring to the cemaat members as novices, the preacher was not trying to disparage their efforts. He was suggesting a trajectory of development. Situating the cemaat's efforts within the dominant sensibilities of the broader Alevi milieu, his comment indicated the way in which such events continue to give the cemaat its impetus, as it aims to engage and transform the existing affective capacities of its Alevi constituents.

CONCLUSION

The ritual events described in this chapter appear to some in Turkey as trivial and to others as scandalous. The emphasis placed on weeping, cursing, and crying is seen as anachronistic and outdated by many Alevis today. To them, it reflects an adherence to religious traditions that appear to be irrelevant to the social and political issues that shape pluralist politics for Alevis today. Yet at the same time, the organization of Alevi ritual within a Shiʻi mosque, led by preachers trained in Iranian seminaries, also strikes many Alevis and non-Alevis alike as both historically inauthentic, evacuating Alevism of its historical particularity, and potentially politically divisive in Turkey at large. For some commentators, the cemaat's promotion of Twelver Shiʻism entails assimilating Alevism to a kind of orthodox religiosity that further stigmatizes most of the Alevi population. The cemaat seems simultaneously insignificant and yet all too threatening. In either case, very few Alevi and non-Alevi commentators have been willing to view the activities of the cemaat as contributing to a pluralist politics.

My purpose in this chapter has been neither to add to the polemics against the cemaat nor to dilute the force of such critiques by arguing that the cemaat in fact actualizes a kind of critical pluralism. Instead, I have interrogated the provocation of the cemaat, which has opened it up to such hostile critique despite its relatively low number of followers. It is inadequate to explain this hostility with the claim that the cemaat advocates a form of religiosity that is foreign to Anatolian Alevism. The practices of devotional mourning emphasized in the cemaat's mosque, in fact, tap into forms of local knowledge and religious sentiment that have long connected communities in Anatolia with Muslims elsewhere. More important, the discursive and affective resources that enable the cemaat's critics to label it as foreign warrant careful examination. I have argued that the reason it has been subject to such critiques is because it calls into question the historicist intelligibility of Alevi religiosity that has found institutional supports for much of the past century. It refuses to mediate religious memory through the genres and performance styles of national historicism. It seeks to counter the naturalized maneuver that renders Alevi ritual recognizable as a trace of the nation's past.

To cite William Connolly's useful phrase once again, the form of devotional subjectivity the cemaat aims to fashion lies outside the "register of legitimate diversity" (Connolly 2005: 68). What is worth pausing over is the extent to which the cemaat seems to locate itself outside of this register and does not, in fact, appear to be particularly interested in finding a slot for itself within it. Indeed, most members of the cemaat do not make the argument that their practices represent the most authentic form of Anatolian Alevi religiosity. Rather, they seek to reject the space of debate oriented around historical authenticity altogether. They appear keenly aware of the thick normative commitments required of participation in such debates, commitments that stretch from a style of reasoning to a form of selfhood, from an aesthetics of public display to modes of religious memorialization and historical consciousness.

I have chosen to focus the concluding chapter of this book on the cemaat and its activities because they point up what we might term the internal limits of pluralism. Most commonly, the limits to pluralism are figured in an external relation: an authoritarian state or governing regime that constrains the space of expression, that silences protest, and that slows the pace of reform. In speaking of an internal limit, I am instead referring to the kind of exclusions that are necessary for a pluralist politics to emerge. In refusing historicist modes of relating to an Alevi past, the cemaat adopts a religious imaginary and a form of devotional subjectivity that are constitutively excluded from discourses of pluralism today. They reveal the forms of affect and knowledge whose excision is presupposed by the dominant registers of legitimate diversity. That constitutive exclusion helps to produce the space of politics in which pluralism has come to be valued and defined.

It is tempting to imagine a maximally inclusive form of pluralism that does not rely on such exclusions and is capable of accommodating various ways of relating to the past without adjudicating among them. I remain skeptical of this hope because it elides the imbrication of contemporary pluralist politics with a longer history of national formation. It allows us to ignore the extent to which contemporary political debate continues to be premised on that formation, even as it claims to attack nationalist ideologies of homogeneity. Imagining pluralism as an ideal of universal inclusion would allow it to appear as an open-ended discourse of political criticism, capable of surmounting its historical limits, but it would thereby fail to adequately interrogate the particular conditions of that critique.

As some of the examples described above demonstrate, the cemaat has not definitively produced a recalibration of affective subjectivity, even within its own ranks. Many of its members prove unable to weep in the months following Muharram. Its efforts are ongoing, uneven, and subject to failure. Such failures suggest that even as members of the cemaat often sidestep the contexts and genres of historicism that have dominated discourses of Alevi identity, they remain in part beholden to norms that orient expressions of public religiosity in Turkey. The fragility of efforts to provoke lamentation in moments that confound conventional expectation reveals the constraints—as institutional as they are psychological—confronted by efforts to extend and intensify the affects of Alevi mourning.

CONCLUSION

IN THE POLITICAL GEOGRAPHY COBBLED together in the aftermath of Ottoman collapse, national Turkish citizenship has held out the democratic promise of equality and liberty, but only by excising, eliminating, and politically dispossessing entire populations that had previously held stable positions under imperial rule. The expansion of rights of citizenship continuously entailed volatile negotiations over how citizenly belonging ought to be defined and by means of whose exclusion. This dynamic—universalizing political rights amid ongoing debates about who to exclude from the designation of citizen—constitutes a historical condition of democratic politics in the republican nation-state.[1]

For some intellectuals today, a critical public discourse on this history is imperative for the future of Turkish democracy. Taner Akçam, a professional historian of the late Ottoman Empire, asserts that "any effort towards democratization in [the Middle East] today, must begin with a dialogue about history and, most important, the ensemble of events that transpired during the transition from Empire to Republic. Only such a process will complete Turkey's real transition from Empire to a normal Republic" (2004: 9). Akçam has written numerous books that focus on the political violence that led to the formation of the Turkish nation-state, and in particular he has gained notoriety for being among the first historians of Turkish origin to recognize the killing of Armenians in 1915 as a genocide. This position has not been an easy or a safe one to assume, and some ultranationalists have threatened to assassinate him. In Akçam's assessment, what is at stake in history writing is not just a particular political position within a broader field, but the very possibility of a "normal Republic" and, ultimately, of democracy itself.

Akçam is not alone in this assessment. In recent years, the notion that Turkey must face up to and confront its history (*tarihle yüzleşmek*) has started to be employed in a vast array of contexts: rights claims made by minorities; debates among jurists about writing a new constitution; public arguments about laws that penalize the "denigration" of the Turkish nation, its founding figures, and state institutions; and demands by historians that the state open classified archives. Democratic futures are increasingly imagined by means of a historical reckoning with the violence of the nation-state's formation.

For some groups, this reckoning has taken the form of redefining national history. For instance, Islamist activists and political leaders in the 1990s countered official accounts of Turkish history by publicly commemorating events that the republican state had long elided, such as the Ottoman conquest of Constantinople (Çınar 2005), or by excavating images of early republican leaders that counter dominant understandings of their jacobin secularity and instead exhibit their piety (Özyürek 2006). For others, such as members of the religious community known as the Dönme, historical revision has required a rethinking of their own commitments to Kemalism.[2] In the era of the early republic, many members of this community supported the Kemalist revolution, but the state nevertheless compelled them to eliminate their communal particularities. At various historical moments, they faced extraordinary institutional discrimination if they maintained religious practices that distinguished them from the majority (Baer 2009).[3] Certain individuals of Dönme heritage today feel that it is important to uncover signs of their community's past and to publicly break the silence that shrouds their communal identity (Neyzi 2002).

It is striking that in the past few decades, as the historical critique of the republican state has been fostered, theorized, and elaborated at some length, many Alevi groups have written themselves into the statist narratives of historical belonging that have fallen under critical scrutiny. This is especially surprising given the fact that the incorporation of Alevis into accounts of Turkish modernity has not been smooth or peaceful, but has been shaped by episodes of extraordinary violence in both the early and late decades of the twentieth century. Many Alevis experienced Turkish modernity neither as its progenitors nor as its defiant challengers. They have often been summoned to declare themselves unstintingly loyal to the nationalist ideologies of the

Kemalist project precisely when these ideologies are being subjected to wide-spread critique.

The Alevi case requires that we reconsider the political significance of history. The question is not simply whether new histories can help to produce a normal republic. That formulation begs the question of how the norm itself is established, by means of what criteria, and with what effects. In following the struggles of various Alevi groups, I have sought to explore how history itself has helped to create normative strictures of citizenly belonging. The use of history motivates a dense assemblage of emotional sensibilities, expressive practices, and forms of knowledge that constitute the normative conditions of political subjectivity. Alevis, whose entry into the public sphere is now being lauded as a sign of pluralization, are often compelled to draw upon speech genres and aesthetic styles that the state established and regulated in the process of its formation. They have found new opportunities for political participation, but the social forms and historical practices that facilitate this participation are themselves undergirded by entrenched epistemologies of the nation.

The practices that inscribe Alevi religiosity within the narratives of national history continue to evolve and take new institutional form. Since 2007, as part of what was termed a "democratic opening," the ruling government under the auspices of the AKP has sponsored public performances of Alevi commemorations of the battle of Karbala. It also hosted a series of workshops for Alevi intellectuals and leaders to meet with government officials. With an eye to meeting the criticisms of EU observers, AKP politicians often claim that this pluralist agenda is unprecedented in a context in which the Turkish state has long insisted that its citizenry is ethnically and religiously homogeneous.

Alevis themselves have tended to remain deeply skeptical of both the motivations and the results of AKP's democratic opening.[4] The skepticism is, undoubtedly, a result of various factors. Alevis have long been suspicious of AKP and its association with Islamist networks, intellectuals, and organizations. Many Alevi groups felt excluded or only superficially incorporated in the public events and workshops sponsored by the ruling party. Also important is the fact that the presence of government officials at public displays of Alevi ritual is not particularly new. As I have stressed throughout this book, the participation of these officials encouraged Alevi visibility in urban settings from which the community has long been marginalized, but it also entrenched an apparatus of disciplinary supervision in the context of ostensibly autonomous Alevi gatherings.

The recent democratic initiatives have been selective. While AKP leaders have been willing to continue the tradition established in the 1980s and 1990s of governmental participation in public displays of Alevi ritual, they have been unwilling to entertain a historical dialogue on contentious issues like the Armenian genocide. The government's democratic initiative in this sense continues to reproduce certain forms of institutionalized silencing.

The point is not that the government has been biased or otherwise insincere in its recent efforts to counter state-enforced silences, but that institutionalized silences have never been imposed in equal measure across the heterogeneous landscape of contemporary Turkey. Fatma Müge Göçek insists upon this point, arguing that historical silence is itself differentially distributed. It is worth quoting her at length:

> [N]ot all groups produce or are allocated the same silence; the size and shape of the silence is closely connected to the power location of the social group in question. The silence of the leftist, mostly Turkish-Muslim, intellectuals has been the best-documented one in Turkish republican history. This has been the case because these intellectuals form an integral part of the dominant national group of secularized Turks. The silence of the Kurdish ethnic minorities and the Alawite [Alevi] religious minorities, however, is less articulated. Even less developed is the public discussion of the silence of the Turkish-Armenian and other non-Muslim minorities. (Göçek 2011: 194)

Historical silences reflect and further entrench social stratifications that asymmetrically structure the national body.

One consequence of Göçek's intervention is that any account of pluralist politics must attend, first and foremost, to the differential location of various groups in the actual landscape of power, rather than assuming that different religious and ethnic communities encounter one another as interlocutors with equal capacities for public speech. The ethnographic analysis presented in this book reinforces this point. From a position of relative marginality, urban Alevis have tentatively grappled with new possibilities for giving voice to their community's history, even as they have been subjected to forms of discrimination and violence. Alevi efforts to discourse about themselves in public have neither entirely dismantled nor entirely submitted to the institutionalized silencing of their community's religious and historical identity.

Yet the material in this book also suggests the need to rethink the dichotomy of silence and voice that structures much of the analysis of the politics of history. For Alevis, some of whom have indeed found a degree of space to write about their historical identity, the question cannot simply be one of countering silence; rather, it concerns the practices, aesthetic media, and discursive technologies—in short, the forms of historical vocality—that are available to them and that they are required to adopt in order to be recognizable as engaged in a contest about the historical past. Only some ways of relating to the past are advocated, championed, and redeemed as contributing to public life and the common good. Others—exemplified by an instance of cursing the oppressors of Husayn in a public display of Alevi ritual (chapter 5)—are ignored, reproached, or occluded.

The government's "democratic opening" only accentuates the importance of investigating and analytically specifying which forms of relating to the past are institutionally promoted as contributions to democratic citizenship. Given the rapidly shifting terrain of institutional discourse, it is crucial to ask not only about the liberating potentials of historical knowledge but about the mobilization of this form of knowledge in new modalities of governance.

The notion of a "confrontation with history" carries a strong political charge. In the aftermath of decades of state-sanctioned forgetting, the call for a history released from state control represents a political demand for the remembrance of pasts that have been violently demolished. It enables a practice of historical countermemory that endows scholarship on Armenian, Kurdish, Alevi, and other minority pasts with critical force. Historical discourse may indeed be necessary for promoting Turkey's democratic future, but I am struck by the prestige accorded to historical knowledge, the authority it wields, and the social range of its application. It establishes not only the standards for argumentation within the disciplines of professional scholarship in Turkey but also arrogates to itself the task of authenticating the way that Alevis ought to relate to their religious narratives and the pasts those narratives articulate. It seems at once to provide a global standard of rational argumentation and to secure locally entrenched disciplines of national belonging. Only certain forms of subjectivity and emotion and certain styles of reasoning and narrative are validated as capable of historical dialogue. How, then, are we to reconcile the pluralist-democratic aim of producing minority histories with the fact that existing institutional powers arbitrate over that validation?

Rather than identifying historical criticism with the consolidation of a "normal Republic," as Akçam proposes, we might instead ask, what forms of critique challenge the normative formation of republican politics? The urgency of the question becomes apparent when, as a historian or anthropologist, one encounters Alevi intellectuals, such as Cafer Solgun, who question the iconographic dispensation that has enabled public displays of collective historical identity (chapter 5), or groups that repudiate altogether the genre of social history as a mode of narrating Alevi pasts (chapter 6). Such stances are critical of historicist practices and the political authority that underwrites them. They challenge the criteria of legitimacy imposed by statist discourses of national unity and security. The dede's denunciation of the aesthetics of Alevi visibility (chapter 4) did not directly target the practice of historicization, but it shared with those critical positions an interest in interrogating the processes that have rendered Alevism recognizable through institutionally regimented forms of plurality.

The positions adopted by these individuals and groups are by no means identical or motivated by the same goals, but at least in some cases, they elicit a sense of public outrage or scandal whose political significance is worth underscoring. Solgun faced death threats, and the Alevi-Shi'i cemaat has often been repudiated as a threatening sign of the Iranian state's revolutionary ideology. In their own ways, Solgun and the cemaat disturb the aesthetics of public display that has defined the conditions of free assembly, and they contest the genres of public voice that have enabled but also regimented the conditions of free speech. Disputing institutionalized conditions of visibility and voice, these social actors and groups scrutinize the conditions under which their questioning itself can be aired in public and posed for national deliberation. They politicize, we might say, the conditions of possibility of politics.

A scandalous encounter may seem untenable as a ground of political engagement. In speaking against the regnant conditions of political belonging, these Alevi critics are questioning the narrative and iconographic practices that have secured a political voice for an otherwise marginalized community. The critics interfere with the institutionally available form of vocality. Their provocations amplify rather than resolve the tensions of pluralism. As a mode of political action, this form of critique is potentially self-undermining. What, after all, is the status of a political act that puts at risk its own political voice?

The tension operative in these critical acts acquires a pressing salience when it arises within contexts where political subjectivity was given definition by means of tremendous violence, as in many of the national states that suc-ceeded the Ottoman Empire. A critique of the articulation of violence and political voice demands a form of inquiry that draws attention to the costs of becoming recognizable as belonging to the nation and to the limits of what is sayable within the existing field of politics. These critics probe the limits of their political empowerment, not only as a function of constraints that restrict their entry in public life, but as a function of the discursive and aesthetic incitements that provoke and produce their participation. They do not simply reveal the inadequacies of Kemalist renditions of modernity. To arrive at a critique of that ideological imaginary, they have had to call into question the available signs of their own modernity. The ambiguity of critical discourses that challenge the conditions of their own empowerment is perhaps also their strength. They model a form of democratic practice that queries the exclusions of national citizenship by contesting the grounds of their inclusion.

NOTES

Chapter 1

1. The Treaty of Lausanne employs the term "non-Muslim" to refer to minorities in Turkey, and yet it has consistently been interpreted as entailing protections only for Orthodox Greeks, Armenians, and Jews. Smaller Christian groups such as Syriacs, Chaldeans, Assyrians, and Nestorians have not been historically protected by the treaty (Oran 2007).

2. The town of Hacıbektaş is an important location within the geography of contemporary Alevi society and politics. It is named after a medieval Anatolian saint, Hacı Bektaş-ı Veli, revered by many Alevis. The town is also the site of the largest annual Alevi gathering.

3. The substance of legal protection has varied over time. While the category of religious identity was paramount in debates about Ottoman citizenship in the mid-nineteenth century, issues of gender equality—for instance, with regard to divorce, inheritance, and voting rights—only came to be protected in the twentieth century.

4. For accounts of the use of emergency powers in the United States before and after the Cold War, see Lobel 2001–2002 and Buck-Morss 2000. Agamben 2005 provides a comparative history of emergency powers in the United States and several western European contexts.

5. Arendt maintained that the nation-state itself lost its coherence in this process: "The nation-state cannot exist once its principle of equality before the law has broken down. Without this legal equality, which originally was destined to replace the older laws and orders of feudal society, the nation dissolves into an anarchic mess of over- and underprivileged individuals" (Arendt 1966: 290). One might question Arendt's presumption that the nation-state has ever, in any actual historical context, enshrined equality without remainder. On this point, see Balibar 1991 and Rancière 2010.

6. Arat 1997 similarly argues that feminist criticisms of the early Republican state contribute to a liberalization of the project of modernity.

7. Scholars disagree on how this transformation came to pass—some emphasize concerted reorientation in the intellectual and political thought of Islamist groups (Yavuz 2009; Silverstein 2010), while others highlight their responsiveness to practical exigencies and political constraints (Turam 2006; Tuğal 2009).

8. Özyürek 2006 offers an extended account of the range of practices adopted by secularist political groups. See also Tambar 2009 for a discussion of the ambivalence of secularist political identity, which in recent decades has attempted to constitute itself as a mode of popular politics, even as it continues to depend on the political interventions of state apparatuses such as the military and the Constitutional Court.

9. Such numbers are not easy to verify because the state's statistical bureau does not distinguish Alevis from the Sunni majority in the national census.

10. Scholars who depict Alevism as the concatenation of various religious traditions often rely on the concept of syncretism. See Dressler 2010 for a critique of the notion of syncretism in the study of religion in Turkish Anatolia.

11. Bilici 1998 and Ocak 2004 offer similar typologies of the positions defended by various Alevi groups. Massicard 2005b provides a detailed sociological comparison of various prominent stances.

12. Mélikoff 1992 argues that the use of the term "Alevi" to designate certain rural Anatolian populations only emerged in the nineteenth century. While I have flagged the analytical insufficiencies of "Alevi" as a gloss for a range of communities, I nonetheless make use of the category in this book without further qualification in order to avoid cumbersome repetition.

13. On the emergence of an Islamist elite to rival the secularist establishment, see White 2002; Potuoğlu-Cook 2006.

14. The party was referred to as the Unity Party of Turkey (Türkiye Birlik Partisi). See Massicard 2005a for more detail.

15. Perhaps the most widespread and pernicious myth refers to the idea that Alevis partake in incestuous orgies after extinguishing candles in one of the community's central ritual practices, the *ayin-i cem*. A number of Alevi interlocutors informed me that, on occasion, Sunni co-workers and classmates had confronted them with this particular accusation. Public performances of Alevi ritual are meant, in part, to refute this myth.

16. For detailed accounts of these events, see Eral 1995 and Şahhüseyinoğlu 1999.

17. Violence in the 1990s included events in Sivas in 1993 in which a gathering of Alevis and left-leaning Alevi supporters was attacked by a mob of right-wing demonstrators, and in Istanbul in 1995, when police shot into crowds of Alevi protestors and supporters, shouting anti-Alevi insults and threats. For an account of these events, see Bruinessen 1996.

18. This definition of historicism itself draws from a deep tradition of scholarship. Schiffman 1985 notes that Friedrich Meinecke, an early investigator of the birth of historicism in western Europe, defined the concept in similar terms: a historical object, in his view, is determined in its individuality by the unique context of its emergence, and it needs to be examined not as fulfilling a predetermined form but as developing according to changing circumstances.

19. Ottoman concerns with history writing do not, however, begin in the nineteenth century. Cornell Fleischer (1986: 237) details efforts by Ottoman statesmen to compose historical chronicles in the sixteenth century and notes that an official Ottoman historiography came into existence in the seventeenth century. The genealogy of history writing in the Ottoman Empire remains outside the scope of this study.

20. Ersanlı 2002 offers a detailed evaluation of the politics of early republican historiography.

21. In his famous nineteenth-century lecture, Ernest Renan ([1882] 1990: 11) made the point explicitly: "Forgetting, I would even go so far as to say historical error, is a crucial factor in the creation of a nation, which is why progress in historical studies often constitutes a danger for [the principle of] nationality."

22. The notion of alternative or multiple modernities has been employed by several scholars of Islamic politics in Turkey. See Göle 1997; 2000; Çınar 2005; Keyman 2007. For a critique of the concept in relation to the Turkish case, see Ahıska 2003.

23. The term "Kemalism" is used in Turkey to refer to the state-led regime of modernization launched by Mustafa Kemal Atatürk and his supporters.

24. Whether this notion of historical time ought to be labeled as "secular" is the topic of some debate. Demonstrating that religious movements in Lebanon have conceptualized their devotional and religious narratives within a linear, chronological framework, Deeb 2009 disputes that national history is necessarily secular, a claim made famous by Benedict Anderson's *Imagined Communities* ([1983] 1991). Wedeen 2008 similarly argues that notions of historical time that are commonly found in nationalisms around the globe are not necessarily secular. Asad's use of the phrase "secular history" avoids some of the problems associated with works such as Anderson's: where Anderson presupposes the binary of the secular and the religious as a ground of analysis, Asad argues for an investigation of how the boundary between the two is defined in particular contexts. As I read Asad, the notion of "secular history" is not meant to be exclusive of religion, but is meant to indicate the temporal framing that defines the intelligibility of "religion" as a discursive object.

25. "Unlike the early 1950s, when it was sometimes said that the heart of Turkey was in its 40,000 villages, all of Turkey today has become a town, one great provincial complex" (Meeker 1994a: 39).

Chapter 2

1. The words *hanım* and *amca* are terms of respect, used in relation to women and men respectively who are older than the speaker. *Hanım* in particular carries connotations of formality, and it was in deference to Ayfer's role at the Alevi organization that I used the term. Throughout the book, I have changed the names of my interlocutors in order to respect their privacy and preserve their anonymity.

2. I observed these events in the provincial town of Çorum and its surrounds. Events that I witnessed in larger metropoles such as Ankara often sparked participation from larger and denser crowds. Several hundred attendees seemed common rather than exceptional. Proportionate to the size of Alevi communities in those cities, however, such numbers are still rather small.

3. A number of scholars argue that the notion of "anachronism" was crucial to the formation of a distinctively modern form of historical consciousness in western Europe. See, e.g., Burke 1969; Fasolt 2004; Koselleck 2004; Woolard 2004. Davis 2008 cautions that this historiography of historicism runs the risk of naturalizing the dichotomy between medieval and modern views of time, eliding the politics of the periodizing framework. On the concept of modernity as a politically invested narrative structure, see also Chakrabarty 2000; Keane 2007.

4. For extended descriptions of Shiʻi accounts of early Islamic history, see Ayoub 1978; Momen 1985; Pinault 1992, 2001.

5. But see Erdemir 2005 for a description of one recent attempt by Alevis in Istanbul at theatrical commemoration, which as Erdemir contends is notably anomalous in this context.

6. Following Durkheim, A. R. Radcliffe-Brown offered a similar assessment, arguing that "ceremonial weeping" functioned "to affirm the existence of a social bond between two or more persons" (1948: 240).

7. I explore the growth in written narratives of Alevi religious history in chapter 5.

8. For a critique of the concept of "objectification" as it has been used in discussions of contemporary Islamic politics, see Tambar 2012.

9. On the notion of "public religion," see Casanova 1994.

10. *Teyze* literally means aunt (specifically, mother's sister), but it is commonly used to denote a female addressee older than the speaker, even in the absence of kin relations.

11. "[The Kemalist] view of history stressed a rapid and radical break between the past and the present, a movement to a new location in historical time. . . . The Kemalists wanted to achieve a dramatic exit from one historical dynamic to another, to pass quickly from what they considered an uncivilized period to a civilized one, to relegate backwardness to the dustbin of history and to become, as a nation, contemporary (*asri*)" (Parla and Davison 2004: 123).

12. Christopher Dole (2006, 2012) makes an analogous point in his analysis of debates about the status of religious healers in Turkey. Such healers were often berated by early republican ideologues as reactionary remnants of the Ottoman era and contrasted with the secular rationality ascribed to biomedicine. Today, the validity of religious, or "traditional," healing continues to be debated, and the ideological staging of modernity remains central: "The attempt to eliminate the *cinci hoca* [the religious

healer] in the name of the modern has transformed into a reliance upon their presence so that they can be disavowed" (Dole 2006: 32).

13. The saz is a lute, often employed in Turkish folk music but also central to the performance of Alevi rituals.

14. The "democratic opening" also led to a series of workshops where state officials, political party leaders, and representatives of the Alevi community were meant to openly discuss social and political problems facing the community. Many Alevi organizations bitterly complained that these workshops were superficial, non-inclusive, and failed to lead to concrete political change.

Chapter 3

1. For critiques of early nationalist studies of Alevism, see Ocak 2004; Bahadır 2005.

2. These were not, however, the first modern studies of Alevism. Christian missionaries preceded Ottoman intellectuals in their efforts.

3. The reform process was a major overhaul both of structures of governance and of cultural imaginaries of citizenship. It has been the subject of a tremendous amount of scholarship, which I do not have the space to exhaustively evaluate. The standard accounts include Berkes 1964; Lewis 1968. Compared to these accounts, a growing body of recent scholarship has been more critical of the teleological presumptions of modernization theory. See, e.g., Fortna 2002; Hanioğlu 2008.

4. For an overview of the legal history, see Findley 2010: 91–94; Rodrigue 2013.

5. European forms of knowledge in the human sciences were also increasingly incorporated by Ottoman intellectuals. M. Şükrü Hanioğlu notes that the Ottoman Empire in the nineteenth century possessed a wealth of distinguished historians, but the "writing and conception of history" itself began to change when the Ottoman Academy of Sciences commissioned Ahmed Cevdet Pasha to "contextualize documents [and] historicize developments"; "the resulting work—with its historiosophical introduction, its situation of Ottoman history in the context of European and world history, its attempts to fashion analytical frameworks for developments that transcended mere chronology, and its overall critical approach—leaves no doubt that Ahmed Cevdet Pasha was a historian in an entirely new mode" (Hanioğlu 2008: 98).

6. Much of the debate about whether the deportation and killing of Armenians constituted "genocide" turns on the question of whether the Ottoman leadership followed an ideology of extermination, strictly pursuing a blueprint for genocide, or pragmatically responded to a context of global war. See Bloxham 2003 for a critique of the dichotomy of "ideology" versus "pragmatism" in the historiography of Ottoman state violence. Michael A. Reynolds (2011: 152) highlights the political stakes of the Armenian expulsion from Anatolia, arguing that "the goal of the deportations was

if not the extermination of the Armenian community, then the devastation of it such that it could no longer have a credible claim to Eastern Anatolia."

7. "Hanefi" refers to the school of Islamic law adopted by the Ottoman state, and claimed today by most ethnic Turks in Turkey. Most Sunni Kurds in Turkey claim to follow the Shafiʿi school of Sunni Islam.

8. Zürcher 2005 provides a helpful portrait of the early nationalist leaders, laid out in terms of their social, political, economic, and educational backgrounds, noting that none of the principal actors were graduates of traditional religious seminaries.

9. Noting the at once descriptive and constructive nature of this project, Andrew Davison (1998: 111) argues that Gökalp "believed that Turkey's national sociologists ought to combine a thoroughly positivist study of the objective conditions of social reality (including an explanation of factors accelerating or retarding growth) with a prescription for a conceptual apparatus for living in them. It was the national sociologists' duty to 'discover the elements of national conscience in the unconscious level and bring them up to the conscious level' and thus best adapt culture to its place in civilization."

10. The term *kızılbaş* refers to Alevis. It has a long history and often carries pejorative connotations, particularly when employed by members of the Sunni majority.

11. Cf. Nadia Abu El-Haj's (2001) discussion of the elective affinity between the positivist epistemologies of Israeli archaeology, which has sought to excavate material and observable signs of an ancient Jewish presence, and the cultural politics of the Israeli state.

12. As noted in chapter 2, the Twelve Imams are the patrilineal descendants of Muhammad's cousin Ali ibn Abi Talib. The Imams are viewed by the Shiʿa as possessing divinely endowed spiritual gifts, a claim that Sunni schools of Islamic law do not accept.

13. Sait wrote with patronizing flair: "[Alevis] continue to wait for the Mehdi, the emergence of the occulted Twelfth Imam. How sad our poor Alevis would be if they understood that it is a Jewish and Christian theory that leads them to destroy themselves in this dream" (Sait [1926] 2000: 120).

14. The doctrine of love for the Twelve Imams is referred to as *tevella* (Arabic, *tawalla*) and hostility toward their oppressors as *teberra* (Arabic, *tabarraʾ*). The Shiʿi doctrine of teberra licenses expressions of hostility toward those that Ali and his descendants opposed. Evidence of doctrinally prescribed ritual cursing can be found in a number of historical Shiʿi communities. Juan Cole (1988: 239–244), for instance, describes the way in which acts of ritual cursing both expressed and instigated communal violence between Sunnis and Shiʿas in the nineteenth-century Indian state of Awadh. As to whether acts of cursing should continue in the face of escalating societal tensions, one prominent Indian Shiʿi jurist argued that the "Shiʿi ruler [of Awadh] should address any public disturbances by suppressing them rather than by forsaking

the ritual prescribed by the faith," holding "cursing the caliphs to be as necessary a ritual obligation for Shi'is as sounding the call to prayer or slaughtering the cows of Hindus" (Cole 1988: 242).

15. Markus Dressler's (2013) discussion of Adem, on which I have relied here, is largely centered on an analysis of a m-onograph, *Türkmen Aşiretleri*, that was originally published under the pseudonym of a German Orientalist (Frayliç and Ravlig [1918] 2008). According to Dressler (2013: 133–134), the name Habil Adem was itself a pseudonym, and his real name was Naci İsmail Pelister. Dressler's book provides an excellent analysis of late Ottoman and early republican studies of Alevism.

16. Karakaya-Stump (2004: 331) similarly argues that nationalist writings would, in this regard, echo earlier missionary formulations: "[D]espite their obviously contrasting conclusions, all these later [Turkish nationalist] approaches to Alevism held in common with the missionary writings, first, the same preoccupation with the question of origins, secondly, the conceptualization of Alevism as a syncretism."

Chapter 4

1. Not all Alevi organizations seek state recognition. Some have openly called for the closing down of the state's Directorate of Religious Affairs, arguing that no religious community, tradition, or practice ought to receive funding from state coffers.

2. On the privatization of television in Turkey, see Öncü 1995.

3. On the closure of Kurdish political parties, see Koğacıoğlu 2003, 2004. Watts 2010 provides a detailed analysis of the struggle of Kurdish political groups to operate within the domain of legitimized party politics.

4. For a critique of liberal theories of pluralism that normatively aim for consensus, see Mouffe 2005, which foregrounds the hegemonic dimensions of deliberative discourse and argues that pluralist politics is constrained, rather than promoted, by procedures that encourage the reconciliation of differences through the achievement of reasoned consensus, contra Jürgen Habermas's *Between Facts and Norms* (1998).

5. "[I]t was not until 1946 that modern Turkey gave democracy its first real trial. The government of the Republican People's Party led by İsmet İnönü allowed other political parties to be formed and to compete for power in the general election of that same year" (Dodd 1990: 8).

6. The term *kızılbaş* is a reference to the Alevi community. See also chap. 3, n. 10.

7. Many of these legal restrictions on political activity were removed with constitutional amendments in 1995 and 2001 (Özbudun and Gençkaya 2009).

8. General elections were held in 1983, marking the beginning of a transfer from military to civilian rule. It is difficult to speak of a complete end to military involvement in politics for several reasons. First, military personnel were retained in positions of political leadership—most notably, General Evren became president of Tur-

key. Second, the 1982 Constitution strengthened the political role of the military-led National Security Council. Third, from the late 1980s (following the PKK uprising) to 2002, states of emergency were continually proclaimed in the largely Kurdish provinces of the southeast, and after 2002, certain regions that had previously been under a state of emergency were designated "security zones." Finally, as Altınay 2004 details, a cultural ethos of militarism continues to be firmly entrenched within dominant conceptions of Turkish nationalism.

9. Cihan Tuğal (2009: 94–101) argues that currents of Islamic internationalism (*ümmetçilik*) that were on the rise in the 1980s have largely been marginalized in the course of the past two decades and absorbed by the dominant trends of Turkish nationalism.

10. Charles Hirschkind describes the production of a national listening audience in Egypt. He argues that the construction of a nation-state in Egypt not only required legal and bureaucratic interventions but also reshaped the "sensory epistemologies" of the populace (2006: 41).

11. The *düvaz* explicitly mention the spiritual exploits of the Twelve Imams. The *mersiye* focus on the tragedies of the battle of Karbala, in which Husayn was martyred.

12. For a critique of Eickelman and Piscatori's conceptualization of "tradition," see Agrama 2012: 10–17. See also Meyer 2008 for a broader critique of symbolic or interpretive approaches to the study of religion. Meyer advances an approach that foregrounds the material and sensory dimensions of aesthetic media in the formation of religious subjectivities.

13. On the semiotic and cultural process of circulation, see Lee and LiPuma 2002; Gaonkar and Povinelli 2003; Gal 2003.

14. The significance of the instrumentation must not be underestimated. On the symbolic and ethical importance of the saz and the bağlama in imaginaries of the Turkish nation, see Stokes 1992 and Bryant 2005.

15. Aykan Erdemir makes a similar point in his discussion of urban cem ceremonies: "In urban cemevis, it was no longer possible to recreate the exclusivity or the social intimacy one would find in village ceremonies. The anonymity of the crowd in cities transformed Alevi worship from an intimate gathering with family, relatives, and fellow villagers, into a crowded ceremony with suspicious strangers" (2005: 945).

16. Generally, civil society groups adopt the status either of *vakıf* or *dernek*. A vakıf is an association based on an allotment of property rather than membership, whereas a dernek is formed by a group of individuals, organized around a common purpose or interest (White 2002: 200–201). For an insightful ethnographic unpacking of how contemporary Alevi groups employ the concept of civil society, see Walton 2013.

Chapter 5

1. Bozkurt is careful to note that many Alevi communities had been exposed to at least some form of modern schooling since the 1940s, with the introduction of state-led Village Institutes in Alevi villages. Kieser 2007 argues that, for at least some eastern Anatolian Alevis, this state-led modernization of education was not the only or even the first exposure to modern schooling. Some of these communities had encountered modern forms of education in the early twentieth century through contact with neighboring Armenian Christians. Kieser's work opens up the possibility of constructing a countergenealogy of Alevi modernity from the one sanctioned by the Turkish state, an extraordinary intellectual project, which I cannot take up in this book.

2. On the use of icons in Shi'i Islam, see Flaskerud 2010. The iconography employed has changed over time. Flaskerud suggests that the single portraiture of Ali, which Zehra teyze had owned but concealed, is of relatively recent vintage. Its exact origin remains obscure, but it most likely derives from mid-nineteenth-century India or Iran. Irène Mélikoff (1998: 270) indicates that images of Ali and the Twelve Imams found at Alevi festivals today are imported from Iran.

3. For a critical analysis of such public presentations, see Sinclair-Webb 1999.

4. Dole (2012: 110) describes Atatürk's iconization in certain forms of Alevi practice as "ironic," given Atatürk's own hostility toward Islamic popular traditions, including those found in many Alevi settings. Dole goes on to argue that state power and "exilic forms of religious authority" have ambiguously intersected from the start in secular Turkey (110–111).

5. The relationship between Alevis and the Bektaşi brotherhood raises complex historiographical problems. In the discursive vernacular of present-day Turkey, the two are often coupled if not equated, and the phrase "Alevi-Bektaşi" is colloquially used with such frequency as to suggest a necessary link. Indeed, many Alevi groups perform practices associated with the Bektaşi brotherhood, such as the *cem* ritual, and many such Alevis also identify with the Bektaşi tradition of the "four stages" (or "doors") of religious experience (Shankland 2003: 85). Yet, according to some scholars, the historical sociology of the Bektaşi brotherhood is distinct from that of the Alevi communities in Anatolia. Abdülbâki Gölpınarlı argues that the terms "Alevi" and "Bektaşi" denote two distinct social orders—the former referring to endogamous, rural communities, the latter to an urban institution whose membership was based not on descent but on rites of initiation. "We cannot call Alevism a Sufi order [*tarikat*] because any man can enter whichever tarikat he wants. But someone whose mother and especially father are not Alevi cannot enter into Alevism" (Gölpınarlı 1969: 277). For a more sophisticated historical account of the relationship between Alevis and the Bektaşi order, see Karakaya-Stump 2008. For more on the history and rituals of the Bektaşi brotherhood, see Birge 1937; Faroqhi 2003; Mélikoff 1992, 1998; Ocak 2004.

6. The *semah* and the *cem* are central ritual practices within the Alevi community. For detailed discussion of the political significance of these practices in the present day, see chapter 4.

7. The *mevlit* is a ritual practice that commemorates the birth of the Prophet Muhammad, although it is enacted at various times during the calendar year (Tapper and Tapper 1987).

8. See, e.g., some of the translated excerpts of İsmet Özel in Meeker 1994b.

9. On the conceptual distinction between the political geography of the nation and that of the Muslim *umma*, see Asad 2003: 195–200.

10. One scholar of contemporary Alevi writings notes, "The introductory chapters in many books generally endeavor to prove that Alevism dates from the times of Ali" (Vorhoff 1998: 237).

11. Muawiya was one of Ali's chief political rivals. He was the first caliph of the Umayyad dynasty, which Shi'is hold responsible for the oppression faced by most of the Twelve Imams.

12. As Çınar 2005 and Özyürek 2006 show, official narratives of the Turkish nation have been further bolstered by annual public events that commemorate the foundation of the nation-state. They have also been contested by alternate commemorative events fostered by Islamist political parties that gained power over local municipalities in the 1990s.

13. In September 2011, the state announced that it would begin incorporating materials about Alevism into school textbooks (*Radikal* 2011). It is as yet too soon to predict the effects of this policy shift. In Germany, Alevis successfully managed to inscribe Alevism as a religion distinct from Sunni Islam in school materials (Sökefeld 2008: 189ff.).

14. The contrast here is with Sunni schools of thought that emphasize the example of the Prophet's companions rather than his kin. For a discussion of how this hadith report indexes sectarian differences, see Fischer and Abedi 1990: 120.

15. For more detail on the ritual acts of cursing and weeping, see chapter 2.

16. On the Dersim events, see Bruinessen 1994 and Watts 2000.

17. The two exceptions were the Progressive Republican Party, founded in 1924 and closed down after nineteen months, and the Free Republican Party, formed in 1930 and closed down after four months.

18. For an elaboration of Solgun's views on the inscription of Alevism in Kemalist political narratives, see his book length treatment, Solgun 2011.

19. For some of the responses by Alevi leaders to Solgun's remarks, see *Demokrat Haber* 2011.

Chapter 6

1. While noting the relatively low number of participants, it is worth recognizing certain qualifications that indicate the difficulty in pinning down the actual number of adherents in the cemaat. For one, the number of attendees rises to several hun-

dred on special religious holidays. More important, the cemaat also hosts an Internet forum that reaches audiences throughout Turkey's global diaspora, especially in western Europe. Moreover, local participants in Çorum often have relatives living abroad, and whether through economic remittances, kinship ties, or more socially informal connections, cemaat members engage in transnationally extended transactions that give them an international audience. Finally, from the late 1980s onward, the cemaat has produced pamphlets and newsletters that it distributes in neighboring provinces. One result has been the development of small Alevi communities in other regions of central and eastern Turkey that have begun organizing themselves as Shi'i congregations in emulation of the cemaat in Çorum. Nonetheless, the number of individuals associated with the cemaat is still only a minor fragment of the broader Alevi community.

2. The cemaat's mosque conforms to the historical norm of most mosques in Turkey, which have tended to be gender-restricted. However, it is worth noting that the past ten years have shown a marked growth in the number of state-trained female preachers in Turkey. This development has worked against historical gender imbalances in the Directorate of Religious Affairs and "the male-gendered spatiality of Turkish mosques" (Hassan 2011: 460).

3. On the local salience of this hadith passage, see the example of the *Şükrancılık cemi* event in chapter 5.

4. The cemaat's Shi'i call to prayer inserts two phrases not found in the call delivered by state mosques, including one that mentions the name of Ali: "I bear witness that Ali is the deputy of God." The morning and afternoon calls are recited at the same time as the state's call to prayer, but in the evening, the cemaat's call is issued 10 to 15 minutes after the latter. Additionally, in accord with Shi'i traditions, it is only recited three times a day, rather than the five that Sunnis recite.

5. In his assessment of the contemporary Islamic revival, Olivier Roy highlights the growing prominence of emotional discourses on morality, salvation, and end-times. While Roy's observation resonates with the discussion here, he concludes rather simplistically that for such movements "feelings are more important than knowledge" (2004: 31). As the material presented here reveals, any dichotomy between emotions and knowledge is untenable in movements like these, inasmuch as they simultaneously seek to convey information about moral narratives and to transform the sensibilities and affects through which such narratives can be experienced.

6. According to Shi'i tradition, the practice of gathering for the sake of praising Husayn's valor and excoriating his killers originates in a speech given by Zaynab, Husayn's sister and one of the survivors of the battle of Karbala, only forty days after her brother's death. The wide variety of literary and ritual forms now found across the Shi'i world historically developed in succeeding centuries, beginning in the Abbasid period, during which time pro-Alid sentiments were promoted by the state (Nakash

1993; Hussain 2005). Soteriological traditions of weeping are not restricted to Shiʿism; Sunni traditions of weeping, unrelated to Karbala lamentations, have a lengthy and rich history. See, e.g., Jonathan Berkey's (2001: 48–50) description of the significance attributed to weeping for one's sins in popular preaching in the medieval Near East.

7. In several important respects, the genre of the preacher's discourse was not, in fact, a sermon (*hutbe*). A number of features distinguished it from the latter. First, it was not delivered on Friday, which is the requisite day for a sermon. Second, the preacher's discourse at the meclis gatherings was restricted to the topic of Karbala, rather than to the broader ethical and social concerns that form subjects of sermons. Finally, whereas attendance at Friday prayers is obligatory for men, attendance at these Muharram sessions was not.

8. The words used by the preacher, *yürek* and *ciğer*, carry emotional but also physiological connotations that are difficult to translate directly into English. Çiğer, for instance, can refer to the liver, but it can also be used in phrases such as the one employed by the preacher in which a burning liver signifies an experience of passion. One anthology of Ottoman lyric poetry notes, "In the usual metaphoric physiology of love, the inside, the heart/liver of the beloved, is set aflame by love. The liver is roasted (becomes a kebab) in the conflagration, the heart is singed and scarred by burns, the throat becomes like a chimney from which hot and smoky sighs emerge in a shower of sparks" (Andrews, Black, and Kalpaklı 2006: 165). I follow Andrews, Black, and Kalpaklı in translating these terms with "heart," rather than "liver," in order to conform to ordinary English usage. I thank Burcu Karahan for providing me with this reference.

9. On the doctrine of *teberra*, see chap. 3, n. 14.

10. Elsewhere, I elaborate a conception of affect in terms of its iterability—that is, "the possibility of inciting emotive sensibilities across empirically variable contexts in ways that permit their repetition, recognition, and cultivation" (Tambar 2011: 485).

Conclusion

1. This exclusionary condition of political rights is not particular to Turkey. Balibar 1991 reflects more generally on the modes of exclusion that have achieved historical articulation in the nation-state form. See also Mouffe 2000's conceptualization of the forms of closure that democratic politics in a modern state requires.

2. The Dönme are sometimes referred to as Sabbateans. They are followers of Sabbatai Sevi, a seventeenth-century Jewish rabbi who claimed that he was the messiah. The term *dönme* literally means "convert" and refers to the fact that Sabbatai Sevi converted to Islam. His followers maintained a Muslim identity in public but conserved communally distinctive practices in private. As Baer 2009 details, this ambiguity only became politically problematic in the late Ottoman and republican periods.

3. The most notorious instance is the Capital Levy (1942–1944), which compelled non-Muslims to pay higher taxes than Muslims. Leyla Neyzi (2002: 146) notes that the tax effectively replaced the non-Muslim bourgeoisie of Istanbul with a bourgeoisie of Muslim origin.

4. In one recent survey, 59.8 percent of Alevi respondents answered yes to the question, "Is AKP's Alevi opening a policy of Sunnification?" (Köse 2010: 148).

BIBLIOGRAPHY

Abu El-Haj, Nadia. 2001. *Facts on the Ground: Archaeological Practice and Territorial Self-Fashioning in Israeli Society*. Chicago: University of Chicago Press.

Abu-Lughod, Lila. 1993. "Islam and the Gendered Discourses of Death." *International Journal of Middle East Studies* 25, 2: 187–205.

Abu-Lughod, Lila, and Catherine Lutz. 1990. "Introduction: Emotion, Discourse, and the Politics of Everyday Life." In *Language and the Politics of Emotion*, ed. Catherine Lutz and Lila Abu-Lughod, 1–23. New York: Cambridge University Press.

Agamben, Giorgio. 2005. *State of Exception*. Translated by Kevin Attell. Chicago: University of Chicago Press.

Aghaie, Kamran Scot. 2004. *The Martyrs of Karbala: Shi'i Symbols and Rituals in Modern Iran*. Seattle: University of Washington Press.

Agrama, Hussein Ali. 2012. *Questioning Secularism: Islam, Sovereignty, and the Rule of Law in Modern Egypt*. Chicago: University of Chicago Press.

Ahıska, Meltem. 2003. "Occidentalism: The Historical Fantasy of the Modern." *South Atlantic Quarterly* 102, 2–3: 351–379.

Akçam, Taner. 2004. *From Empire to Republic: Turkish Nationalism and the Armenian Genocide*. New York: Zed Books.

Akin, Erkan, and Ömer Karasapan. 1988. "The Turkish-Islamic Synthesis." *Middle East Report* 153: 18.

Akşit, Bahattin. 1998. "İçgöçlerin Nesnel vs Öznel Toplumsal Tarihi Üzerine Gözlemler: Köy Tarafından Bir Bakış." In *Türkiye'de İçgöç*, ed. Ahmet İçduygu, 22–37. Istanbul: Türkiye Ekonomik ve Toplumsal Tarih Vakfı.

Altınay, Ayşe Gül. 2004. *The Myth of the Military Nation: Militarism, Gender, and Education in Turkey*. New York: Palgrave Macmillan.

And, Metin. 1979. "The Muharram Observances in Anatolian Turkey." In *Ta'ziyeh: Ritual and Drama in Iran*, ed. Peter Chelkowski, 238–254. New York: New York University Press.

Anderson, Benedict. (1983) 1991. *Imagined Communities: Reflections on the Origin and Spread of Nationalism*. New York: Verso.

Anderson, Jon. 2003. "New Media, New Publics: Reconfiguring the Public Sphere of Islam." *Social Research* 70, 3: 887–906.

Andrews, Walter G., Najaat Black, and Mehmet Kalpaklı, eds. 2006. *Ottoman Lyric Poetry: An Anthology.* Expanded ed. Seattle: University of Washington Press.

Appadurai, Arjun. 2006. *Fear of Small Numbers: An Essay on the Geography of Anger.* Durham, NC: Duke University Press.

Arat, Yeşim. 1997. "The Project of Modernity and Women in Turkey." In *Rethinking Modernity and National Identity in Turkey,* ed. Sibel Bozdoğan and Reşat Kasaba, 95–112. Seattle: University of Washington Press.

Arendt, Hannah. 1966. *The Origins of Totalitarianism.* New York: Harcourt, Brace, & World.

Asad, Talal. 1993. *Genealogies of Religion: Discipline and Reasons of Power in Islam and Christianity.* Baltimore: Johns Hopkins University Press.

———. 2003. *Formations of the Secular: Christianity, Islam, Modernity.* Stanford: Stanford University Press.

Ayoub, Mahmoud. 1978. *Redemptive Suffering in Islam: A Study of the Devotional Aspects of 'Ashura' in Twelver Shi'ism.* New York: Mouton.

Baer, Marc David. 2009. *The Dönme: Jewish Converts, Muslim Revolutionaries, and Secular Turks.* Stanford: Stanford University Press.

Bahadır, İbrahim. 2005. "Türk Milliyetçi Söyleminde Şamanizm ve Alevilik." *Kırkbudak: Anadolu Halk İnançlar* 1, 4: 5–26.

Bakhtin, Mikhail. 1981. *The Dialogic Imagination: Four Essays.* Translated by Caryl Emerson and Michael Holquist. Austin: University of Texas Press.

———. 1986. "The Problem of Speech Genres." In *Speech Genres and Other Late Essays.* Translated by Vern W. McGee, 60–102. Austin: University of Texas Press.

Balibar, Étienne. 1991. "Racism and Nationalism." In id. and Immanuel Wallerstein, *Race, Nation, Class: Ambiguous Identities,* 37–67. New York: Verso.

Bauman, Richard. 1986. *Story, Performance, and Event: Contextual Studies of Oral Narrative.* Cambridge: Cambridge University Press.

Bauman, Zygmunt. 1992. *Intimations of Postmodernity.* New York: Routledge.

Berkes, Niyazi. 1964. *The Development of Secularism in Turkey.* Montreal: McGill University Press.

Berkey, Jonathan. 2001. *Popular Preaching and Religious Authority in the Medieval Near East.* Seattle: University of Washington Press.

Bhabha, Homi. 1994. "DissemiNation: Time, Narrative and the Margins of the Modern Nation." In id., *The Location of Culture,* 139–170. New York: Routledge.

Bilici, Faruk. 1998. "The Function of Alevi-Bektashi Theology in Modern Turkey." In *Alevi Identity: Cultural, Religious, and Social Perspectives,* ed. Tord Olsson, Elizabeth Özdalga, and Catharina Raudvere, 51–62. Istanbul: Numune Matbaasi.

Birdoğan, Nejat. 1990. *Anadolu'nun Gizli Kültürü Alevilik.* Hamburg: Hamburg Alevi Kültür Merkezi Yayınları.

Birge, John Kingsley. 1937. *The Bektashi Order of Dervishes.* London: Luzac.

Belge, Ceren. 2006. "Friends of the Court: The Republican Alliance and Selective Activism of the Constitutional Court in Turkey." *Law and Society Review* 40, 3: 653–692.

Bloxham, Donald. 2003. "The Armenian Genocide of 1915–1916: Cumulative Radicalization and the Development of a Destruction Policy." *Past and Present* 181: 141–191.

Bora, Tanıl, and Kemal Can. 1991. *Devlet, Ocak, Dergah: 12 Eylül'den 1990'lara Ülkücü Hareket.* Istanbul: İletişim Yayınları.

Bozarslan, Hamit. 1999. "Le phénomène milicien: Une composante de la violence politique en Turquie des années 1970." *Turcica* 31: 185–244.

———. 2002. "L'alévisme et l'impossible équation du nationalisme en Turquie." In *Nationalismes en mutation en Mediterranée orientale*, ed. Alain Diekhoff and Riva Kastoryano, 133–152. Paris: CNRS.

Bozkurt, Fuat. 1990. *Aleviliğin Toplumsal Boyutları.* Istanbul: Yön Yayıncılık.

———. 1998. "State-Community Relations in the Restructuring of Alevism." In *Alevi Identity: Cultural, Religious and Social Perspectives*, ed. Tord Olsson, Elisabeth Özdalga, and Catharina Raudvere, 85–96. Istanbul: Swedish Research Institutes.

———. 2000. *Çağdaşlaşma Sürecinde Alevilik.* Istanbul: Doğan Kitapçılık.

Brink-Danan, Marcy. 2010. "Names That Show Time: Turkish Jews as 'Strangers' and the Semiotics of Reclassification." *American Anthropologist* 112, 3: 384–396.

———. 2011. "Dangerous Cosmopolitanism: Erasing Difference in Istanbul." *Anthropological Quarterly* 84, 2: 439–474.

Brubaker, Rogers. 1996. *Nationalism Reframed: Nationhood and the National Question in the New Europe.* Cambridge: Cambridge University Press.

Bruinessen, Martin van. 1994. "Genocide in Kurdistan? The Suppression of the Dersim Rebellion in Turkey (1937–1938) and the Chemical War Against the Iraqi Kurds (1988)." In *Genocide: Conceptual and Historical Dimensions*, ed. George J. Andreopoulos, 141–170. Philadelphia: University of Pennsylvania Press.

———. 1996. "Kurds, Turks and the Alevi Revival in Turkey." *Middle East Report* 200: 7–10.

Bryant, Rebecca. 2005. "The Soul Danced into the Body: Nation and Improvisation in Istanbul." *American Ethnologist* 32, 3: 222–238.

Buck-Morss, Susan. 2000. *Dreamworld and Catastrophe: The Passing of Mass Utopia in East and West.* Cambridge, MA: MIT Press.

Burke, Peter. 1969. *The Renaissance Sense of the Past.* New York: St. Martin's Press.

Çağaptay, Soner. 2006. *Islam, Secularism, and Nationalism in Modern Turkey: Who is a Turk?* New York: Routledge.

Casanova, José. 1994. *Public Religions in the Modern World.* Chicago: University of Chicago Press.

Chakrabarty, Dipesh. 2000. *Provincializing Europe: Postcolonial Thought and Historical Difference.* Princeton, NJ: Princeton University Press.

Chatterjee, Partha. 2004. *The Politics of the Governed: Reflections on Popular Politics in Most of the World.* New York: Columbia University Press.

Chelkowski, Peter, ed. 1979. *Ta'ziyeh: Ritual and Drama in Iran.* New York: New York University Press.

Çınar, Alev. 2005. *Modernity, Islam, and Secularism in Turkey: Bodies, Places, and Time.* Minneapolis: University of Minnesota Press.

Cole, Juan. 1988. *Roots of North Indian Shi'ism in Iran and Iraq: Religion and State in Awadh, 1722–1859.* Berkeley: University of California Press.

———. 2002. *Sacred Space and Holy War: The Politics, Culture, and History of Shi'ite Islam.* New York: I. B. Tauris.

Comaroff, John, and Jean Comaroff. 1991. *Of Revelation and Revolution: Christianity, Colonialism, and Consciousness in South Africa,* vol. 1. Chicago: University of Chicago Press.

———. 2004. "Criminal Justice, Cultural Justice: The Limits of Liberalism and the Pragmatics of Difference in the New South Africa." *American Ethnologist* 31, 2: 188–204.

Connolly, William. 2005. *Pluralism.* Durham, NC: Duke University Press.

Copeaux, Étienne. 1997. *Espaces et temps de la nation turque: Analyse d'une historiographie nationaliste, 1931–1993.* Paris: CNRS.

Davis, Kathleen. 2008. *Periodization and Sovereignty: How Ideas of Feudalism and Secularization Govern the Politics of Time.* Philadelphia: University of Pennsylvania Press.

Davison, Andrew. 1998. *Secularism and Revivalism in Turkey: A Hermeneutic Reconsideration.* New Haven, CT: Yale University Press.

de Certeau, Michel. 1988. *The Writing of History.* Translated by Tom Conley. New York: Columbia University Press.

Deeb, Lara. 2006. *An Enchanted Modern: Gender and Public Piety in Shi'i Lebanon.* Princeton, NJ: Princeton University Press.

———. 2009. "Emulating and/or Embodying the Ideal: The Gendering of Temporal Frameworks and Islamic Role Models in Shi'i Lebanon." *American Ethnologist* 36, 2: 242–257.

Demokrat Haber. 2011. "Cafer Solgun tepkilere ne dedi?" 8 December 2011, www.demokrathaber.net/guncel/cafer-solgun-tepkilere-ne-dedi-h5497.html.

———. 2012. " 'Biz de Solgun gibi düşünüyoruz': Dersimli aydın ve sanatçılar, Cafer Solgun'a tehditlere tepki gösterdi," 9 January 2012, www.demokrathaber.net/guncel/biz-de-solgun-gibi-dusunuyoruz-h6188.html.

Deringil, Selim. 1990. "The Struggle against Shiism in Hamidian Iraq: A Study in Ottoman Counter-Propaganda." *Die Welt des Islams* 30, 1–4: 45–62.

Dodd, C. H. 1990. *The Crisis of Turkish Democracy*. 2nd ed. Huntingdon, UK: Eothen Press.

Dole, Christopher. 2006. "Mass Media and the Repulsive Allure of Religious Healing: The *Cinci Hoca* in Turkish Modernity." *International Journal of Middle East Studies* 38, 1: 31–54.

———. 2012. *Healing Secular Life: Loss and Devotion in Modern Turkey*. Philadelphia: University of Pennsylvania Press.

Dressler, Markus. 2008. "Religio-Secular Metamorphoses: The Re-Making of Turkish Alevism." *Journal of the American Academy of Religion* 76, 2: 280–311.

———. 2010. "How to Conceptualize Inner-Islamic Plurality/Difference: 'Heterodoxy' and 'Syncretism' in the Writings of Mehmet F. Köprülü (1890–1966)." *British Journal of Middle Eastern Studies* 37, 3: 241–260.

———. 2013. *Writing Religion: The Making of Turkish Alevi Islam*. Oxford: Oxford University Press.

Duara, Prasenjit. 1995. *Rescuing History from the Nation: Questioning Narratives of Modern China*. Chicago: University of Chicago Press.

Dündar, Fuat. 2001. "İttihat ve Terakki Etnisite Araştırmaları." *Toplumsal Tarihi* 91, 16: 43–50.

Durkheim, Emile. 1995. *The Elementary Forms of Religious Life*. Translated by Karen Fields. New York: Free Press.

Eickelman, Dale, and James Piscatori. 1996. *Muslim Politics*. Princeton, NJ: Princeton University Press.

Eissenstat, Howard. 2005. "Metaphors of Race and Discourse of Nation: Racial Theory and State Nationalism in the First Decades of the Turkish Republic." In *Race and Nation: Ethnic Systems in the Modern World*, ed. Paul Spickard, 239–256. New York: Routledge.

Ellington, George. 2004. "Urbanization and the Alevi Religious Revival in the Republic of Turkey." In *Archeology, Anthropology and Heritage in the Balkans and Anatolia: The Life and Times of F. W. Hasluck, 1878–1920*, vol. 1, ed. David Shankland, 369–401. Istanbul: Isis Press.

Eral, Sadık. 1995. *Çaldıran'dan Çorum'a Anadolu'da Alevi Katliamları*. Istanbul: Ant Yayınları.

Erdemir, Aykan. 2005. "Tradition and Modernity: Alevis' Ambiguous Terms and Turkey's Ambivalent Subjects." *Middle Eastern Studies* 41, 6: 937–951.

Ersanlı, Büşra. 2002. "The Ottoman Empire in the Historiography of the Kemalist Era: A Theory of Fatal Decline." In *The Ottomans and the Balkans: A Discussion of Historiography*, ed. Fikret Adanır and Suraiya Faroqhi, 115–154. Leiden: Brill.

Erseven, İlhan Cem. 1990. *Aleviler'de Semah*. Ankara: Ekin Yayınları.

Ertürk, Nergis. 2011. *Grammatology and Literary Modernity in Turkey*. Oxford: Oxford University Press.

Euben, Roxanne. 1999. *Enemy in the Mirror: Islamic Fundamentalism and the Limits of Modern Rationalism.* Princeton, NJ: Princeton University Press.

European Commission. 2004. *2004 Regular Report on Turkey's Progress toward Accession.* Brussels: Commission of the European Communities.

———. 2008. *Turkey 2008 Progress Report.* Brussels: Commission of the European Communities.

Evren, Kenan. 1982. *Türkiye Cumhuriyeti Devlet Başkanı Orgeneral Kenan Evren'in Yeni Anayasayı Devlet Adına Resmen Tanıtma Programı Gereğince Yaptıkları Konuşmalar.* Ankara: TBMM Basımevi.

Fabian, Johannes. 1983. *Time and the Other: How Anthropology Makes its Object.* New York: Columbia University Press.

Faroqhi, Suraiya. 2003. *Anadolu'da Bektaşilik.* Translated by Nasuh Barın. Istanbul: Simurg.

Fasolt, Constantin. 2004. *The Limits of History.* Chicago: University of Chicago Press.

Feld, Steven. 1990a. *Sound and Sentiment: Birds, Weeping, Poetics, and Song in Kaluli Expression.* Philadelphia: University of Pennsylvania Press.

———. 1990b. "Wept Thoughts: The Voicing of Kaluli Memories." *Oral Tradition* 5, 2–3: 241–266.

Findley, Carter Vaughn. 2010. *Turkey, Islam, Nationalism, and Modernity: A History, 1789–2007.* New Haven, CT: Yale University Press.

Fischer, Michael. 1980. *Iran: From Religious Dispute to Revolution.* Madison: University of Wisconsin Press.

Fischer, Michael, and Mehdi Abedi. 1990. *Debating Muslims: Cultural Dialogues in Postmodernity and Tradition.* Madison: University of Wisconsin Press.

Flaskerud, Ingvild. 2010. *Visualizing Belief and Piety in Iranian Shiism.* New York: Continuum.

Fleischer, Cornell. 1986. *Bureaucrat and Intellectual in the Ottoman Empire: The Historian Mustafa Ali (1541–1600).* Princeton, NJ: Princeton University Press.

Fortna, Benjamin. 2002. *Imperial Classroom: Islam, the State, and Education in the Late Ottoman Empire.* Oxford: Oxford University Press.

Foucault, Michel. 1984. "Nietzsche, Genealogy, History." In *The Foucault Reader*, ed. Paul Rabinow, 76–100. New York: Pantheon Books.

———. 1991. "Governmentality." In *The Foucault Effect: Studies in Governmentality*, ed. Graham Burchell, Colin Gordon, and Peter Miller, 87–104. Chicago: University of Chicago Press.

Frayliç, Dr. [pseud.], and Mühendis Ravlig. (1918) 2008. *Türkmen Aşiretleri.* Edited by Ali Cin, Haluk Kortel, and Haldun Eroğlu. Istanbul: İQ Kültür Sanay Yayıncılık.

Gal, Susan. 2003. "Movements of Feminism: The Circulation of Discourses about Women." In *Recognition Struggles and Social Movements: Contested Identities,*

Agency and Power, ed. Barbara Hobson, 93–118. Cambridge: Cambridge University Press.

Gaonkar, Dilip Parameshwar, and Elizabeth Povinelli. 2003. "Technologies of Public Forms: Circulation, Transfiguration, Recognition." *Public Culture* 15, 3: 385–397.

Göçek, Fatma Müge. 2011. *The Transformation of Turkey: Redefining State and Society from the Ottoman Empire to the Modern Era.* New York: I. B. Tauris.

Göle, Nilüfer. 1997. *Forbidden Modern: Civilization and Veiling.* Ann Arbor: University of Michigan Press.

———. 2000. "Snapshots of Islamic Modernities." *Dædalus* 129, 1: 91–117.

———. 2002. "Islam in Public: New Visibilities and New Imaginaries." *Public Culture* 14, 1: 173–190.

Gölpınarlı, Abdülbâki. 1969. *Türkiye'de Mezhepler ve Tarikatler.* Istanbul: Gerçek Yayınevi.

Goluboff, Sascha. 2008. "Patriarchy through Lamentation in Azerbaijan." *American Ethnologist* 35, 1: 81–94.

Göner, Özlem. 2005. "The Transformation of Alevi Collective Identity." *Cultural Dynamics* 17, 2: 107–134.

Gültekin, Ahmet Kerim, and Yüksel Işık. 2005. "Diyanet İşleri Başkanı Prof. Dr. Ali Bardakoğlu'yla Söyleşi." *Kırkbudak: Anadolu Halk İnançları Araştırmaları* 1, 3: 4–23.

Habermas, Jürgen. 1998. *Between Facts and Norms: Contributions to a Discourse Theory of Law and Democracy.* Translated by William Rehg. Cambridge, MA: MIT Press.

Hale, Charles R. 2002. "Does Multiculturalism Menace? Governance, Cultural Rights and the Politics of Identity in Guatemala." *Journal of Latin American Studies* 34, 3: 485–524.

Hale, William. 1994. *Turkish Politics and the Military.* New York: Routledge.

Hanioğlu, M. Şükrü. 2008. *A Brief History of the Late Ottoman Empire.* Princeton, NJ: Princeton University Press.

Hankins, Joseph Doyle. 2012. "Maneuvers of Multiculturalism: International Representations of Minority Politics in Japan." *Japanese Studies* 32, 1: 1–19.

Hart, Kimberly. 2009. "The Orthodoxization of Ritual Practice in Western Anatolia." *American Ethnologist* 36, 4: 735–749.

Hassan, Mona. 2011. "Women Preaching for the Secular State: Official Female Preachers (*Bayan Vaizler*) in Contemporary Turkey." *International Journal of Middle East Studies* 43, 3: 451–473.

Hefner, Robert. 2001. "Public Islam and the Problem of Democratization." *Sociology of Religion* 62, 4: 491–514.

Henkel, Heiko. 2005. " 'Between Belief and Unbelief Lies the Performance of Salat':

Meaning and Efficacy of a Muslim Ritual." *Journal of the Royal Anthropological Institute* 11: 487–507.

Heper, Metin. 1985. *The State Tradition in Turkey.* Walkington, UK: Eothen Press.

Hirschkind, Charles. 2006. *The Ethical Soundscape: Cassette Sermons and Islamic Counterpublics.* New York: Columbia University Press.

Hobsbawm, Eric. 1983. "Introduction: Inventing Traditions." In *The Invention of Tradition*, ed. Eric Hobsbawm and Terence Ranger, 1–14. Cambridge: Cambridge University Press.

Hürriyet. 2004. "Alevilerden AB'ye tepki: Azınlık değiliz." October 14, webarsiv.hurriyet.com.tr/2004/10/14/536757.asp.

Hürriyet Daily News. 2011. "Turkish Prime Minister Erdoğan apologizes for Dersim killings." November 23, archive.hurriyetdailynews.com/n.php?n=turkish-prime-minister-erdogan-apologizes-for-dersim-killings-2011-11-23.

Hussain, Ali J. 2005. "The Mourning of History and the History of Mourning: The Evolution of Ritual Commemoration of the Battle of Karbala." *Comparative Studies of South Asia, Africa, and the Middle East* 25, 1: 78–88.

Hyder, Syed Akbar. 2006. *Reliving Karbala: Martyrdom in South Asian Memory.* Oxford: Oxford University Press.

Imber, C. H. 1979. "The Persecution of the Ottoman Shiʿites According to the Mühimme Defterleri, 1565–1585." *Der Islam* 56: 245–273.

İnalcık, Halil. 1994. *The Ottoman Empire: The Classical Age, 1300–1600.* London: Phoenix.

Kaplan, Sam. 2006. *The Pedagogical State: Education and the Politics of National Culture in Post-1980 Turkey.* Stanford: Stanford University Press.

Karakaya-Stump, Ayfer. 2004. "The Emergence of the Kızılbaş in Western Thought: Missionary Accounts and Their Aftermath." In *Archeology, Anthropology and Heritage in the Balkans and Anatolia: The Life and Times of F. W. Hasluck, 1878–1920*, vol. 1, ed. David Shankland, 329–353. Istanbul: Isis Press.

———. 2008. "Subjects of the Sultan, Disciples of the Shah: Formation and Transformation of the Kizilbash/Alevi Communities in Ottoman Anatolia." Ph.D. diss., Harvard University.

Keane, Webb. 2007. *Christian Moderns: Freedom and Fetish in the Mission Encounter.* Berkeley: University of California Press.

Kehl-Bodrogi, Krisztina. 2003. "Atatürk and Alevis: A Holy Alliance?" In *Turkey's Alevi Enigma: A Comprehensive Overview*, ed. Paul J. White and Joost Jongerden, 53–69. Leiden: Brill.

Keyder, Çağlar. 1997. "Wither the Project of Modernity? Turkey in the 1990s." In *Rethinking Modernity and National Identity in Turkey*, ed. Sibel Bozdoğan and Reşat Kasaba, 37–51. Seattle: University of Washington Press.

Keyman, E. Fuat. 2007. "Introduction: Modernity and Democracy in Turkey." In

Remaking Turkey: Globalization, Alternative Modernities, and Democracy, ed. E. Fuat Keyman, xv–xxviii. Lanham, MD: Lexington Books.

Kieser, Hans-Lukas. 2004. "Alevilik as Song and Dialogue: The Village Sage of Meluli Baba (1892–1989)." In *Archeology, Anthropology and Heritage in the Balkans and Anatolia: The Life and Times of F. W. Hasluck, 1878–1920,* vol. 1, ed. David Shankland, 355–368. Istanbul: Isis Press.

————. 2007. "The Anatolian Alevis' Ambivalent Encounter with Modernity in Late Ottoman and Early Republican Turkey." In *The Other Shiites: From the Mediterranean to Central Asia,* ed. Alessandro Monsutti, Silvia Naef, and Farian Sabahi, 41–57. Bern: Peter Lang, 2007.

Kirişci, Kemal. 2000. "Disaggregating Turkish Citizenship and Immigration Practices." *Middle Eastern Studies* 36, 3: 1–22.

Koğacıoğlu, Dicle. 2003. "Dissolution of Political Parties by the Constitutional Court in Turkey: Judicial Delimitation of the Political Domain." *International Sociology* 18, 1: 258–276.

————. 2004. "Progress, Unity, and Democracy: Dissolving Political Parties in Turkey." *Law and Society Review* 38, 3: 433–462.

Köse, Talha. 2010. "The AKP and the 'Alevi Opening': Understanding the Dynamics of the Rapprochement." *Insight Turkey* 12, 2: 143–164.

Koselleck, Reinhart. 2004. *Futures Past: On the Semantics of Historical Time.* Translated by Keith Tribe. New York: Columbia University Press.

Küçük, Murat. 2003. "Mezhepten Millete: Aleviler ve Türk Milliyetçiliği." In *Modern Türkiye'de Siyasi Düşünce: Milliyetçilik,* 901–910. Istanbul: İletişim Yayınları.

Kushner, David. 1977. *The Rise of Turkish Nationalism, 1876–1908.* London: Frank Cass.

Lapidus, Ira. 1997. "Islamic Revival and Modernity: The Contemporary Movements and the Historical Paradigms." *Journal of the Economic and Social History of the Orient* 40, 4: 444–460.

Lawrence, Bruce. 1998. *Shattering the Myth: Islam beyond Violence.* Princeton, NJ: Princeton University Press.

Lee, Benjamin, and Edward LiPuma. 2002. "Cultures of Circulation: The Imaginations of Modernity." *Public Culture* 14, 1: 191–213.

Lewis, Bernard. 1968. *The Emergence of Modern Turkey.* Oxford: Oxford University Press.

Livaneli, Zülfü. 2005. "Bu Ülkede Alevi Olmak." *Vatan Gazetesi,* June 8.

Lobel, Jules. 2001–2002. "The War on Terrorism and Civil Liberties." *University of Pittsburgh Law Review* 63: 767–790.

Lutz, Catherine. 1988. *Unnatural Emotions: Everyday Sentiments on a Micronesian Atoll and Their Challenge to Western Theory.* Chicago: University of Chicago Press.

Mahmood, Saba. 2001. "Rehearsed Spontaneity and the Conventionality of Ritual: Disciplines of Salat." *American Ethnologist* 28, 4: 827–853.

———. 2005. *Politics of Piety: The Islamic Revival and the Feminist Subject.* Princeton, NJ: Princeton University Press.

Malkki, Liisa. 1995. *Purity and Exile: Violence, Memory, and National Cosmology among Hutu Refugees in Tanzania.* Chicago: University of Chicago Press.

Mandel, Ruth. 1990. "Shifting Centers and Emergent Identities: Turkey and Germany in the Lives of the Turkish *Gastarbeiter.*" In *Muslim Travelers: Pilgrimage, Migration, and the Religious Imagination,* ed. Dale Eickelman and James Piscatori, 153–174. Berkeley: University of California Press.

———. 2008. *Cosmopolitan Anxieties: Turkish Challenges to Citizenship and Belonging in Germany.* Durham, NC: Duke University Press.

Mardin, Şerif. 2006. "Some Consideration on the Building of an Ottoman Public Identity in the Nineteenth Century." In *Religion, Society, and Modernity in Turkey,* 124–134. Syracuse, NY: Syracuse University Press.

Margulies, Ronnie, and Ergin Yıldızoğlu. 1984. "Trade Unions and Turkey's Working Class." *Middle East Report* 121: 15–31.

Markoff, Irene. 1986. "The Role of Expressive Culture in the Demystification of a Secret Sect of Islam: The Case of the Alevis of Turkey." *World of Music* 28, 3: 42–56.

Massicard, Élise. 2005a. "Alevism in the 1960s: Social Change and Mobilisation." In *Alevis and Alevism: Transformed Identities,* ed. Hege Irène Markussen, 109–135. Istanbul: Isis Press.

———. 2005b. *L'Autre Turquie: Le mouvement aléviste et ses territoires.* Paris: Presses universitaires de France.

———. 2006. "Claiming Difference in a Unitarist Frame: The Case of Alevism." In *Turkey Beyond Nationalism: Towards Post-Nationalist Identities,* ed. Hans-Lukas Keiser, 74–82. New York: I. B. Tauris.

Massignon, Louis. 1969. "La notion du vœu et la dévotion musulmane à Fatima." In id., *Opera minora: Textes, recueillis, classés et présentés, avec une bibliographie,* vol. 1, ed. Y. Moubarac, 573–591. Paris: Presses universitaires de France.

Massumi, Brian. 2002. *Parables for the Virtual: Movement, Affect, Sensation.* Durham, NC: Duke University Press.

Meeker, Michael. 1994a. "Oral Culture, Media Culture, and the Islamic Resurgence in Turkey." In *Exploring the Written: Anthropology and the Multiplicity of the Writing,* ed. Eduardo Archetti, 31–64. Oslo: Scandinavian University Press.

———. 1994b. "The Muslim Intellectual and His Audience: A New Configuration of Writer and Reader among Believers in the Republic of Turkey." In *Cultural Transitions in the Middle East,* ed. Şerif Mardin, 153–188. Leiden: Brill.

———. 2002. *A Nation of Empire: The Ottoman Legacy of Turkish Modernity.* Berkeley: University of California Press.

Mélikoff, Irène. 1992. *Sur les traces du soufisme turc: Recherches sur l'Islam populaire en Anatolie*. Istanbul: Isis.

———. 1998. *Hadji Bektach: Un mythe et ses avatars*. Leiden: Brill.

Mervin, Sabrina. 2000. *Un réformisme chiite: Ulémas et lettrés du Gabal 'Amil (actuel Liban-Sud) de la fin de l'Empire ottoman à l'indépendance du Liban*. Paris: Karthala; Beirut: CERMOC; Damascus: IFEAD.

Meyer, Birgit. 2008. "Religious Sensations: Why Media, Aesthetics, and Power Matter in the Study of Contemporary Religion." In *Religion: Beyond a Concept*, ed. Hent de Vries, 704–723. New York: Fordham University Press.

Milli Güvenlik Konseyi Genel Sekreterliği. 1981. *12 Eylül Öncesi ve Sonrası*. Ankara: Türk Tarih Kurumu Basımevi.

Milliyet. 2009. "MHP'den Alevi Açılımı." June 9, www.milliyet.com.tr/Siyaset/HaberDetay.aspxaType=HaberDetay&KategoriID=4&ArticleID=1104777&Date=10.0 6.2009&b=MHPden%20Alevi%20acilimi.

Mitchell, Timothy. 1991. *Colonising Egypt*. Berkeley: University of California Press.

———. 2000. "The Stage of Modernity." In *Questions of Modernity*, ed. id., 1–34. Minneapolis: University of Minnesota Press.

Momen, Moojen. 1985. *An Introduction to Shi'i Islam: The History and Doctrines of Twelver Shi'ism*. Oxford: Oxford University Press.

Mouffe, Chantal. 2000. *The Democratic Paradox*. New York: Verso.

———. 2005. *On the Political*. New York: Routledge.

Nakash, Yitzhak. 1993. "An Attempt to Trace the Origin of the Rituals of Ashura." *Die Welt des Islams* 33, 2:161–181.

Navaro-Yashin, Yael. 2002. *Faces of the State: Secularism and Public Life in Turkey*. Princeton, NJ: Princeton University Press.

Neyzi, Leyla. 2002. "Remembering to Forget: Sabbateanism, National Identity, and Subjectivity in Turkey." *Comparative Studies in Society and History* 44, 1: 137–158.

Nokta Dergisi. 1990. "Mollaların Hedefi: Aleviler." July 15.

Nur, Rıza. 1967. *Hayat ve Hatıratım*, vol. 3. Istanbul: Altındağ Yayınevi.

Ocak, Ahmet Yaşar. 1991. "Les réactions socio-religieuses contre l'idéologie officielle ottomane et la question de *zendeqa vs ilhâd* (hérésie et athéisme) au XVIe siècle." *Turcica* 21–23: 71–82.

———. 2004. *Türk Sufiliğine Bakışlar: Türkiye'de Tarihin Saptırılması Sürecinde*. Istanbul: İletişim Yayıncılık.

Öncü, Ayşe. 1995. "Packaging Islam: Cultural Politics on the Landscape of Turkish Commercial Television." *Public Culture* 8: 51–71.

Oran, Baskın. 2007. "The Minority Concept and Rights in Turkey: The Lausanne Peace Treaty and Current Issues." In *Human Rights in Turkey*, ed. Zehra Kabasakal Arat, 35–56. Philadelphia: University of Pennsylvania Press.

Öz, Baki. 2001. *Alevilik Nedir?* Istanbul: Der Yayınları.

Özbudun, Ergun. 1988. *Türk Anayasa Hukuku*. Ankara: Yetkin Yayınları.

———. 2012. "Turkey—Plural Society and Monolithic State." In *Democracy, Islam, and Secularism in Turkey*, ed. Ahmet T. Kuru and Alfred Stepan, 61–94. New York: Columbia University Press.

Özbudun, Ergun, and Ömer F. Gençkaya. 2009. *Democratization and the Politics of Constitution-Making in Turkey*. Budapest: Central European University Press.

Öztürkmen, Arzu. 2002. " 'I Dance Folklore.' " In *Fragments of Culture: The Everyday of Modern Turkey*, ed. Deniz Kandiyoti and Ayşe Saktanber, 128–146. New Brunswick, NJ: Rutgers University Press.

———. 2005. "Staging a Ritual Dance Out of Its Context: The Role of an Individual Artist in Transforming the Alevi Semah." *Asian Folklore Studies* 64: 247–260.

Özyürek, Esra. 2006. *Nostalgia for the Modern: State Secularism and Everyday Politics in Turkey*. Durham, NC: Duke University Press.

———. 2009a. "Beyond Integration and Recognition: Diasporic Constructions of Alevi Muslim Identity between Germany and Turkey." In *Transnational Transcendence: Essays on Religion and Globalization*, ed. Thomas Csordas, 121–144. Berkeley: University of California Press.

———. 2009b. "Convert Alert: German Muslims and Turkish Christians as Threats to Security in the New Europe." *Comparative Studies in Society and History* 51, 1: 91–116.

Palmié, Stephan. 2013. "Historicist Knowledge and Its Conditions of Impossibility." In *The Social Life of Spirits*, ed. Ruy Blanes and Diana Espírito Santo, 218–240. Chicago: University of Chicago Press.

Parla, Ayşe. 2011a. "Labor Migration, Ethnic Kinship, and the Conundrum of Citizenship in Turkey." *Citizenship Studies* 15, 3–4: 457–470.

———. 2011b. "Undocumented Migrants and the Double Binds of Rights Claims." *differences: A Journal of Feminist Cultural Studies* 22, 1: 64–89.

Parla, Taha. 1985. *The Social and Political Thought of Ziya Gökalp, 1876–1924*. Leiden: Brill.

Parla, Taha, and Andrew Davison. 2004. *Corporatist Ideology in Kemalist Turkey: Progress or Order?* Syracuse, NY: Syracuse University Press.

Pinault, David. 1992. *The Shiites: Ritual and Popular Piety in a Muslim Community*. New York: St. Martin's Press.

———. 2001. *Horse of Karbala: Muslim Devotional Life in India*. New York: Palgrave Macmillan.

Poovey, Mary. 1995. *Making a Social Body: British Cultural Formation, 1830–1864*. Chicago: University of Chicago Press.

Potuoğlu-Cook, Öykü. 2006. Beyond the Glitter: Belly Dance and Neoliberal Gentrification in Istanbul. *Cultural Anthropology* 21, 4: 633–660.

———. 2010. "The Uneasy Vernacular: Choreographing Multiculturalism and Dancing Difference Away in Globalised Turkey." *Anthropological Notebooks* 16, 3: 93–105.

Povinelli, Elizabeth. 2002. *The Cunning of Recognition: Indigenous Alterities and the Making of Australian Multiculturalism*. Durham, NC: Duke University Press.

———. 2011. *Economies of Abandonment: Social Belonging and Endurance in Late Liberalism*. Durham, NC: Duke University Press.

Radcliffe-Brown, A. R. 1948. *The Andaman Islanders*. Glencoe, IL: Free Press.

Radikal. 2011. " 'Alevilik' Ders Kitaplarına Girdi." September 8, www.radikal.com.tr/ Radikal.aspx?aType=RadikalDetayV3&ArticleID=1062700&Date=03.12.2011&C ategoryID=86.

Rancière, Jacques. 1999. *Disagreement: Politics and Philosophy*. Translated by Julie Rose. Minneapolis: University of Minnesota Press.

———. 2010. "Who Is the Subject of the Rights of Man?" In id., *Dissensus: On Politics and Aesthetics*, trans. Steven Corcoran, 62–75. New York: Continuum.

Renan, Ernest. (1882) 1990. "What Is a Nation?" In *Nation and Narration*, ed. Homi Bhabha, 8–22. New York: Routledge.

Reynolds, Michael A. 2011. *Shattering Empires: The Clash and Collapse of the Ottoman and Russian Empires, 1908–1918*. Cambridge: Cambridge University Press.

Rodrigue, Aron. 2013. "Reflections on Millets and Minorities: Ottoman Legacies." In *Turkey between Nationalism and Globalization*, ed. Riva Kastoryano, 36–46. New York: Routledge.

Roy, Olivier. 2004. *Globalized Islam: The Search for a New Ummah*. New York: Columbia University Press.

Şahhüseyinoğlu, H. Nedim. 1999. *Yakın Tarihimizde Kitlesel Katliamlar: Malatya, K. Maraş, Çorum, Sivas Katliamların İçyüzüne Dönük bir İnceleme*. Ankara: İtalik Kitaplar.

Şahin, Şehriban. 2005. "The Rise of Alevism as a Public Religion." *Current Sociology* 53, 3: 465–485.

Şahin, Teoman. 1995. *Alevilere Söylenen Yalanlar: Bektaşilik Soruşturması*. Ankara: Armağan Kitap ve Yayınevi.

Sait, Baha. (1918) 2000. "Anadolu'da İçtimai Zümreler ve Anadolu İçtimaiyatı." In id., *Türkiye'de Alevi-Bektaşi, Ahi ve Nusayri Zümreleri*, ed. İsmail Görkem, 79–90. Ankara: T.C. Kültür Bakanlığı Yayınları.

———. (1926) 2000. "Türkiye'de Alevi Zümreleri: Tekke Aleviliği-İçtimai Alevilik." In id., *Türkiye'de Alevi-Bektaşi, Ahi ve Nusayri Zümreleri*, ed. İsmail Görkem, 111–122. Ankara: T.C. Kültür Bakanlığı Yayınları.

Salvatore, Armando. 1997. *Islam and the Political Discourse of Modernity*. Reading, UK: Ithaca Press.

Salzmann, Ariel. 1999. "Citizens in Search of a State: The Limits of Political Participation in the Late Ottoman Empire." In *Extending Citizenship, Reconfigur-*

ing States, ed. Michael Hanagan and Charles Tilly, 37–66. New York: Rowman & Littlefield.

Şapolyo, Enver Behnan. 1964. *Mezhepler ve Tarikatlar Tarihi*. Istanbul: Türkiye Yayınevi.

Schiffman, Zachary. 1985. "Renaissance Historicism Reconsidered." *History and Theory* 24, 2: 170–182.

Şener, Cemal. 1989. *Alevilik Olayı: Toplumsal bir Başkaldırının Kısa Tarihçesi*. Istanbul: Yön Yayıncılık.

Seremetakis, Constantina Nadia. 1991. *The Last Word: Women, Death, and Divination in Inner Mani*. Chicago: University of Chicago Press.

Shankland, David. 2003. *The Alevis in Turkey: The Emergence of a Secular Islamic Tradition*. New York: Routledge Curzon.

Shryock, Andrew. 1997. *Nationalism and the Genealogical Imagination: Oral History and Textual Authority in Tribal Jordan*. Berkeley: University of California Press.

———. 2004. "Other Conscious / Self Aware: First Thoughts on Cultural Intimacy and Mass Mediation." In *Off Stage / On Display: Intimacy and Ethnography in the Age of Public Culture*, ed. id., 3–28. Stanford: Stanford University Press.

Silverstein, Brian. 2003. "Islam and Modernity in Turkey: Power, Tradition, and Historicity in the European Provinces of the Muslim World." *Anthropological Quarterly* 76, 3: 497–517.

———. 2005. "Islamist Critique in Modern Turkey: Hermeneutics, Tradition, Genealogy." *Comparative Studies in Society and History* 47, 1: 134–160.

———. 2010. *Islam and Modernity in Turkey*. New York: Palgrave Macmillan.

Sinclair-Webb, Emma. 1999. "Pilgrimage, Politics and Folklore: The Making of Alevi Community." *Annales de l'Autre Islam* 6: 259–274.

———. 2003. "Sectarian Violence, the Alevi Minority, and the Left: Kahramanmaraş 1978." In *Turkey's Alevi Enigma: A Comprehensive Overview*, ed. Paul J. White and Joost Jongerden, 215–235. Leiden: Brill.

Soileau, Mark. 2005. "Festivals and the Formation of Alevi Identity." In *Alevis and Alevism: Transformed Identities*, ed. Hege Irene Markussen, 91–108. Istanbul: Isis Press.

———. 2006. "Humanist Mystics: Nationalism and the Commemoration of Saints in Turkey." Ph.D. diss., University of California, Santa Barbara.

Sökefeld, Martin. 2008. *Struggling for Recognition: The Alevi Movement in Germany and in Transnational Space*. New York: Berghahn Books.

Solgun, Cafer. 2011. *Alevilerin Kemalizm'le İmtihanı*. Istanbul: Timaş Yayınları.

Spencer, Robert F. 1958. "Process and Intellectual Current: Durkheim and Atatürk." *American Anthropologist* 60, 4: 640–657.

Starrett, Gregory. 1998. *Putting Islam to Work: Education, Politics, and Religious Transformation in Egypt*. Berkeley: University of California Press.

Stokes, Martin. 1992. *The Arabesk Debate: Music and Musicians in Modern Turkey.* Oxford: Clarendon Press.

———. 1996. "Ritual, Identity and the State: An Alevi (Shi'a) Cem Ceremony." In *Nationalism, Minorities and Diasporas: Identities and Rights in the Middle East,* ed. Kirsten Schultz, Martin Stokes, and Colm Campbell, 188–202. New York: I. B. Tauris.

Sullivan, Winnifred Fallers. 2005. *The Impossibility of Religious Freedom.* Princeton, NJ: Princeton University Press.

Tambar, Kabir. 2009. "Secular Populism and the Semiotics of the Crowd in Turkey." *Public Culture* 21, 3: 517–537.

———. 2011. "Iterations of Lament: Anachronism and Affect in a Shi'i Islamic Revival in Turkey." *American Ethnologist* 38, 3: 484–500.

———. 2012. "Islamic Reflexivity and the Uncritical Subject." *Journal of the Royal Anthropological Institute* 18, 3: 652–672.

Tapper, Nancy, and Richard Tapper. 1987. "The Birth of the Prophet: Ritual and Gender in Turkish Islam." *Man,* n.s., 22, 1: 69–92.

Taraf. 2011. "Cafer Solgun: Atatürk'ün resmi kalkacak." December 5, taraf.com.tr/nese-duzel/makale-cafer-solgun-ataturk-un-resmi-cemevinden-kalkacak.htm.

Toprak, Binnaz. 1996. "Civil Society in Turkey." In *Civil Society in the Middle East,* vol. 2, ed. Augustus Richard Norton, 87–118. Leiden: Brill.

Trouillot, Michel-Rolph. 1995. *Silencing the Past: Power and the Production of History.* Boston: Beacon Press.

———. 2003. *Global Transformations: Anthropology and the Modern World.* New York: Palgrave Macmillan.

Tuğal, Cihan. 2009. *Passive Revolution: Absorbing the Islamic Challenge to Capitalism.* Stanford: Stanford University Press.

Turam, Berna. 2006. *Between Islam and the State: The Politics of Engagement.* Stanford: Stanford University Press.

Turan, İlter. 1988. "Political Parties and the Party System in Post-1983 Turkey." In *State, Democracy and the Military: Turkey in the 1980s,* ed. Metin Heper and Ahmet Evin, 63–80. New York: Walter de Gruyter.

Türkyılmaz, Zeynep. 2009. "Anxieties of Conversion: Missionaries, State and Heterodox Communities in the Late Ottoman Empire." Ph.D. diss., University of California, Los Angeles.

Ülker, Erol. 2005. "Contextualising 'Turkification': Nation-Building in the Late Ottoman Empire, 1908–1918." *Nations and Nationalism* 11, 4: 613–636.

Üngör, Uğur Ümit. 2011. *The Making of Modern Turkey: Nation and State in Eastern Anatolia, 1913–1950.* Oxford: Oxford University Press.

Urban, Greg. 1988. "Ritual Wailing in Amerindian Brazil." *American Anthropologist* 90, 2: 385–400.

Vorhoff, Karin. 1998. "'Let's Reclaim our History and Our Culture!' Imagining Alevi Community in Contemporary Turkey." *Die Welt des Islams* 38, 2: 220–252.

Walton, Jeremy. 2013. "Confessional Pluralism and the Civil Society Effect: Liberal Mediations of Islam and Secularism in Contemporary Turkey." *American Ethnologist* 40, 1: 182–200.

Warner, Michael. 2002. *Publics and Counterpublics*. New York: Zone Books.

Watts, Nicole. 2000. "Relocating Dersim: Turkish State-Building and Kurdish Resistance, 1931–1938." *New Perspectives on Turkey* 23: 5–30.

———. 2010. *Activists in Office: Kurdish Politics and Protest in Turkey*. Seattle: University of Washington Press.

Wedeen, Lisa. 2008. *Peripheral Visions: Power, Publics, and Performance in Yemen*. Chicago: University of Chicago Press.

White, Jenny. 2002. *Islamist Mobilization in Turkey: A Study in Vernacular Politics*. Seattle: University of Washington Press.

Wilce, James. 2008. *Crying Shame: Metaculture, Modernity, and the Exaggerated Death of Lament*. Malden, MA: Wiley-Blackwell.

———. 2009. *Language and Emotion*. Cambridge: Cambridge University Press.

Woolard, Kathryn. 2004. "Is the Past a Foreign Country? Time, Language Origins, and the Nation in Early Modern Spain." *Journal of Linguistic Anthropology* 14, 1: 57–80.

Yavuz, M. Hakan. 2003a. *Islamic Political Identity in Turkey*. Oxford: Oxford University Press.

———. 2003b. "Media Identities for Alevis and Kurds in Turkey." In *New Media in the Muslim World*, 2nd ed., ed., Dale Eickelman and Jon Anderson, 180–199. Bloomington: Indiana University Press.

———. 2009. *Secularism and Muslim Democracy*. Cambridge: Cambridge University Press.

Yörükan, Yusuf Ziya. 1998. *Anadolu'da Aleviler ve Tahtacılar*. Edited by Turhan Yörükan. Ankara: T.C. Kültür Bakanlığı.

Zaman. 2004a. "Alevi vakfı: Diyanet kaldırılırsa çatışma çıkar." October 13, www.zaman.com.tr/haber.do?haberno=100961.

———. 2004b. "Ankara: AB ile 'azınlık' tanımlarımız birbirinden farklı." October 8, www.zaman.com.tr/haber.do?haberno=99367.

———. 2004c. "Doğan'dan şaşırtan açıklama: Alevilik islamın dışındadır." October 1, www.zaman.com.tr/haber.do?haberno=96746.

———. 2011a. "Aleviler ve Sünniler, Kerbela gecesinde buluştu: Birliğimizi bozamayacaklar." December 5, www.zaman.com.tr/haber.do?haberno=1210388&keyfield=616C657669.

———. 2011b. "CHP'li Hüseyin Aygün: Dersim Katliamının sorumlusu devlet ve CHP'dir." November 10, www.zaman.com.tr/haber.do?haberno=1200334#.

————. 2011c. "K. Maraş'ta hoşgörü iftarı." December 8, www.zaman.com.tr/haber. do?haberno=1211819&keyfield=616C657669.

Zarinebaf-Shahr, Fariba. 1997. "Qizilbash 'Heresy' and Rebellion in Ottoman Anatolia during the Sixteenth Century." *Anatolia Moderna, Yeni Anadolu* 7: 1–15.

Zürcher, Erik. 2001. *Turkey: A Modern History.* New York: I. B. Tauris.

————. 2005. "How Europeans Adopted Anatolia and Created Turkey." *European Review* 13, 3: 379–394.

INDEX

Abdülhamid II (1876–1909), 62–63
Abu-Lughod, Lila, 150
Adem, Habil, 71, 183n15
aesthetics: media, 78, 92–106, 153, 173, 184n12; political, 92–100, 105–6, 136, 171, 175; public ritual performance, 21, 22, 78, 81–82, 91–106, 153, 167, 171, 174. *See also* iconography; senses
affect: anthropology of, 34, 150; iterability of, 162, 164, 188n10; morality and, 146–47, 151, 155–56, 162–66, 187n5; subjectivity, 22, 151, 167–68, 171, 173. *See also* emotion, ritual
agency, political, 29, 140, 143–44
ahl al-bayt, 30, 129. *See also* Muhammad's family
Akçam, Taner, 169–70, 174
AKP (Justice and Development Party/Adalet ve Kalkınma Partisi), 8, 10, 51, 134, 171–72, 189n4
Alevis, 2–4, 9–10, 53; and Armenians, 73, 185n1; and Bektaşi, 9, 53, 113, 144–45, 185n5; census, 178n9; citizenship, 21, 55, 56, 64; civilizing project, 71; civil society groups, 53–54, 83–84, 96–97, 101, 104–5, 108, 110, 127–28, 133, 138–51, 184n16; Çorum, 23–28, 36–40, 44, 81, 96–97, 109–10, 116–17, 139–68; education, 3, 10–11, 25, 73, 107–8, 120, 144, 185n1; ethnic groups among, 9; as ethnic Turks, 66–67; ethnographic studies of, 65–75, 181n2; founding of nation-state, 4, 9–10, 11, 12, 16, 19, 134–35; German, 37, 102; historiography, 68, 108–9, 115–49, 167; iconography, 110–15; inclusion, 12–14, 91; intellectuals, 28, 44, 83, 119, 120–23, 132, 141–49, 174–75; *kızılbaş*, 66, 87, 182n10, 183n6; knowledge object, 58, 62, 65–76; Kurds, 9, 10, 133–34; leftist, 10–11, 15, 24, 87, 90, 114, 117; and modernity, 11–20, 29, 37, 40–44, 71, 108,

111–12, 121, 128, 136, 170–71, 185n1; nationalists and, 9–10, 55–75, 104–5, 111, 113–14, 170–71; Ottomans and, 20–21, 56, 58, 64, 67; political participation, 10–12, 26; population, 9, 24–25; Protestant missionaries and, 72–73, 183n16; religious identity, 9, 12, 53–54, 62, 72–75, 91, 107, 144–49; rural, 9, 10, 23, 39, 107, 128, 178n12; and Shi'ism, 9, 18–19, 22, 25, 27, 30–31, 68–70, 122, 123, 140–46, 149, 152, 166; Sunnis differentiated, 31, 36–37, 69–70, 187n4; Tahtacıs, 9, 69–71
Alevis—rituals, 4, 17–20; 55, 186n6; and discipline, 30–34; festivals, 97–99, 104; and national unity, 44–58, 75, 77–106, 133; saz music, 47, 96, 97, 181n13, 184n14; *semah*, 81–82, 94, 95–104, 117; as worship *(ibadet)*, 77, 79–83, 97–104, 153. *See also cem*; mourning
Alevis—violence against, 112, 172; apology for, 134–35; Atatürk iconography and, 136–37; civil, 11, 86–92; Dersim, 10, 133–37; and exclusion, 11, 12, 13, 170; governmentality and, 85–92; inclusion and belonging and, 12, 13, 14; Kahramanmaraş, 51–52; mosques involved in, 152–53; nation-building, 10, 133–37; public performance and, 78, 84, 172; right-wing/MHP, 8, 24, 87–88, 91, 113, 178n17; rituals and national unity and, 50, 51–52, 54, 58; sectarian, 11, 24, 26, 51–52, 84–92, 105–6, 110, 120–21, 152–53
Alevis—youth: activism, 10, 15; *cem*, 82–83, 93, 101–4; vs. relevance of ritual, 20, 36, 38–40; *semah*, 83, 93, 95–104, 117
Ali ibn Abi Talib, 30–31, 69–70, 72, 123, 148–49, 186nn10,11; in call to prayer, 152, 187n4; iconography, 4, 109–12, 114, 125, 129, 185n2; love for *(Ali sevgisi)*, 149–50; *Nahj al-Balagha*, 149; Ramadan memo-

Stanford Studies in Middle Eastern and Islamic Societies and Cultures

Diana Allan, *Refugees of the Revolution: Experiences of Palestinian Exile*
2013

Shira Robinson, *Citizen Strangers: Palestinians and the Birth of Israel's Liberal Settler State*
2013

Joel Beinin and Frédéric Vairel, editors, *Social Movements, Mobilization, and Contestation in the Middle East and North Africa*
2013 (Second Edition), 2011

Ariella Azoulay and Adi Ophir, *The One-State Condition: Occupation and Democracy in Israel/Palestine*
2012

Steven Heydemann and Reinoud Leenders, editors, *Middle East Authoritarianisms: Governance, Contestation, and Regime Resilience in Syria and Iran*
2012

Jonathan Marshall, *The Lebanese Connection: Corruption, Civil War, and the International Drug Traffic*
2012

Joshua Stacher, *Adaptable Autocrats: Regime Power in Egypt and Syria*
2012

Bassam Haddad, *Business Networks in Syria: The Political Economy of Authoritarian Resilience*
2011

Noah Coburn, *Bazaar Politics: Power and Pottery in an Afghan Market Town*
2011

Laura Bier, *Revolutionary Womanhood: Feminisms, Modernity, and the State in Nasser's Egypt*
2011

Samer Soliman, *The Autumn of Dictatorship: Fiscal Crisis and Political Change in Egypt under Mubarak*
2011

Rochelle A. Davis, *Palestinian Village Histories: Geographies of the Displaced*
2010

Haggai Ram, *Iranophobia: The Logic of an Israeli Obsession*
2009

John Chalcraft, *The Invisible Cage: Syrian Migrant Workers in Lebanon*
2008

Rhoda Kanaaneh, *Surrounded: Palestinian Soldiers in the Israeli Military*
2008

Asef Bayat, *Making Islam Democratic: Social Movements and the Post-Islamist Turn*
2007

Robert Vitalis, *America's Kingdom: Mythmaking on the Saudi Oil Frontier*
2006

Jessica Winegar, *Creative Reckonings: The Politics of Art and Culture in Contemporary Egypt*
2006

Joel Beinin and Rebecca L. Stein, editors, *The Struggle for Sovereignty: Palestine and Israel, 1993–2005*
2006